PHILOSOPHY AND LAW

Karen Lewis
Dec. '87

PHILOSOPHY AND LAW

Edited by

Jules Coleman & Ellen Frankel Paul

BASIL BLACKWELL
for the
Social Philosophy and Policy Center
Bowling Green State University

First Published 1987

Basil Blackwell Limited
108 Cowley Road, Oxford OX4 1JF, England

Basil Blackwell Inc
432 Park Avenue South, Suite 1503,
New York, NY 10016, USA

British Library Cataloguing in Publicaton Data
Philosophy and law.—(Social philosophy & policy, ISSN 0265-0525; v. 4)
I. Coleman, Jules II. Paul, Ellen Frankel
III. Bowling Green State University. *Social Philosophy and Policy Centre*
IV. Series
340′.1 K230

ISBN 0-631-15257-1

Library of Congress Cataloging in Publication Data applied for

Printed in Great Britain by Whitstable Litho, Kent

CONTENTS

INTRODUCTION

Philosophical questions about law have been of perennial interest to both philosophers and lawyers. From the time of Plato forward, some of the principal questions of political philosophy have been what might be called "foundational" questions about law. Do we have a general moral obligation to obey the law? What role do concepts like justice, mercy, and rights properly play in the framing and application of laws? Questions like these lead us to consider, and perhaps to reformulate, the very rationale for using legal coercion to coordinate collective activities and to preserve minimum standards of civility. Less fundamental but equally important are what might be called "practical" questions about particular laws and legal systems. What criteria should be used to interpret constitutions or specific statutes? What standards should judges use to assess harm in civil cases? Questions of this sort, even when they do not lead us back to foundational questions, may nonetheless yield important legal and philosophical insights.

The selections in this volume cover the spectrum from the foundational to the practical. In "Mercy and Legal Justice," Jeffrie G. Murphy explores our conventional understanding of the virtue of mercy. Mercy is ordinarily thought of as an autonomous virtue which, although it is never owed to anyone by right, serves to temper justice and which flows from a character marked by compassion. But this conventional understanding leads to what Murphy calls the "paradox of mercy." Judges are charged by society to carry out the laws and to mete out punishment accordingly. If mercy prompts a judge to punish less severely than justice requires, then the judge has violated his obligation to society. (And if the judge fits the punishment to *the criminal* as well as the crime, he has merely followed the requirements of justice; mercy is redundant in this context.) However, Murphy does construct a "paradigm of private law" in which mercy seems to have a place. Mercy is the civil law litigant's prerogative when he holds a right against another which, through compassion, he decides not to exercise. The litigant waives a right, but he does not violate an obligation. Hence, mercy has a place in the law, but only as a virtue manifested by private persons using the law, not by officials enforcing the law.

In his essay "Law's Halo," Donald Regan explores the connection between law and another important moral concept – that of obligation.

Regan begins with the premise that "there is no general moral obligation to obey the law." However, he does not think that it is enough to say this and no more about the moral significance of law. For even though there is no general obligation to obey the law, it is nonetheless an important part of law's function to create moral obligations of various sorts. Thus, the law is something that a moral agent ought always to consider before acting. And this, in turn, implies that law is more than a necessary evil by which we try to resolve inevitable conflicts and control base human impulses. In Regan's words, "There would be law even in a society of saints".

Philip Soper's contribution also explores the connection between moral obligation and the law. "Choosing a Legal Theory on Moral Grounds" takes up the debate between H.L.A. Hart and Lon Fuller, a quarter-century after it was first joined. Fuller argued that the emergence of evil regimes, especially Nazi Germany, was in some way the consequence of the morally neutral character of legal positivism. Hart, on the other hand, denied that there is any connection between the adoption of legal positivism and morality. As the debate currently stands between positivists and natural law theorists, the former claim superiority for their view as a moral theory, although not necessarily as a theory about the distinction between law and morality (which is how Hart understood his enterprise). Positivists claim that law and morality ought to be construed as separate and distinct because of the practical implications of this view. Natural law theorists, on the other hand, still maintain that construing law and morality as intimately connected is preferable because it sets up a barrier to evil regimes and evil officials. Soper finds both these sets of claims wanting, and argues that there are no adverse consequences to be expected from the adoption of either positivism or natural law theory.

A central feature of virtually any complex legal system is taxation; without taxation, it is difficult to imagine how a society could support the institutions and officials that make up a modern legal system. In "Taxation in a Lockean World," Richard Epstein sets out to determine whether or not taxation is legitimate within the framework of a Lockean moral view. One dilemma immediately presents itself: liberty and taxation seem to be antithetical. In a Lockean world, in which liberty is regarded as a good and coercion an evil, the concession to government of the power to tax seems to allow government to trample on the very liberty that it was established to protect. Epstein's solution to this dilemma is to argue that taxation is an inherent power of sovereignty, but also a limited power. The most important limitations are that taxation be neutral in its application, because it is not the purpose of taxation to shift the relative endowments or practices of individuals, and that taxation should be made as invulnerable to political pressure and manipulation as possible. Epstein contends that a flat tax best meets these criteria.

One means of limiting the power of government, including the power to tax, is a constitution. In recent years a lively debate has flourished in the United States over the manner in which judges ought to interpret the U.S. Constitution. Supreme Court justices, the attorney general, and academics have become involved in this (often heated) controversy. In "Constitutional Interpretation and Original Meaning," David Lyons steps back from the fray and dispassionately examines the arguments of the "originalists," i.e., those who contend that judges should be limited in their exercise of judicial review either by the original intent of the framers of the Constitution or by the actual text of the document. He scrutinizes the writings of some of the leading scholars who endorse some variant of the originalist theory – Paul Brest, Henry Monaghan, Justice William Rhenquist, and Judge Robert Bork – and finds each of their versions of the originalist position riddled with contradictions, and thus unconvincing.

An important component of any modern legal system is the civil law, which allows citizens to initiate legal proceedings to redress what they perceive as wrongs. In "Justice in Settlements," Jules Coleman and Charles Silver examine the presumption of most lawyers, judges, and law professors that it is preferable in terms of public policy to discourage trials and encourage settlements in civil cases. They examine the reasons most frequently given for this preference – that settlements conserve resources and enable parties to resolve their differences amicably – and conclude that these reasons do not give sufficient weight to the role that justice ought to play in a legal system. They argue that if justice requires giving each party his due, then there is little reason to think that settlements result in justice being done. They then proceed to evaluate a more problematical category of cases – those involving class action suits. Here, they focus on the legitimacy of the argument most frequently given by judges for dividing settlements between class members in proportion to the size and strength of their claims, and conclude that the practice cannot be defended on the grounds that are usually given for it.

A relatively new and still relatively rare kind of civil case is the so-called "wrongful life" suit – a suit brought by a person who claims that a medical practitioner or parent was negligent in allowing him to be born at all. In "Wrongful Life and the Counterfactual Element in Harming," Joel Feinberg attempts to resolve some of the complex philosophical issues raised by these suits. He begins by exploring the concept of harm and what it means for one person to harm another. Then he applies this analysis to cases of prenatal harming, including such torts as wrongful birth (actions brought by parents against medical practitioners for compensation for the birth defects suffered by their offspring), wrongful pregnancy (suits brought by parents against medical practitioners for negligence leading to contraceptive failure and unwanted pregnancy), and most problematic of all, wrongful life suits.

Feinberg meticulously examines the five principal objections against recognizing a tort of wrongful life and finds them unconvincing, although he does recognize the conceptual difficulty of assessing damages in cases in which the victim alleges that he would have been better off had he never been born. Feinberg artfully employs the counterfactual test of harming to conclude that it does make sense to award damages to individuals whose birthright to be born with positive life possibilities has been violated at the moment of birth itself.

A more traditional form of civil suit is one brought by a victim of breach of contract. In "Contract Remedies and Inalienable Rights," Randy Barnett examines the traditional remedies available to the victim of breach of contract: legal relief in the form of money damages (the usual outcome) and equitable relief in the form of specific performance or an injunction (the exceptional outcome). Courts generally reserve the remedy of specific performance for cases in which the thing contracted for is unique or nearly so and money damages will therefore not suffice. By applying what he calls a "consent theory of contract," Barnett discerns a greater role for this remedy. His argument turns on a distinction between alienable and inalienable rights, with rights to external resources falling into the former category and rights to one's person or personal service falling into the latter. Thus, Barnett differentiates three categories of contracts with different remedies appropriate to each. In the first – contracts for external resources – the fitting remedy would be that the victim gets from the person in breach the item that he had bargained for in the contract or, if the victim so elects, money damages. Contracts for personal services should not require performance but, rather, money damages. Contracts for corporate services present a more complex problem, which Barnett resolves in favor of specific performance because, he argues, the moral problem which arises in the case of personal service contracts does not arise when it is a corporation that must perform.

The final essay in this volume addresses a fundamental theoretical problem in the realm of legal ethics: Is there any common link between members of the legal profession, that is, a bond that would both set those who practice the law apart from others and distinguish law as a profession from a mere expertise. In "Practical Wisdom and Professional Character," Anthony Kronman observes that all lawyers, no matter how their specializations or occupational tasks may differ, are case-centered: "they deal with specific problems or controversies, with cases, and not merely with abstract propositions." To be case-centered requires that the lawyer possess a special kind of knowledge that Aristotle called *phronesis*, or practical wisdom. To be a lawyer in the true sense, one must posess certain traits of character: he must be a practically wise man, one who is both sympathetic to the interests of others and yet able to detach himself from those interests and perceive the larger picture. These qualities are seen most apparently in the temper of a judge, one rightly so-called. Lawyers must also possess imagination in the Kantian sense, for it is the imaginative faculty which allows a lawyer to see the whole panoply of possible solutions to a client's problems. Kronman concludes that, indeed, lawyers do have a distinctive professional character, and it is a character in which they can take pride.

Ongoing debate on the nature and morality of the legal system and specific laws is an integral part of the process of self-government. The essays in this volume cover a broad range of the moral issues raised by the law and, as such, are an important contribution to that process.

CONTRIBUTORS

Jeffrie G. Murphy is Professor of Philosophy at Arizona State University and has published numerous articles and books in moral, legal, and political philosophy, among them *Evolution, Morality*, and the Meaning of Life; *Kant, The Philosophy of Right*; and *Retribution*, Justice and Violence. He is the coauthor, with Jules Coleman, of *The Philosophy of Law: An Introduction to Jurisprudence*, and the editor of *Civil Disobedience and Violence, An Introduction to Moral and Social Philosophy*, and *Punishment and Rehabilitation*.

Donald Regan is a member of the law faculty and the philosophy department at the University of Michigan. He teaches constitutional law, and moral and political philosophy. His book *Utilitarianism and Co-operation* shared the Franklin J. Matchette Prize for 1979–1980. In 1985–86, on a Guggenheim Fellowship, he completed a monograph about the constitutional limits on state economic regulation and taxation. With that out of his system, he resumed work on a book tentatively titled *Prolegomena to a Theory of the Good: Two Essays on Moral Agency*.

Philip Soper holds a Ph.D. in Philosophy, as well as a law degree from Harvard University, and is Professor of Law at the University of Michigan Law School. He has published widely in the areas of legal, moral, and political philosophy. His recent book, *A Theory of Law*, was published by Harvard University Press in 1985.

Richard A. Epstein is James Parker Hall Professor of Law at the University of Chicago Law School and has published widely in the fields of legal philosophy and economic law. He is the editor of the *Journal of Legal Studies*. This book, *Takings: Private Property and the Power of Eminent Domain* was published by Harvard University Press in 1985.

David Lyons is Professor of Philosophy at the Sage School of Philosophy at Cornell University, as well as Professor of Law at the Cornell Law School. He has published widely in the fields of moral, legal, and political philosophy. His most recent book, *Ethics and the Rule of Law*, was published in 1984 by Cambridge University Press.

Jules Coleman is Professor of Law and Philosophy of the Social Sciences at the Yale Law School. He is the author of many articles on moral, legal, and political philosophy, and the coauthor, with Jeffrie Murphy, of *The Philosophy of Law: An Introduction to Jurisprudence* (Totowa, N.J.: Rowman &

Allanheld, 1984). He is currently completing one book on rational choice aproaches to moral, political, and legal theory, and a second on the philosophy of tort law.

Charles Silver is a former Managing Editor of *Ethics: An International Journal of Social, Political and Legal Philosophy*, a Ph.D. candidate in political science at the University of Chicago, and a student of law at Yale. He is the author of "Negative Positivism and the Hard Facts of Life," *The Monist*, vol. 68 (1985), and "Utilitarian Participation," *Social Science Information*, vol. 23 (1984).

Joel Feinberg is Professor of Philosophy at the University of Arizona in Tucson, and has published widely in the fields of moral, legal, and political philosophy. *Offense to Others*, volume two of his four-volume work, *The Moral Limits of the Criminal Law*, was published in 1985 by Oxford University Press.

Randy E. Barnett is Associate Professor of Law at the Illinois Institute of Technology, Chicago-Kent College of Law. His most recent articles include "A Consent Theory of Contract," in the *Columbia Law Review*, "Pursuing Justice in a Free Society" (two parts), in *Criminal Justice Ethics*, and "Curing the Drug Law Addiction: The Harmful Side-Effects of Legal Prohibition," forthcoming in *Dealing with Drugs*, edited by Ronald Hamowy. He edited a recent symposium on "The Limits of Public Law" in the *Harvard Journal of Law and Public Policy*, and coedited the book *Assessing the Criminal: Restitution, Retribution, and the Legal Process* (1977).

Anthony Kronman is the Edward J. Phelps Professor of Law at the Yale Law School. He has taught for nine years, previously holding positions at the University of Chicago and the University of Minnesota. He holds degrees in law and philosophy from Yale, and did his undergraduate work at Williams College. Professor Kronman is the author of a book on Max Weber, and the coeditor of a casebook on contract law and a collection of readings on the economic analysis of contracts. He is presently working on a book on the nature of practical wisdom and its place in the practice and teaching of law.

MERCY AND LEGAL JUSTICE*

By Jeffrie G. Murphy

> I looked at him. Alive. His lap a puddle of blood. With the restoration of the normal order of matter and sensation, I felt I was seeing him for the first time as a person. The old human muddles and quirks were set flowing again. Compassion, remorse, mercy.
>
> Don DeLillo
> *White Noise*

Internal and External Questions. The most profound questions in ethics, social philosophy, and the philosophy of law are foundational; i.e., they are questions that call the entire framework of our ordinary evaluations into doubt in order to determine to what degree, if at all, that framework can be rationally defended. Such questions, called "external" by Rudolf Carnap, are currently dominating my own philosophical reflections and are forcing me to rethink a variety of positions I have in the past defended.[1]

Because my current thinking about external foundational questions is in such a state of flux, it is with some anxiety that I turn to the "internal" questions that motivate the present essay, i.e., questions that accept "our" ordinary framework of evaluation as a given and seek to explore certain tensions and puzzles within that framework in order to see to what degree that framework is internally coherent. The goal is to attain, if possible, that nirvana of moral epistemology that John Rawls calls "reflective equilibrium."[2] In spite of my increasing skepticism about the value of reflective

* Several persons were kind enough to comment on earlier drafts of this paper, and I wish to thank them here: Lewis Beck, Ray Elugardo, Herbert Granger, Joshua Halberstam, Sterling Harwood, Margaret Holmgren, Lisa Isaacson, David Lyons, and Gareth Matthews. I learned a great deal from each of their comments – far more than the few changes I was able to make in the paper will indicate. Earlier versions of the paper were read at the 1985 Kraemer Lecture at the University of Arkansas, at the 1986 Conference on Law and Philosophy held at the University of Michigan Law School and sponsored by the Bowling Green Social Philosophy and Policy Center, and at the 1986 meeting of the North American Society for Social Philosophy in conjunction with the American Philosophical Association, Central Division, in St. Louis. I am grateful for helpful comments I received from the audiences at these meetings and for helpful comments I received from the editors of *Social Philosophy and Policy*.

[1] See Jeffrie G. Murphy and Jules L. Coleman, *The Philosophy of Law* (Totowa: Rowman and Allenheld, 1984) and Jeffrie G. Murphy, "Retributivism, Moral Education, and the Liberal State," *Criminal Justice Ethics*, vol. 4 (Winter/Spring 1985).

[2] John Rawls, *A Theory of Justice* (Cambridge: Harvard University Press, 1971), pp. 48–51.

equilibrium in foundational moral theory,[3] I am still inclined to believe (a) that internal coherence is relevant to external evaluation and (b) that questions of an internal nature, if properly explored with an appreciation of their limits, can be interesting and important in their own right.[4] Thus, I shall temporarily suppress my initial anxiety and plow ahead on the matter at hand.

Mercy and Justice. We are ordinarily inclined to believe – or at least pay lip service to – the claim that justice and mercy are both moral virtues. We are also inclined to maintain that both of these virtues are characteristic of such lofty objects as God (as conceived in the Judeo-Christian tradition[5]) and of such human all too human objects as legal systems – where in literature and folklore we celebrate (perhaps without fully understanding what we are saying) those judges who can "temper their justice with mercy." As we expect God as cosmic judge to manifest both justice and mercy, so too do we expect this of secular judges. Or so we often say. Shakespeare's two important "comedies of mercy," for example, contain some of the most often quoted sentiments on mercy and justice in our civilization – so often quoted, indeed, that they have attained the status of clichés and may any day find their way onto Hallmark cards or table napkins:

> The quality of mercy is not strain'd;
> It droppeth as the gentle rain from heaven
> Upon the place beneath: it is twice blessed;
> It blesseth him that gives and him that takes:
> 'Tis mightiest in the mightiest; it becomes
> The throned monarch better than his crown;
> His sceptre shows the force of temporal power,
> The attribute to awe and majesty,
> Wherein doth sit the dread and fear of kings;
> But mercy is above this scepter'd sway,—
> It is enthroned in the heart of kings,
> It is an attribute to God himself;

[3] See my "Rationality and Constraints on Democratic Rule," J. Roland Pennock and John W. Chapman, eds., *Nomos XXVIII: Justification* (New York: New York University Press, 1986), pp. 141–164.

[4] See, for example, Joel Feinberg, *Harm to Others* (Oxford: Oxford University Press, 1984). Feinberg explicitly refuses to address foundational issues (taking a kind of "liberalism" as a given) and still manages to enrich our thinking about morality and the criminal law to a profound degree.

[5] "Even God prays. What is His prayer? 'May it be My will that My love of compassion overwhelm My demand for strict justice.'" Mahzhor for Yom Kippur, The Rabbinical Assembly of New York, 439 (from Berakhot 7a).

And earthly power doth then show likest God's
When mercy seasons justice.

(*Merchant of Venice*, IV, I; Portia speaks)

No ceremony that to great ones 'longs,
Not the king's crown, nor the deputed sword,
The marshall's truncheon, nor the judge's robe,
Become them with one half so good a grace
As mercy does.

(*Measure for Measure*, II, II; Isabella speaks)

These passages express some fairly widely held – and closely related – views about mercy: (1) It is an *autonomous* moral virtue (i.e., it is not reducible to some other virtue – especially justice). (2) It is a virtue that tempers or "seasons" justice, something that one adds to justice (the primary virtue) in order to dilute it and perhaps – if one takes the metallurgical metaphor of tempering seriously – to make it stronger. (3) It is never owed to anyone as a right or a matter of desert or justice. It always, therefore, transcends the realm of strict moral obligation and is best viewed as a free gift – an act of grace, love, or compassion that is beyond the claims of right, duty, and obligation. ("The quality of mercy is not [con]strained.") (4) As a moral virtue, it derives its value at least in part from the fact that it flows from a certain kind of *character* – a character disposed to perform merciful acts from love or compassion while not losing sight of the importance of justice. (5) It requires a generally retributive outlook on punishment and responsibility. Mercy is often regarded as found where a judge, out of compassion for the plight of a particular offender, imposes upon that offender a hardship less than his just deserts. This way of conceptualizing mercy requires, of course, that we be operating with a rich concept of "just desert" – some thing that is not easy to come by on a utilitarian/deterrence analysis.[6]

The foregoing suggests that there are certain other virtues or, at least, *desiderata* of moral and legal systems with which mercy often is but should not be confused: excuse, justification, and forgiveness. If a person has actually done the right thing (i.e., his conduct was justified), or if he was not responsible for what he did (i.e., he had a valid excuse), then it would simply be *unjust* to punish him, and no question of mercy need arise – for there is no responsible wrongdoing, and responsible wrongdoing is (it is commonly thought) the proper object of mercy.

[6] Note that this is a list of commonly held views about mercy and its relation to justice. I shall later argue that some of these views – (5) in particular — are distorted or mistaken.

Forgiveness is trickier. As I have argued elsewhere,[7] forgiveness is primarily a matter of changing how one *feels* with respect to a person who has done *oneself* an injury. It is particularly a matter of overcoming, on moral grounds, the *resentment* that a self-respecting person quite properly feels as a result of such an injury. Mercy, though related to forgiveness, is clearly different in at least these two respects. To be merciful to a person requires not merely that one change how one feels about that person but, also, requires a specific kind of action (or omission) – namely, treating that person less harshly than, in the absence of the mercy, one would have treated him. This explains how we can forgive in our heart of hearts but cannot show mercy in our heart of hearts, why we can forgive the dead but cannot show mercy to the dead, and so forth. Also, it is not a requirement of my showing mercy that I be an injured party. All that is required is that I stand in a certain relation to the potential beneficiary of mercy. This relation – typically established by legal or other institutional rules – makes it *fitting* (I purposely speak vaguely here for reasons that will later become clear) that I impose some hardship upon the potential beneficiary of mercy.

The Paradoxes of Mercy. All is not well with the above rosy picture. For the following pattern of argument seems tempting: If mercy requires a tempering of justice, than there is a sense in which mercy may require a departure from justice. (Temperings are tamperings.) Thus, to be merciful is, perhaps, to be *unjust*. But it is a vice, not a virtue, to manifest injustice. Thus, mercy must be not a virtue, but a vice – a product of morally dangerous sentimen tality. This is particularly obvious in the case of a sentencing judge. We (society) hire this individual to enforce the rule of law under which we live. We think of this as "doing justice," and the doing of this is surely his sworn obligation. What business does he have, then, ignoring his obligations to justice while he pursues some private, idiosyncratic, and not publicly accountable virtue of love or compassion?[8] Shakespeare, always sensitive to both sides of complex moral issues, captures this thought well even in the midst of his dramatic sermons on mercy:

[7] "Forgiveness and Resentment," Peter A. French, *et al.*, eds. *Midwest Studies In Philosophy, VII: Social and Political Philosophy* (Minneapolis: University of Minnesota Press, 1982) pp. 503–516.

[8] Note that I describe the judge's job to be that of upholding the *rule of law*. I mean by this the upholding of legal rules that meet certain standards of justice, not the mechanical upholding of any legal rules at all no matter how unjust they may be. Of course, I do not believe that judges should enforce legal rules in the absence of any reflection on the merits of those rules from the point of view of justice. If the rules are unjust, then if the judge has discretion, he should use that discretion to seek to do justice. (If the judge has no discretion and if the rules are terribly unjust, then such drastic acts as resignation or civil disobedience may be in order.) These complexities, however, do not show a need for a special virtue of mercy; and only a highly impoverished view of justice (i.e., that it is simply mechanical rule following) would make one think that these complexities could not be dealt with in terms of a sophisticated theory of justice.

I show [pity] most of all when I show justice,
For then I pity those I do not know,
Which a dismissed offense would after gall;
And do him right that, answering one foul wrong,
Lives not to act another.

(*Measure for Measure*, II, II; Angelo speaks[9])

Perhaps the clearest statements of the paradoxes I want to develop on mercy come from St. Anselm. His worry is about the divine nature – how God can be both just and merciful – but the paradoxes he formulates can easily be adapted to secular and legal concerns. He writes:

> What justice is it that gives him who merits eternal death everlasting life? How, then, gracious Lord, good to the wicked, canst thou save the wicked if this is not just, and thou dost not aught that is not just? (*Proslogium* IX)
>
> But if it can be comprehended in any way why thou canst will to save the wicked, yet by no consideration can we comprehend why, of those who are alike wicked, thou savest some rather than others, through supreme goodness, and why thou dost condemn the latter, rather than the former, through supreme justice. (*Proslogium* XI)

Though Anselm's specific worry is about the divine nature (Are the divine attributes of perfect justice and perfect compassion coherently ascribable to the same being?), he raises a general worry about the concepts of justice and mercy themselves – namely, to what degree (if at all) are they consistent? More specifically: If we simply use the term "mercy" to refer to certain of the demands of justice (e.g., the demand for individuation), then mercy ceases to be an autonomous virtue and instead becomes a part of (is reducible to a part of) justice. It thus beomes obligatory, and all the talk about gifts, acts of grace, supererogation, and compassion becomes quite beside the point. If, on the other hand, mercy is totally different from justice and actually requires (or permits) that justice sometimes be set aside, it then counsels injustice.[10] In short: mercy is either a vice (injustice) or redundant (a part of

[9] The point here, I take it, is that the judge who is influenced by the plight of the offender before him may lose sight of the fact that his job is to uphold an entire system of justice that protects the rights and security of all citizens

[10] A critic has suggested that I am here confusing the unjust with the *non*-just – that I fail to notice that some acts (perhaps some acts of mercy) are non-just (neutral from the point of view of justice) in that they are neither unjust nor required by justice. What bearing might this observation have, even if correct, on the issue of mercy in a criminal law context? None that I can see. To be morally acceptable, a non-just act would at least have to be *permitted* by the rules of justice; but, on standard versions of retributive justice (e.g., Kant's), it is *not* permitted from the moral point of view that persons receive less punishment than, in justice, they deserve. To give them less punishment would be to do an injustice.

justice). (This is a gloss on Anselm's first paradox – from IX. The second paradox – from XI – will be explored in a later section.)

Some Specific Cases and Some Good Journal Articles. Two of the most interesting articles on mercy are those by Alwynne Smart and Claudia Card.[11] Both seek to establish that there is indeed a place for mercy in a world that takes the value of justice seriously, and both (Smart especially) develop a discussion of this general issue in terms of specific cases – cases that are supposed to test and hone our intuitions so that we can be in "reflective equilibrium" about the issues of justice and mercy.

Smart asks that we consider the following pairs of cases – cases that might face a sentencing judge who, we may suppose, has some discretion and is not bound by mandatory sentencing rules:

	A	*B*
(1)	The defendant, convicted of vehicular homicide, had his own child – whom he loved deeply – as his victim.	The defendant has been convicted of killing another person in cold blood
(2)	The defendant is a young and inexperienced criminal.	The defendant is a hardened career criminal.

According to Smart, "we" would all agree that the judge should impose a lighter sentence on those persons under *A* than on those under *B* and that it would be proper, in a perfectly ordinary sense of the word "mercy", to express "our" conviction about what he should do by saying that he should show mercy in those cases.

Let us suppose that Smart is correct here. It is proper for the judge to go easy here, and such easing up would be called by many people (prior to reading this essay) an act of mercy. This still strikes me as philosophically confused and as an obstacle to philosophical clarity on the concept of mercy. If we feel that the judge should go easy in cases under *A*, this is surely because we believe that there is some morally relevant feature that distinguishes these cases from those under *B*. What might this feature be? In (1)

[11] Alwynne Smart, "Mercy," H. B. Acton, ed., *The Philosophy Of Punishment* (New York: St. Martin's Press, 1969), pp. 212–227. (Smart's article originally appeared in *Philosophy*, October 1968). Claudia Card, "Mercy," *Philosophical Review*, vol. XLIII (April 1972), pp. 182–207. Since Smart's essay provides me with a useful starting point from which to develop what I want to say about mercy, I will focus my discussion primarily around her piece and will thus not give Card's rich essay the detailed discussion it deserves. I will comment on it only in passing. Card, like Smart, operates within what I will later call the Criminal Law Paradigm for mercy (a paradigm I will reject) and, also like Smart, she seems to offer a view of mercy that makes it a part of justice (on a sophisticated theory of justice) and not an autonomous moral virtue.

it is no doubt our conviction that the criminal has already suffered a great deal – perhaps even that he has suffered enough – and that the infliction of any additional misery by the state would be gratuitous and cruel.[12] In (2) we are no doubt influenced by the idea that the character of a younger person is less mature and thus less responsible than that of a hardened criminal.[13] But, if this is our thinking, then why talk of mercy here and confuse what we are doing with some moral virtue that requires the tempering of justice? For to avoid inflicting upon persons more suffering than they deserve, or to avoid punishing the less responsible as much as the fully responsible, is a simple – indeed, obvious – demand of *justice*. A basic demand of justice is that like cases be treated alike, and that morally relevant differences between persons be noticed and our treatment of those persons be affected by those differences. This demand for individuation – a tailoring of our retributive reponse to the individual natures of the persons with whom we are dealing – is a part of what we mean by taking persons seriously as persons and is thus a basic demand of justice. One could introduce a sense of "mercy" that means "seeking to tailor our response to morally relevant individual differences." But this would be confusing and dangerous: confusing because it would make us think that the rich literature noted above (Shakespeare, Anselm) was somehow relevant to this; dangerous because it might lead us to suppose that individuation was not owed to persons as a right and was thus somehow optional as a free gift or act of grace. But this would be deeply wrong. The legal rules, if they are just, will base required penal treatment on morally relevant differences *or* they will give judges the discretion to so do; and criminal defendants surely have a *right* that it be this way.[14] One could

[12] The idea that natural suffering can serve as a substitute for legally imposed suffering is complex and perhaps incoherent; see my "Forgiveness and Resentment," p. 509 and note 17.

[13] Perhaps we also think that prison will be harder on them and thus that they may suffer more than they deserve. Perhaps we might also think that young people are more likely to be influenced by the bad environment that prison represents.

The idea that it is immoral to impose a level of suffering out of proper proportion to a person's character is also central to Card's view of mercy. She writes: "Mercy ought to be shown to an offender when it is evident that otherwise (1) he would be made to suffer unusually more on the whole, owing to his peculiar misfortunes, than he deserves in view of his basic character and (2) he would be worse off in this respect than those who stand to benefit from the exercise of their right to punish him (or to have him punished). When the conditions of this principle are met, the offender deserves mercy." ("Mercy," p. 184) Card thus seems explicitly to classify merciful acts as a subcategory of just acts, and not as acts autonomous from justice. But then I fail to understand how she can say (also on p. 184) that "desert of mercy does not give rise to an obligation."

[14] In commenting on an earlier draft of this paper, Lewis Beck raised the question of how the demand for individuation (which I suggest is a demand of justice) can be squared with the common and intuitively compelling metaphor that "justice is blind." The short answer, I think, is this: justice is not to be totally blind but is, rather, to be blind to all aspects of an individual that do not have a bearing on the question of what his just treatment or just deserts really are, e.g., race, sexual attractiveness and willingness, ability to bribe, etc.

talk of mercy here, but why? (One might as well protest strict criminal liability offenses by saying that they are unmerciful.) Judges or lawmakers who are unmindful of the importance of individuated response are not lacking in mercy; they lack a sense of justice.[15] Recall our earlier dilemma: mercy is either a vice or is redundant. The above cases illustrate redundancy.

Smart is sensitive to the fact that not everyone will find her initial cases representative of mercy in any deep or interesting sense, and she thus introduces some additinal cases in an attempt to capture a different and more important kind of mercy. These are cases where (unlike the earlier cases) we agree that some punishment *P* is, *all* relevant things about Jones considered, the just punishment for what Jones has done. Still, on moral grounds, we argue that a punishment less than *P* should be inflicted. We now have a virtue that is not redundant – is not merely reducible to justice. These are the cases:

(1) Jones's family, who need his support very much, would be harmed to an unacceptable degree if *P* is inflicted on Jones. Thus, we ought to show mercy to Jones and inflict less than *P*.
(2) Adverse social consequences will result if *P* is inflicted on Jones. (Perhaps he is a popular leader of the political opposition, and his followers will riot or commit acts of terrorism if *P* is inflicted on Jones.) Thus, we should show mercy to Jones.
(3) Jones has been in jail for a long time and has so reformed that he is, in a very real sense, a "new person." Thus, we should show him mercy and grant him an early release.

These cases strike me as unpersuasive. It strikes me as analytic that mercy is based on a concern for the *defendant's* plight, and this feature is absent in (1) and (2). If we are showing mercy to anyone in (1) it is to Jones's family, and he is simply the indirect beneficiary of the mercy. But even this seems a confusing way to talk. In (1) and (2) one is basically choosing to bring about a net gain in utility. This may be reasonable if a utilitarian moral outlook is reasonable. But these cases would not be interestingly unique given that outlook; and, for reasons sketched above, it is not an outlook in which a concern with mercy as a special virtue would arise.

Case (3) is, of course, very different. But it, like Smart's earlier cases,

[15] Those who desire to talk about mercy in this context probably do so because they have an overly restricted and simplistic conception of justice and thus fail to appreciate all that would be involved in a sophisticated theory of retributive justice and the role of the judiciary in implementing such a theory. It might be worth noting, in this regard, that in our particular legal system most visible law-reforming judicial activism in the cause of greater individuation will take place at the level of a court of appeals. Trial judges (in giving instructions, for example) and trial juries (in refusing to convict, for example) may move toward greater justice in particular cases, but what they do does not become a public and permanent part of the law in the obvious way provided by written opinions of a court of appeals (particularly the Supreme Court).

seems simply a matter of justice. I am suspicious of "new person" talk. However, if there really are cases where we should take it literally, then it is obviously a matter of justice that one not punish one person for the crime of another. Why talk of mercy here? .

In summary: We have yet to find one case of genuine mercy as an autonomous virtue. The cases we have explored represent either virtuous behavior that is simply a matter of justice *or* they represent cases of unjustified sentimentality *or* they represent cases where the demands of justice are thought to be overridden by the demands of utility. Thus some skepticism about mercy seems in order. Judges in criminal cases are obligated to do justice.[16] So too, I would argue, are prosecutors and parole boards in their exercise of discretion.[17] There is thus simply no room for mercy as an autonomous virtue with which their justice should be tempered. Let them keep their sentimentality to themselves for use in their private lives with their families and pets.

A New Paradigm for Mercy.[18] But could all the rich and moving literature of mercy be totally worthless – nothing but propaganda for mindless sentimentality? I think not; and I shall spend the remainder of this essay attempting to think about mercy in a new way – one which may allow us to give it some meaningful life as an autonomous moral virtue.

Thus far we have been operating with what might be called the Criminal Law Paradigm of mercy – thinking of mercy as a virtue that most typically would be manifested by a sentencing judge in a criminal case. This is the paradigm represented in *Measure for Measure*, where Isabella begs that Angelo, a judge in a criminal case involving her brother, will show her brother mercy. It is this paradigm, I have suggested, that is probably a failure.

[16] Recall that by this claim I do not mean that judges are always obligated to enforce any rule no matter how unjust that rule may be. My point is rather this: the focus of a judge, either in enforcing a rule *or* in seeking a way to modify or get around it, is to be on the question of what is required by justice – not on what he may be prompted out of compassion to do.

[17] Special problems may arise for a chief executive or head of state in his exercise of the power of pardon. The "job description" for such an office may, to borrow some language from Aquinas, involve a concern for the common good or common welfare of the community in the executive's care. This might mean that, in deciding whether or not to pardon an individual, the chief executive (unlike a judge) might legitimately draw upon values other than the requirements of justice and thus might legimately ignore the just deserts of an individual and pardon that individual if the good of the community requires it. This whole account, of course, presupposes a political theory of the various offices and roles required by society and a theory of the proper values and decision-making criteria proper to (and perhaps unique to) each of the offices and roles. Space does not allow the articulation, much less the defense, of such a theory here.

[18] This section draws heavily on P. Twambley's important article "Mercy and Forgiveness," *Analysis*, vol. 36 (January 1976), pp. 84–90.

But there is another paradigm – that represented in *Merchant of Venice* – a paradigm that I will call the Private Law Paradigm. In that play, you will recall, the central focus is on a *civil* case – a contract dispute. Antonio has made a bad bargain with Shylock and, having defaulted, is contractually obligated to pay Shylock a pound of his flesh. Portia, acting as judge, asks that Shylock show mercy to Antonio by not demanding the harsh payment.[10]

Note how radically this case differs from the criminal law case. A judge in a criminal case has an *obligation* to do justice – which means, at a minimum, an obligation to uphold the rule of law. Thus, if he is moved, even by love or compassion, to act contrary to the rule of law – to the rules of justice – he acts wrongly (because he violates an obligation) and manifests a vice rather than a virtue. A criminal judge, in short, has an obligation to impose the just punishment; and all of his discretion within the rules is to be used to secure greater justice (e.g., more careful individuation). No rational society would write any other "job description" for such an important institutional role.

But a litigant in a civil suit is not the occupier – in anything like the same sense – of an institutional role. He occupies a private role. He does not have an antecedent obligation, required by the rules of justice, to impose harsh treatment. He rather has, in a case like Shylock's, a *right* to impose harsh treatment. Thus, if he chooses to show mercy, he is simply *waiving a right* that he could in justice claim – not violating an obligation demanded by justice.[20] (Consider here the analogy with the rules of chivalric combat. The fallen knight begs for mercy. He is not asking that the victor violate an obligation to kill him but is, rather, asking that the victor waive a right to kill him.) And there is no contradiction, paradox, or even tension here. I do not necessarily show a lack of respect for justice by waiving my justice-based rights as I would by ignoring my justice-derived obligations.[21] Thus, in the Private Law Paradigm, the virtue of mercy is revealed when a person, out of compassion for the hard position of the person who owes him an obligation, waives the right that generates the obligation and frees the individual of the burden of that obligation. People who are always standing on their rights, indifferent to the impact that this may have on others, are simply intolerable.

[19] Portia serves a complex role in the play. She does not simply represent the virtue of mercy but also stands as a representative of hypocrisy, unjust manipulation, and anti-Semitism.

[20] There may be special problems in cases (defamation?) where tort suits aid in upholding certain socially important rules and protections. In this sense they are not purely private legal matters even though they are handled in the private law rather than in the criminal law. Thus, there may be cases where an individual might feel a public responsiblity to proceed with a private lawsuit.

[21] I say "not necessarily" because there are cases where a refusal to stand on one's rights and demand just treatment would reveal a lack of self-respect and a lack of respect for oneself as a morally relevant object (and thus a lack of respect for the rules of morality themselves). Of course, not every case of standing on one's rights (no matter how trivial) is of this nature.

Such persons cannot be faulted on grounds of justice, but they can certainly be faulted. And the disposition to mercy helps to check these narrow and self-involved tendencies present in each of us.[22] There is thus room for mercy as an important moral virtue with impact upon the law, but it is a virtue to be manifested by private persons using the law – *not* by officials enforcing the law.[23]

Note also that this Private Law Paradigm might help, by analogy, with Anselm's theological puzzle about mercy. Anselm sees a paradox in attributing both justice and mercy to God because he seems to see God as analogous to a judge in a criminal case – as someone with an obligation to enforce certain rules. But surely this is not the only model of God. God (at least on one fairly common view) is not bound by independent rules of obligation with respect to his creatures; for the rules of morality are, on this view, simply His commands. He does, however, have many *rights* with respect to His creatures. Thus, His mercy may be viewed as His deciding, out of love or compassion, to waive certain rights that He has – *not* to violate certain obligations that He has. Anselm's first paradox disappears.

Rationality and the Equal Protection Paradox. Is everything now coherent in the land of mercy? Is its status as an autonomous virtue, different from and tempering justice, intact, ready to be dispensed from our compassionate natures as a free gift or act of grace? Not quite. For Anselm's second paradox now appears to haunt us:

> But if it can be comprehended in any way why thou canst will to save the wicked, yet by no consideration can we comprehend why, of those who are alike wicked, thou savest some rather than others, through supreme goodness, and why thou dost condemn the latter, rather than the former, through supreme justice. (*Proslogium* XI)

[22] Sterling Harwood has suggested to me in correspondence that the tempering metaphor might illuminate if applied to persons and their dispositions rather than to the rules of justice themselves. A person, on this view, should temper his just personality (a dominant disposition to see that justice is done) by developing (if possible) a disposition to be merciful (an openness to being moved by the plight of others to the degree that one will not always demand one's just rights from them). This suggestion seems correct to me. Bishop Butler, in his classic sermons "Upon Resentment" and "Upon the Forgiveness of Injuries" is, of course, brilliant on such topics.

[23] Should judges in civil cases follow Portia's lead and encourage litigants in some cases to show mercy? Perhaps; but there are problems here. The desire to settle cases and avoid the human and financial costs of litigation is certainly a reasonable one; but, as Jules Coleman and Charles Silver have argued elsewhere in this volume, there are serious social costs involved in settlement as well, e.g., the cost of not having the law clarified in the way that actual litigation makes possible.

Anselm here seems to be raising a kind of "equal protection" paradox: If God (or any other rational being) shows mercy, then the mercy must not be arbitrary or capricious, but must rather rest upon some good reason – some morally relevant feature of the situation that made the mercy seem appropriate. Compassion and love are, after all, cognitively loaded emotions; they are not sensations like headaches or tickles. Thus, they are the sorts of reactions for which reasons may be given; and where reasons are given, it is possible to distinguish good from bad reasons, relevant from irrelevant ones. ("I showed him mercy because he was so sick" has a kind of sense lacking in "I showed him mercy because he was so handsome.") But once a reason, always a reason. And does not the Principle of Sufficient Reason require that if I, as a rational being, showed mercy to Jones because of characteristic *C*, then it is presumably required of me (rationally required, not morally required) that I show comparable mercy to *C*-bearing Smith?[24] But if so, then what becomes of all this grace/free gift talk when applied to mercy? (Of course, there can even be reasons for gifts: "It is your birthday.") Is it nothing more than this: I am not ever required to show mercy, but if I show it even once then I am rationally required to show it to all relevantly similar persons? But if I show mercy for a reason (which must be the case, if mercy is not simply capricious) does not that reason then *require* that I show mercy whenever I recognize the presence of that reason? The showing of mercy may not be an obligation in the strong sense (based on rights), but it may be something I *ought-for-a-reason* to do. In that case it cannot *totally* be a free act of grace. Some of Anselm's second paradox thus remains.

Internal and External Again.[25] Let me briefly return to the worry about foundations. It seems to be the case that "we" (all well brought up, educated, middle-class intellectuals?) see justice to be the primary value with respect to law, but that we also want to find some place for mercy as a secondary virtue to temper or otherwise have some effect on justice. It is interesting to inquire into why we think this and into whether our common pattern of thought is rationally justified.

Suppose that Gilbert Harman is right about ethics: our moral views are simply conventions that result from tacit bargains struck between the weak and poor and the rich and powerful – bargains where each attempts to

[24] For a discussion of the Principle of Sufficient Reason (a rational being will not prefer one thing over another without basing that preference upon some relevant difference between the things) and equal protection, see my "Justifying Departures from Equal Treatment," *Journal Of Philosophy* (October 1984), pp. 587–593.

[25] This section of the paper was greatly improved by some comments and suggestions of Ray Elugardo.

maximize his self-interest while still securing the vital benefits of social cooperation.[26] This might be a start toward explaining some of our ordinary views about justice and mercy. Justice – the regular enforcement of the rules that make social stability (and thus social life) possible – will be a strong priority of all parties to the bargain – whether rich or poor, strong or weak. Not all will have the same stake in these rules, but all (or almost all) will have a high stake. Thus, it is not difficult to see why conventions of justice should have a very high priority. Mercy, however, is a different matter. It is more likely to be needed by the poor and weak than by the rich and powerful, and thus it is easy to see why it is present (some level of it is perhaps required to secure the cooperation and compliance of the disadvantaged) but also easy to see why it does not have the dominant role that justice has – why it only tempers justice but never replaces or supersedes it.

The bargaining model of moral conventions might also provide a start toward dealing with Anselm's second paradox – namely, if I show mercy to *C*-bearing Jones, how can I consistently (morally?) fail to show mercy to equally *C*-bearing Smith? If moral conventions are viewed as agreements based on rational self-interest, then the impact *on me* of my continued showings of mercy would become relevant. Thus, what relevantly distinguishes the Jones case from the Smith case will not be some feature that distinguishes Jones from Smith but, rather, some feature that distinguishes the impact on me of mercy to Jones from the impact on me of mercy to Smith. The mere fact that Jones got there first (or I noticed him first) might then make a great deal of difference. I show mercy to Jones, who is pitiful to degree *P*, and thus forgive his debt to me of five dollars. Smith, who is also pitiful to degree *P*, also owes me five dollars. I do not show him mercy, however, because, though I can afford the loss of five dollars, I cannot afford the loss of ten. Also, I may begin to fear – quite legitimately — that if I start to make a practice of showing mercy instead of simply showing it every now and then when the spirit moves me, I will be taken for an easy mark in future dealings with those who might attempt to exploit my perceived good will. Thus, if rational persons thought that once having shown mercy they would be stuck with making a regular practice of it, they might be inclined never to show it at all. But since, as I argued above, there are reasons why rational agents would agree to conventions establishing some level of mercy, they would not want to adopt a principle of mercy that would give rational persons incentives never to show it. And thus they would probably agree with the

[26] Gilbert Harman, "Justice and Moral Bargaining," *Social Philosophy And Policy*, vol. 1 (Autumn 1983), pp. 114–131. Similar views may also be found in such otherwise diverse thinkers as Hume, Marx, and Nietzsche.

adoption of mercy as what Kant called an imperfect duty – a duty that admits of wide latitude in the time and manner of its fulfilment.[27]

And what does all this have to do with rational justification? I am not sure. But I suppose that, with respect to any bargain or convention, if it is the case that it represents, for each party, the best deal he could have struck for himself under the circumstances, then it may be called rational in some minimal sense. This may not be much (not what Kant, for example, would like the connection between morality and rationality to be), but it strikes me as a more impressive argument for a moral view than the argument that the view would put Mr. and Mrs. Front Porch in a state of reflective equilibrium with respect to their moral intuitions. But this is a very complex issue and should be – and will be – left to be pursued in another context.

Philosophy, Arizona State University

[27] For a stimulating argument that Kantian conclusions can be generated from egoistic premises and that central Kantian doctrines can be rationally reconstructed on the basis of models that initially seem anti-Kantian, see David Gauthier, "The Unity of Reason: A Subversive Reinterpretation of Kant," *Ethics*, vol. 96 (October 1985), pp. 74–88. As Lisa Isaacson has pointed out to me, the analysis presented in this final section of the paper will probably not help with the paradoxes of divine mercy, for it is probably not reasonable to view God's morality as a result of a bargain He strikes with humanity in order to advance His interests.

LAW'S HALO

By Donald H. Regan

Like many people these days, I believe there is no general moral obligation to obey the law.[1] I shall explain why there is no such moral obligation – and I shall clarify what I mean when I say there is no moral obligation to obey the law – as we proceed. But also like many people, I am unhappy with a position that would say there was no moral obligation to obey the law and then say no more about the law's moral significance.[2] In our thinking about law in a reasonably just society, we have a strong inclination to invest law with a sort of moral halo. It does not *feel* right to suggest that law is a morally neutral social fact, nor to suggest that law is merely a useful social technique.

In this essay, I shall try to account in part for law's moral halo. (Let me emphasize "in part"; I do not purport to say everything that could be said.) Because I share the widespread inclination to invest law with this halo, I shall not be interested in a merely historical account of how we come to see law with a halo – a pure "error theory" of law's halo, if you will. I want to justify the halo. On the other hand, the main way to justify the halo is to get clear just what law's moral significance is. It is unlikely that at the end of the process of clarification the halo will have exactly the shape or luminance that it had at the beginning.

Obviously, if we are going to clarify law's moral significance, we must have some general moral presuppositions. I shall write as if I were an act-utilitarian. That is, I shall assume that an act is right if and only if it produces at least as good consequences throughout the universe as any other act available to the agent. In truth, I am not an act-utilitarian. For reasons I have explained elsewhere, I think the act-utilitarian view about the structure of the maximization decision required of a moral agent is oversimplified.[3] But

[1] *Cf.* M. B. E. Smith, "Is There a Prima Facie Obligation to Obey the Law?," *Yale Law Journal*, vol. 82 (1973), pp. 950–976; Joseph Raz, *The Authority of Law* (Oxford: Clarendon Press, 1979), pp. 233–249.

[2] *Cf.* Philip Soper, "The Moral Value of Law," *Michigan Law Review*, vol. 84 (1985), pp. 63–86; Raz, *The Authority of Law*, pp. 250–261. Notice that Raz, like me, wants to be on both sides of the fence. Indeed, from the point of view of the reader who likes his questions and answers writ large, it may seem I have little to say that Raz has not already said. But there are enough differences of detail, of emphasis, and of general perspective that I hope the repetition of major themes may be justified.

[3] See my *Utilitarianism and Co-operation* (Oxford: Clarendon Press, 1980), especially ch. 2.

of the standard utilitarian theories, act-utilitarianism is nearest the truth; and it will do for present purposes. There is another issue, of course, about just what consequences count as good consequences which the moral agent is to maximize. My axiological views, like my views on the structure of maximization, are nonstandard in important respects; I am an "ideal utilitarian" and, speaking generally, my views are those of G. E. Moore. But again, that need not concern us in this essay. With one exception, which will be sufficiently marked when it appears, the particular claims I rely on about what is good and what is bad will be uncontroversial.

What follows is divided into three sections, in which I shall discuss three aspects of law's moral significance. In the first section, I shall explain that even though there is no moral obligation to obey the law, it is nonetheless a very important part of law's function to create moral obligations, in various senses. In the second section, I shall explain why, even though there is no moral obligation to obey the law, the law is nonetheless something a moral agent ought always to take into account before acting. In the third section, I shall point out that law is not a mere necessary evil. It is, as Aristotle thought, a good in itself – the natural capstone of human development in a certain aspect. There would be law even in a society of saints.

I. HOW SOME LAWS CREATE MORAL OBLIGATIONS

Notice the title of this section. The topic is how *some* laws create moral obligations. Just as there is no moral obligation to obey the law in general, so there are many individual laws, including many mandatory laws directly regulating private behavior, which neither create moral obligations nor are intended to. But there are also many laws which do create moral obligations, in various senses, and which are intended to. The main business of this section is to get clear how those laws work.

Let us start with a simple example, the law that says one should stop at a red traffic light and proceed only on a green light. It is clear that I often have a moral obligation to stop at a red light. I have that obligation (when I have it) because if I do not stop, I will cause an accident and injure someone. Why will I cause an accident if I do not stop? Because someone else who has a green light will be driving through the intersection, expecting me to stop. Why will that other party be expecting me to stop? In large measure because the law requires me to stop. In sum, the existence of the law has created the moral obligation.

(I said the other party will be expecting me to stop "in large measure because the law requires me to stop." I do not mean to suggest that the other person expects me to be regulating my behavior with regard to red lights primarily by the occurrent thought that the law requires me to stop at them. I will stop partly out of habit, partly out of prudence, partly out of direct concern for others, and perhaps partly out of respect for the law; and the other party, if she stopped to think, would know all this. But even so, the law about traffic lights played an important causal role in bringing about the situation where habit, prudence, concern for others, and so on, conspire to make me stop. The law therefore played an important causal role in creating and justifying the other party's expectation that I will stop.)

At one level, my moral obligation to stop at the red light can be explained without any reference at all to the law. I should stop because of the injurious consequences of not stopping, given other people's expectations and behavior. Still, the law was crucial in creating the relevant expectations and, thus, in bringing it about that my moral obligations with regard to traffic lights are what they are. And it was the main *purpose* of the law, if not to create the moral obligations (since the mere existence of moral obligations can hardly be thought to be a good in itself), then to create the organization of communal expectations and behavior that the moral obligations fall out of.

The law about traffic lights solves a coordination problem. It is representative of a vast range of other cases in which laws solve, and are intended to solve, other coordination problems. The example is simple; the function it points to is as important as any function law serves.[4]

Now, the observation that many laws solve coordination problems may seem too obvious to bother with. In fact, I shall have no choice but to say some obvious things in the course of trying to get straight just what it is of moral significance that law does for us. But for what it is worth, my observation may be a bit less obvious than it seems, inasmuch as I would reject most of the thinking that conventionally surrounds the idea that laws somehow solve coordination problems.

The idea that laws solve coordination problems most often crops up in connection with the "fair-play" argument for a general moral obligation to obey the law. But I differ with fair-play theorists on at least three grounds. In the first place, I do not think there is any *basic* moral obligation of "fair-play," that is, of holding up one's end in fair cooperative arrangements. Insofar as there are particular obligations which suggest this general fair-play obligation, they are generated by utilitarian considerations. (This obviously is a topic too large to argue about here.) In the second place, fair play theorists tend to believe that achieving coordination often requires non-act-utilitarian behavior. They suggest, implicitly or explicitly, that we ought to hold up our end in some cooperative scheme *instead of* doing the act-utilitarian thing, because general act-utilitarian behavior would destroy coordination entirely.

[4] *Cf.* Raz, *The Authority of Law*, pp. 246–249. (Raz's ideas on law as a technique of achieving cooperation are emphatically not the object of my criticisms in the next few paragraphs of text.)

This is simply a mistake. The red-light example is by no means the best example for showing that this is a mistake, but notice that even in that example my stopping at a red light while someone else drives through the intersection is not only the behavior that coordination requires, it is also thoroughly act-utilitarian.[5]

Finally, even if there were an obligation of fair play which sometimes required non-act-utilitarian behavior, that would not entail a general moral obligation to obey the law, for the simple reason that the law might sometimes enact unfair cooperative schemes. Once we decide that some particular act required by some law is not required by fairness, then the fact that the law requires it provides no reason at all for doing it (not just a reason that is overridden, but no reason at all). Nor can we avoid this point by saying the legal system is a single overarching cooperative scheme which we should abide by so long as it is reasonably fair. There is no ground for thinking we have any basic obligation to follow all the details of a scheme, when those details are unrelated to fairness or perhaps even positively unfair, just because the scheme is reasonably fair as a whole.[6]

Of course, if there were a basic obligation of fair play, then the fair-play theorist could say the same thing about law that I say from the act-utilitarian perspective: he could say that many laws create *particular* moral obligations by setting up *particular* fair cooperative schemes which, once they are brought into existence, morally demand participation. But this would still be a case of laws creating moral obligations; it would not demonstrate the existence of a general moral obligation to obey the law.

In the last two paragraphs, which dealt with the relation between a hypothetical obligation of fair play and a general moral obligation to obey the law, I have gotten a bit ahead of myself by assuming some ideas I shall develop more carefully when I explain from the act-utilitarian point of view why there is no moral obligation to obey the law even though many laws create moral obligations. To reemphasize the main point made so far: the red-light example discussed above is a case in which law is intended to and does create moral obligations in the course of solving a coordination problem, without reference to any general moral obligation to obey the law and without requiring any non-act-utilitarian behavior.

Let us turn now to a different red-light example. Imagine that you are driving in a flat desert. You approach an intersection, and you are facing a red light. Sometimes there is traffic at this intersection (that accounts for the presence of the traffic light), but on this occasion you can see that there is no other car within a mile in any direction. The law unequivocally requires that

[5] For further discussion of the compatibility of coordination and act-utilitarian behavior, see my *Utilitarianism and Co-operation*, especially chs. 3, 4.

[6] For further discussion, see Smith, "Is There a Prima Facie Obligation," pp. 954–958.

you stop and wait for the light to change. Habit, or even prudence (in the form of uncertainty about whether there is a police helicopter overhead) may lead you to stop and wait for the light. But you have no moral obligation to stop or, having stopped, to wait. (When I say there is no moral obligation, I am not relying on a distinction between morality and prudence. For convenience, let us assume there is in fact no police helicopter. Now you have no moral obligation and no prudential "obligation" either.) There is simply *no reason at all*, moral or prudential, to stop at the light.

This case shows that there is no moral obligation to obey the law. The law requires you to stop and wait at the red light in the desert. If there is in fact no moral reason at all to stop and wait in the case as I have described it, then obviously the fact that stopping is required by law is not a moral reason to stop. But if the illegality of not stopping is not a moral reason to stop, then there cannot be a moral obligation (not even a *prima facie* moral obligation) to obey the law. What could we possibly mean by saying there was a moral obligation to obey the law, if that did not at least entail that the illegality of an act was *some* moral reason for avoiding the act? The fact I am pointing to when I say there is no moral obligation to obey the law is just this: there are some cases where a particular act is illegal but where there is no moral reason at all to avoid that act.

In a sense, of course, my argument begs the question. I simply *assert* that when you are faced with the red light in the desert in the circumstances I have imagined, you have no moral reason to stop. But in that sense, every argument from an example must beg the question. The point of examples is to help us see things clearly. My assumption is that one who reflects on my example (and, if necessary, on well-known refutations of various positive arguments for the existence of a general moral obligation to obey the law) will see, in the end, that there is in fact no moral reason at all to stop — in which case my other conclusions follow.[7]

Perhaps it will help if we compare the case of the red light in the desert with my original case of the red light at an intersection where there was cross traffic. In the original red-light case, I said I had a moral obligation to stop, which the law in fact created. But even in connection with the original case, I said something which might have prepared us for my conclusion about the red light in the desert. I said that my obligation to stop when there was traffic could be explained without any reference to the law. Once we have pointed

[7] My argument here obviously owes much to Smith, "Is There a Prima Facie Obligation," pp. 969–971. Just for completeness, I will stipulate, if the reader wishes, that no one observes my disobedience at the red light in the desert (so I cannot be setting a bad example); there is no danger of my present disobedience weakening my own resolve to obey other laws when obedience would have good consequences; and so on. All of this to guarantee that there really is no reason for obedience in this case.

out that there is oncoming traffic, that the person faced with a green light will be expecting me to stop, and that if I do not stop there will be an accident, then we have done all that needs to be done to account *logically* for the existence and the full strength of my moral obligation to stop. The obligation is completely accounted for, and the law has not been mentioned.

As I have said before, the law is part of the *causal* explanation for the existence of the circumstances that account logically for the obligation. Specifically, the law is part of the causal explanation of why the driver with the green light expects me to stop, which in turn is part of the explanation of why, if I do not stop, there will be an accident. And because the law is part of the causal explanation of the facts that constitute the logical explanation for the moral obligation to stop, the law is in an obvious sense part of the causal explanation for the existence of the obligation. But precisely because the law contributes only causally, and not logically, to the existence of the obligation, there may be cases, like the case of the red light in the desert, where it just turns out that the law does not actually cause the sort of facts that are logically related to the existence of a moral obligation. When that happens, there is a law, and there is legal obligation, but there is no moral reason at all to do as the law requires. The law has not caused the existence of a moral obligation in the way that it often does.[8]

It may not be entirely clear just what I mean by distinguishing between the law's being logically related to the existence of moral obligation and its being only causally related. By way of clarification, let me introduce a distinction between what I shall call "intrinsic" and "indicative" reasons.

Consider the original red-light case, in which I am confronted with a red light and there is oncoming traffic. In the final analysis, the reason I should stop is that if I do not stop, I will cause physical injury or, at least, property damage. The fact that some act will cause physical injury (let us concentrate on that) is always a morally relevant reason for avoiding that act. This reason may be outweighed. There may be competing moral reasons for doing the act which are more significant than the reason against doing the act constituted by the fact that it will cause physical injury. But even if the physical-injury reason is outweighed, it always counts. This sort of reason is what I call an "intrinsic reason" for action.

The illegality of driving through a red light, in contrast, is not an intrinsic reason for stopping. It is an indicative reason. Indicative reasons, as their name suggests, indicate the likely presence of intrinsic reasons. The fact that I am coming up to a red light at a traffic intersection is some indication

[8] It might occur to the reader that laws could not create any expectations at all, and therefore the law on traffic lights could not create a moral obligation even in the red-light-in-traffic case, unless people *believed* there was a moral obligation to obey the law. This is a mistake, for reasons I shall adumbrate in section III (without being able to develop them at length).

that there is an intrinsic reason for me to stop at that intersection (such as the intrinsic reason that I will cause physical injury if I do not stop). But the indicative reason does not guarantee the existence of any intrinsic reason at all, as we have seen in the case of the traffic light in the desert, in which the indicative reason turns out to be illusory. The force of the indicative reason may evaporate completely once we consider more facts. An indicative reason may be canceled, annulled. (Remember that no additional facts can make the force of an *intrinsic* reason evaporate. An intrinsic reason cannot be canceled or annulled; it can only be outweighed.)

In sum, intrinsic reasons are reasons which are logically connected with the existence of obligation, which is why they always count, while indicative reasons merely indicate the likely presence of particular intrinsic reasons. An intrinsic reason does not entail the existence of an obligation-all-things-considered. It entails a sort of a *prima facie* obligation, or a moral pressure. But, unlike an indicative reason, it *entails* such a *prima facie* obligation or moral pressure; it does not merely tend to suggest it.

(The distinction between intrinsic and indicative reasons is not a distinction peculiar to utilitarian analysis. Even deontologists will have use for such a distinction. So far as I can see, the main point of W. D. Ross's invention of *prima facie* obligations was to have a category of moral considerations with the same logical relation to obligations-all-things-considered as these things I prefer to call intrinsic reasons. Needless to say, even though utilitarians and deontologists both have use for the distinction between intrinsic and indicative reasons, they will differ on what reasons are to count as intrinsic and what as merely indicative. That is a matter of the substance of one's moral theory.)

One last point, lest my attempt to clarify cause new confusion. Intrinsic reasons are reasons that are logically connected with the existence of moral obligations, and what I meant earlier when I said the law was not logically related to moral obligation was just that illegality is not an intrinsic moral reason for avoiding an action. But as the counterpoise to my earlier claim that law was not logically related to moral obligation, I said that law was (often) causally related; and as the counterpoise to my more recent observation that illegality is not an intrinsic moral reason for action, I have said that law is an indicative reason. Obviously, being causally related to moral obligation is not exactly the same thing as being an indicative reason. It is because law is causally related to moral obligation in many red-light cases that it is an indicative reason in such cases. But something could be an indicative moral reason for action without making any causal contribution to the existence of the relevant moral obligation. Indeed, laws are often indicative reasons in this totally noncausal way, as we shall see in the example I now turn to.

Imagine that agricultural scientists discover that a recently introduced growth-enhancing chemical used on watermelons causes serious injury to people who ingest it. Accordingly, an appropriate regulatory agency forbids further use of the chemical. This is a case in which the law is a very significant indicative moral reason for not using the chemical even though the law makes no causal contribution to the existence of the intrinsic reasons for not using the chemical.

Someone might suggest that the regulation here does contribute to the intrinsic reasons for not using the chemical. The existence of the regulation encourages buyers of watermelons to expect that the chemical has not been used, and this encourages them to eat the watermelons, which is what will cause harm if the chemical has been used. But the expectations here do not play the same role in the explanation of why the chemical should not be used that the expectations surrounding red lights play in the explanation of why we should stop at them. If we assume that the only reason for growing watermelons is for human consumption, then regardless of the number of people who will actually buy and eat the contaminated watermelons, there is no possible gain, and some possible cost, from using the dangerous chemical. So, regardless of the number of people who will actually buy and eat the contaminated watermelons, the chemical should not be used. If the existence of the regulation proscribing the chemical generates expectations in some knowledgeable consumers that the chemical will not be used, that may increase the *number* of consumers who are at risk if the chemical is used. And in that sense, the weight of the intrinsic reasons for not using the chemical is increased. But we can give a complete explanation of why the chemical should not be used without reference to consumer expectations or to the regulation which generates them.

However, even though the regulation does not create the intrinsic reasons for avoiding the chemical, it can still be an important indicative reason. It may well be the regulation which first brings the dangerousness of the chemical to the watermelon growers' attention. The significance of the regulation is increased if we reflect that the promulgators of the regulation are likely to be much more expert than the growers on the matter of dangerousness. Doubting growers should almost certainly bow to the regulators' expertise. So the ban on the chemical is an extremely significant indicative reason to abandon the chemical, from the growers' point of view.

If we distinguish between objective and subjective obligation – where objective obligation is detemined by the facts of the case regardless of what the agent knows about the facts, while subjective obligation is defined as what the agent's objective obligation would be if the facts were as he believes them, or should reasonably believe them, to be – then even though the regulation which forbids the use of the growth-enhancing chemical does not create the *objective* moral obligation to abandon the chemical, still it creates a strong subjective obligation to abandon it. And it is the purpose of the law to create this subjective obligation, in just the same sense in which it is the purpose of the law about red lights to create the objective (and incidentally subjective) obligation to stop at them in most circumstances.

For the sake of a certain sort of completeness, I shall discuss one last example, a law that regulates private behavior in a very important way but that creates neither objective nor subjective moral obligation. Consider the law against murder. So long as people are disposed to commit murder, the law forbidding murder is important. (I assume there is some deterrent effect.) But the law against murder makes no contribution to our moral obligations not to commit murder. The explanation of why murder is (almost always) objectively wrong does not depend at all on expectations generated by the law against murder. (As with the ban on the growth-enhancing chemical for watermelons, the existence of a law against murder might lull some potential murder victims into a false sense of security and might thereby increase the number of opportunities which present themselves to a would-be murderer. But the law still contributes nothing to the explanation of why any particular murder is wrong.) Nor does the law against murder affect our subjective obligation not to commit murder. We know murder is wrong without needing the law to inform or remind us.

Let me quickly summarize what our examples have shown about law's relation to moral obligation, before I add a couple of final observations.

(1) There is no general moral obligation to obey the law, not even a *prima facie* obligation. This is shown by the fact that there can be cases in which an act is illegal but in which there is no intrinsic moral reason at all for avoiding it. (The red light in the desert.) The illegality of the act is not itself an intrinsic moral reason for avoiding the act.

(2) Some laws create objective moral obligations. That is to say, some laws contribute causally to the existence in certain circumstances of intrinsic moral reasons for adopting or avoiding the behavior the law requires or forbids. (The red light in traffic.) Furthermore, it is often part of the purpose of such laws to create such intrinsic reasons.

(3) One and the same law may create objective moral obligation (intrinsic reasons) in some cases to which it applies but not in other cases to which it applies. (The law about red lights.) This is what we would expect if we remember that law's contribution to the existence of intrinsic reasons is causal, not logical.

(4) Some laws create indicative reasons for action (subjective obligation). Laws which create important indicative reasons may include both laws which sometimes create intrinsic reasons (the law about red lights) and laws which do not create intrinsic reasons (the watermelon growth-enhancing

chemical regulation). It is often part of the purpose of a law to create indicative reasons for action.

(5) Some important laws regulating private behavior create no moral obligation of any kind, objective or subjective. They create neither intrinsic nor indicative reasons. (The law against murder.) This can be true even though there is a weighty moral obligation which coincides in content with the legal obligation the law imposes.

Now, as to the final observations: First, once we understand how laws can create moral obligations, we see further that laws can create moral obligations of widely varying strengths. The law that limits how long one may park at the same parking meter creates a genuine moral obligation, but a vastly weaker obligation than is created by the law about red lights when there is cross traffic.

In his well-known argument against the existence of a moral obligation to obey the law, M. B. E. Smith assumes implicitly that *if* there is something reasonably denominated "the moral obligation to obey the law," then it must be of the same strength in all cases in which it is relevant.[9] (Of course, the other reasons for or against some action may vary from case to case, so the obligation to obey the law will sometimes prevail and sometimes be defeated even though its strength is constant.)

For myself, I think Smith's assumption is a fair one: if what we are talking about really is just the moral obligation "to obey the law," then it would seem that the obligation ought to have the same strength whether the law is about parking meters or about murder. Notice I am not claiming that *all* obligations must be of constant strength in all cases. Consider, say, the obligation to avoid doing harm. Harm is something that comes in degrees, so it is both natural and sensible to talk about an obligation to avoid doing harm that comes in varying strengths. But illegality is not like harm; illegality does not come in degrees. We normally think that an act either is illegal, or it is not. We may not be certain which it is; but degrees of certainty are not the same as degrees of legality. So, it is specifically the supposed obligation to obey the law about which I am suggesting that it seems it ought to have a constant strength.

If, as Smith and I suggest, any "obligation to obey the law" ought to have a constant strength, then the fact that different laws so obviously create (moral) obligations of different strengths is evidence for the claim that even though laws do create moral obligations, the obligations are not sensibly regarded as instances of a general moral obligation to obey the law. (Without contradicting myself, I can add that *if* one is going to argue for a moral obligation to obey the law, then one ought to claim that that obligation comes

[9] Smith, "Is There a Prima Facie Obligation," pp. 970–971.

in varying strengths. Such is the claim of John Finnis, for example, who is to that extent on the right track — though Finnis does not adequately explain, to my mind, how it is that one and the same obligation "to obey the law" can vary in its strength from case to case.)[10]

Finally, although I have argued that there is no general moral obligation to obey the law, what I have said about the various ways in which laws can create moral obligations may tend to explain, historically and psychologically, the occurrence of loose talk about such a general moral obligation. And what I have to say in the remaining sections may add to the explanation.

II. HOW A MORAL AGENT SHOULD ALWAYS TAKE THE LAW INTO ACCOUNT

I have pointed out that individual laws are often indicative moral reasons for action. In fact, there is a sense in which illegality in general is a moral indicator: in a reasonably just modern society, an agent should not do an act which she knows to be illegal without giving thought to the question why the act is illegal and making sure that she has taken whatever it is the law is trying to accomplish adequately into account.

The argument for this claim is obvious enough. In a reasonably just modern society most laws have comprehensible purposes; most of the laws with comprehensible purposes are aimed at promoting genuine goods or avoiding genuine harms; and many of the laws aimed at promoting genuine goods or avoiding genuine harms are actually reasonably designed to accomplish their ends. Given all of that, it is worth an agent's time (morally) to give thought to possible explanations of the illegality of some action she is considering before she actually does the act, in order to make sure the law does not suggest some relevant consideration she might otherwise have overlooked or underestimated.[11]

Notice the various things I have *not* said in the course of explaining how illegality in general is a moral indicator. (1) I have not said that if the agent knows some act is illegal, that makes it more probable than not that the act in question is immoral. My claim is not about probabilities at all. (2) I have not

[10] John Finnis, *Natural Law and Natural Rights* (Oxford: Clarendon Press, 1980), pp. 314–320. Incidentally, Finnis is also one of the few people who have recognized that *promises* create obligations of widely varying strengths (p. 308). This obvious but neglected fact about promises moves me to deny that there is anything sensibly referred to as "the obligation to keep promises," just as I deny that there is an obligation to obey the law. Of course promises, like laws, are often intended to and often do create moral obligations; but that is a different claim.

[11] My claim here obviously resembles Raz's claim that a citizen might "trust" the lawmaking and judicial institutions of a generally good legal system (*The Authority of Law*, p. 245). But Raz seems primarily to suggest trust as a permissible reason for obedience, whereas my emphasis is on what the citizen is morally required to do before she disobeys.

said that if the agent knows some act is illegal, then she should not do the act unless she can adduce some positive moral reason for doing it. The agent might know the act is illegal but might decide on the basis of additional facts that the illegality indicates no actual intrinsic moral reason for avoiding the act. (3) I have not even said (or I have not meant to say) that an agent must not act illegally until she is sure she has figured out just why the act she is considering is illegal and just how important are any intrinsic moral reasons which the illegality indicates. Depending on the other reasons for and against an action, there may be wide variation in how much thought or investigation is required in order to have taken the illegality adequately into account. (4) Finally, I have not contradicted my claim in the previous section that the law against murder creates no significant indicative reason. My claim in this section entails that an agent who knows murder is illegal should not commit murder until she is reasonably sure she knows what the point of the law against murder is; but since no sane person could lose track of the point of the law against murder, the law against murder is not a *significant* indicative moral reason in any sane agent's thinking. Nor is it intended to be.

Once we are clear about all the things I have not said, it may seem that what I have said is very weak. From one perspective it is indeed weak, weak to the point of vanishing. What I have said does not give illegality any intrinsic moral weight; nor does it guarantee that illegality always indicates a reason of any intrinsic moral weight.

From another perspective, however, the claim I have made is a strong one. It is a claim about the moral significance of illegality *in general*. The significance is merely subjective and cautionary; but it attaches to illegality across the board (in a reasonably just modern society).

I suspect that not infrequently in ordinary discourse the real force of reminders that some act is illegal is to encourage the agent to look again at certain consequences she may have slighted in her deliberations. And I suspect that this subjective and cautionary moral relevance of illegality in general helps to account for our inclination to say there is a general moral obligation to obey the law.

III. LAW IN A SOCIETY OF SAINTS

Brief as it is, this section will begin with a coherent theme and then degenerate into a loosely connected miscellany of observations. The coherent theme is this: Our inclination to say there is a moral obligation to obey the law may actually reflect an inchoate understanding that law is a valuable institution in a very deep sense. Law is not merely a necessary evil, a social technique for holding in check the selfish and criminal tendencies that abound in any actual society. Rather, law would have a role even in a society of saints.

Perhaps it is not obvious why the fact that law would have a role in a society. But I think it does. If there would be no law in an ideal society – if law were nothing more than a tool of social engineering for mitigating present evils – then it would seem more natural to many people to say that present evils — then it would seem more natural to many people to say that law can be ignored when the goals of the law can be better promoted by ignoring the law than by obeying it. On the other hand, if law has a role in an ideal society, that seems to give law an intrinsic value, for which we show proper respect by asserting a moral obligation, even in our imperfect society, to obey the law.

The tendency I have just suggested is not a necessary feature of our psychology; there is even a contrary tendency. With some people, feelings about the fragility of social organization in our actual, very unsaintly, world probably contribute more to the desire to assert a moral obligation to obey the law than do any considerations of the ideal. Still, for many other people the idea that law has a role in an ideal society would suggest, through the mediation of the idea that law is therefore morally valuable, that we have an obligation to obey the law.

As to how it is that law has a role in an ideal society, notice that because I am a utilitarian, my notion of an ideal society is much more ideal than many people's notion. On one common (nonutilitarian) view, people have conflicting goals inevitably and essentially. The "ideal" society is one in which everyone subordinates his pursuit of his own particular goals to principles of justice which are designed to palliate and channel the unavoidable conflict. In this ideal society, law presumably has an important role, but it is no part of my project to specify just what that role is. In my ideal society, my society of (utilitarian) saints, there is no fundamental conflict at all. But even so, there is a need for institutions to disseminate information about the consequences of various actions and to organize cooperation; and as we have seen, these are functions the law can and does perform (both in our very imperfect actual society and in the ideal).

I would go so far as to claim that informed and self-conscious cooperation is an intrinsically valuable activity of great importance. (Here is the one point at which I make a possibly controversial axiological claim.) Since cooperation in large schemes between strangers can only be organized by the law (or by some essentially analogous social institution), law is an essential means to achieving something of intrinsic value. I think law remains a means; but one might well suggest that the more nearly society approaches the ideal, the harder it is to distinguish meaningfully between obedience to law and participation in a large-scale cooperative scheme[12] – and if we cannot

[12] *Cf.* J. L. Mackie, "Obligations to Obey the Law," *Virginia Law Review*, vol. 67 (1981), pp. 143–158, 150.

distinguish at all, then we must admit that *in this context* obedience to law takes on intrinsic value and becomes morally obligatory.

Whether or not we think obedience to law as such becomes obligatory in my ideal society, it is certainly (and perhaps paradoxically) true that the better the society, the higher will be the proportion of laws that create moral obligations. This is not simply because a better society will have better and wiser legislators. It is rather because the better the society, the less need there will be for laws which enforce totally independent moral obligations, such as the law against murder. In a very imperfect society, even the laws promulgated by a perfectly wise legislator would often create no moral obligation at all. Much effort would be devoted to stopping murder and the like. The better the society, the higher the proportion of laws that will be devoted to creating cooperative schemes and providing information for well-disposed but non-omniscient citizens to act on. In short, the higher will be the proportion of laws that *create* moral obligation.

Another feature of the ideal society that leads to a mild paradox about the relation between legal and moral obligation is this. In an ideal society, where individuals are not only well-motivated in general terms but can be counted on to use the subjectively most appropriate rules of thumb for estimating consequences in whatever situations they find themselves, all laws would contain act-utilitarian excusing conditions. Driving through the red light in the desert would be permitted if the circumstances made it a reasonable choice. (In our actual society laws do not normally have act-utilitarian excusing conditions because individuals cannot be trusted not to abuse such excusing conditions, whether intentionally or by unconscious self-preference; and the administrative burden of separating the excused (or justified) violations from the unexcused case by case, if the act-utilitarian excuse were allowed, would be too great. In the ideal society, however, people can be trusted not to abuse the excusing conditions. Indeed, we would never need to review the individual's choice; anyone who thought he was excused (having, of course, taken the law into account) would be excused – perhaps only subjectively, but if so, then still in a sufficiently strong sense so that there would be no point in punishing the act even though it was objectively wrong.)

But if every law includes an act-utilitarian excusing condition, then there will never be a case where legal and moral obligation diverge. Someone might suggest that this casts doubt on the claim that in the ideal society there is no moral obligation to obey the law.[13] For myself, I do not see any problem for the claim that there is no moral obligation to obey the law (except, perhaps, the problem I have already mentioned, viz., the difficulty of dis-

[13] This possibility was raised by Philip Soper in a discussion of my paper.

tinguishing between obedience to law and participation in a large cooperative scheme). It is true that we could not *prove* the nonexistence of a moral obligation to obey the law by adducing an actual case where there was legal obligation but no moral reason at all to comply (as we did with the red-light-in-the-desert case in our imperfect society, where laws do not contain act-utilitarian excusing conditions). But that does not mean we could not still *see* that there was no moral obligation to obey the law, either by bringing forward hypothetical cases from an imperfect society or by just seeing, on moral reflection, that it is not legality or illegality that is fundamentally morally significant. Incidentally, if we could not prove the nonexistence of the moral obligation to obey the law in my ideal society, we equally could not prove that it was important to recognize or to posit such an obligation, since one would never have any legal obligation which was not duplicated in content by some moral obligation which might be caused by the law but which was logically explicable without any reference to the law.

On a related point, it might seem that we need at least a general *belief* in the moral obligation to obey the law to explain how law could produce cooperation at all. Why do we assume other people will do their part in the legally stipulated scheme if not because we assume they will think they are obligated? The answer, which I cannot develop here, is that if all the potential participants in the scheme are well-motivated and understand the law as indicating a superior pattern of joint behavior which it would be desirable for all to adopt, then there is no reason why the existence of the law as an indicator should not produce new mutually coherent intentions and expectations of cooperative behavior on all sides, without the help of any notion that the law as such obligates.

The discussion of this section should have made it clear why I did not mention in the first section certain actual but uninteresting ways in which laws may create moral obligation. From a utilitarian point of view, once a law is passed one may have a number of moral reasons to obey it: disobedience may lead to punishment, which is a bad consequence one has an obligation to avoid even when it occurs to oneself; justified disobedience may set an example for others which will be misinterpreted and will stimulate unjustified disobedience; any instance at all of lawbreaking may create resentment and similar painful feelings in other people who obey the law and want the law to be obeyed all the time; even justified disobedience might conceivably contribute to a lawbreaking disposition in the agent which would lead to unjustified lawbreaking on other occasions; and so on. These are all moral reasons for doing what the law requires which come into existence only with the adoption of the law, so they are in a sense moral reasons which the law creates. But these reasons would not exist in a society of saints. Nor is creating these reasons ever the ultimate purpose behind the adoption of any particular law, even in an imperfect society. So, the modes of legal creation of moral obligation that I have focused on are the modes that are essential to law's function.

A CONCLUDING REMINDER OF OUR STARTING POINT

I am at least as conscious as the reader of the fact that this essay has been a potpourri mixing moderately precise argument and rather impressionistic "suspecting" and "suggesting." My excuse is the nature of the question from which we started: Why, given that there is no general moral obligation to obey the law, are we not content simply to say there is no obligation and have done with it? Why does law have a halo? Why does an attitude of "respect for law" (Joseph Raz's phrase, though I mean to use it more loosely than he) seem to some extent required and not merely permissible, as Raz suggests?[14] The moderately precise argumentation in this essay has been about what law's connections with moral obligation really are, in both imperfect and ideal societies. The impressionistic bits have been about how the real connections of law and moral obligation generate law's halo. Halos, for better or worse, resist precise analysis.

Law and Philosophy, University of Michigan

[14] Raz, *The Authority of Law*, pp. 249, 260.

CHOOSING A LEGAL THEORY ON MORAL GROUNDS

BY PHILIP SOPER

I. INTRODUCTION

Twenty-five years is roughly the time that has elapsed since the exchange between H. L. A. Hart and Lon Fuller[1] and the subsequent revival in this country of the natural law/positivism debate.[2] During this time, a curious thing has happened to legal positivism. What began as a conceptual theory about the distinction between law and morality has now been turned, at least by some, into a moral theory. According to this theory, the reason we must see law and morality as separate is not (at least not entirely) because of the logic of our language, but because of the practical implications of holding one or the other of the two traditional views in this area. The natural law theorist, it is said, can connect law and morality only at the cost of investing official directives with undeserved moral authority, thus encouraging obedience where there should be none. The natural law position should therefore be rejected – and the positivist's accepted – on moral grounds.[3]

What makes this position doubly curious is the contrast it presents with the moral implications that previously surrounded this debate. Hart's claim about the separation of law and morals was initially presented as a neutral theory about the concept of law; it was not presented as a moral or political theory. Moreover, it was Fuller in the earlier debate who claimed to occupy the moral high ground by suggesting that evil regimes like Nazi Germany were in some way a consequence of German positivism. Hart took pains to deny this alleged connection between positivism and the emergence or viability of unjust states. But he did so again largely by emphasizing the

[1] See Hart, *Positivism and the Separation of Law and Morals*, 71 Harv. L. Rev. 593 (1958); Fuller, *Positivism and Fidelity to Law – a Reply to Professor Hart*, 71 Harv. L. Rev. 630 (1958).

[2] The debate continued with the subsequent publication of Hart's influential book, The Concept of Law (1961), and Fuller's The Morality of Law (1964, rev. ed. 1969). For Fuller's own description of the various "rounds" in this exchange, see the revised edition of the latter at 188 ("A Reply to Critics").

[3] See MacCormick, *A Moralistic Case for A-Moralistic Law*, 20 Valparaiso L. Rev. 1, 9–10, *passim*; *id.*, H. L. A. Hart (1981), at 159–62. MacCormick's precise argument, which differs somewhat from the above characterization, is quoted below.

morally neutral character of the positivist's theory, which leaves open the question whether to obey the laws of such a state.[4]

In this paper I examine these moral claims about the consequences of choosing a particular legal theory. My general conclusion will be a skeptical one. I argue that the particular moral argument recently advanced for legal positivism fails: there are no adverse practical consequences to be expected from viewing law and morality as connected. I do not, however, conclude that honors for the morally superior theory must therefore be returned to the natural law theorist, for it is equally clear, I think, that no unhappy consequences attend adoption of the positivist's view either. The upshot, if I am correct, is that no practical consequences of any kind or, at least, not of the kind that concerns ordinary moral theory, attend this debate at all.

This conclusion implies, not that the debate is verbal or meaningless, but that its resolution must be sought in the cognitive arena, rather than the moral one. The importance of the debate arises from the long-standing concern to understand the *existing* connections between such basic concepts as justice, law, authority, and obligation. Of course, we may seek such understanding because our ultimate interests are moral and involve the question what ought to be done. Moreover, because morality itself is such a difficult concept, we will undoubtedly find that comparing "legal" and "moral" obligation helps us to define and understand the features of both. In these respects, moral interests may guide and motivate the inquiry, even though the inquiry itself remains primarily conceptual.[5] In the last part of this paper, I describe this enterprise more fully and consider its relationship to moral and political theory.

II. THE MORAL CASE FOR POSITIVISM

The moral argument for legal positivism, briefly described above, has been most explicitly advanced by Neil MacCormick:

> The practical argument is that states, governments, wielders of power in general, will in practice be able to manipulate the idea of "law." If we insist that nothing is really "law" unless it passes a

[4] To be sure, Hart did suggest that these moral issues would be clarified by keeping law and morality separate. But that claim falls short of the new moral arguments being advanced on behalf of positivism which predict not just moral confusion, but actual immoral conduct (an undermining of the "sovereignty of conscience"), as the consequence of failing to preserve the distinction. See MacCormick, *A Case for A-Moralistic Law*, at 10.

[5] By "conceptual," I do not mean that the goal is to set out complete conditions for the proper use of "law" or "legal system." The critical agenda for legal theory, which may be related to this definitional one, is conceptual clarification: probing what we mean by both morality and law in order to see whether the moral claims we make in the name of law are consistent. See note 27, *infra*. Of course in conducting this enterprise, one may find that one is inevitably engaged in substantive moral argument: i.e., by "conceptual" I do not mean to suggest that a sharp distinction can be drawn between "meta" and substantive inquiries.

> substantive moral test as well as a "formal sources" test, we risk *enhancing* the moral aura which states and governments can assume, even if our true hope is to cut out of the realm of "law" evil and unjustifiable acts of legislation and of government.
>
> The argument of last resort here is an argument for the final sovereignty of conscience, and how best to preserve it. . . . [A] powerful case, and perhaps a sufficiently powerful case, can be made out for the positivist position on purely practical and moral grounds. For my own part, I do not believe that any sufficient case can be made out which does not at least include these moral and practical grounds, these arguments for conceptually buttressing the sovereignty of moral conscience.[6]

MacCormick's argument is attractive because it includes a claim about the final sovereignty of conscience which is both important and correct: "[E]very order of positive law or positive morality ought always to be subjected to the critical judgment of an enlightened morality . . . ."[7] This claim, however, is only one half of the argument. The other half – in my view, the incorrect half – is the claim that the way to get people to adopt this critical attitude toward state authority is to insist on the conceptual distinction between legal validity and moral value.

To see why the conceptual distinction is unlikely to affect ordinary attitudes and behavior, imagine two hypothetical citizens. One, call him Gandhi, is ideally conscientious; the other, call him Eichmann, is not. By *conscientious*, I mean that Gandhi already possesses the morally desirable trait of testing all legal demands by reference to critical morality before deciding what to do. Eichmann, in contrast, never appraises law but always complies, just as a soldier might unquestioningly comply with a superior's orders.[8]

[6] N. MacCormick, *A Case for A-Moralistic Law*, at 10–11. MacCormick previously advanced this view as a tentative interpretation of Hart's own position, see *id.*, H. L. A. Hart, at 160 (referring to Hart, Concept of Law, at 206). But as the text notes, Hart's arguments were always primarily conceptual, rather than moral. It is not without interest that someone like MacCormick who, with some minor variations, carries on in the positivist tradition of Hart, finds it necessary now to turn to normative arguments to defend that tradition. The discomfort that leads to this turn of events may be due to the inability of the positivist to connect law *conceptually* with the normative implication that "law" justifies coercion. Compare P. Soper, A Theory of Law (1984).

[7] MacCormick, H. L. A. Hart, at 162.

[8] Such automatic compliance could, of course, be due to a conscientiously held moral theory according to which laws were thought always to have overriding moral authority. That would be an incorrect moral theory, but would still qualify citizen Eichmann as conscientious, however wrong. I assume for purposes of the argument that Eichmann's compliance is unthinking and not the result of a moral judgment about either the content or legitimacy of law. It should also be clear that when I describe Gandhi as subjecting the demands of law to the inspection of critical morality, I do not mean to deny that Gandhi's view of critical morality may permit or require compliance with some laws even though Gandhi believes them to be misguided or wrong in their content.

How is the behavior of either Gandhi or Eichmann affected by the choice between natural law and positivism?

Begin with positivism. Assume that Gandhi and Eichmann both live in a society that has accepted the positivist's claim about the distinction between law and morality. The few natural law theorists who remain are treated like flat-earthers, with bemused tolerance, while all others accept without question that legal validity is determined without reference to moral tests. How will Gandhi and Eichmann behave? Gandhi, of course, will behave as he always has, subjecting the claims of law to the test of critical morality, so the critical case is that of Eichmann. But Eichmann, by hypothesis, is unconscientious. He does not critically appraise the demands made on him, but defers his judgment to others – either out of fear, laziness, or the ease of going along. Eichmann too, then, will behave as he always does, complying with the law automatically without engaging in critical reflection.

Does behavior change if we now imagine a revolt in legal theory? All citizens (including Gandhi and Eichmann) now believe and are taught that nothing is law if it does not meet certain minimum moral requirements, as well as formal tests for validity? Eichmann, of course, continues to obey without thinking as always, so the critical case is now that of Gandhi. But Gandhi's behavior doesn't change either, since he reacts not to what legislators and judges claim is the case, but to what his moral conscience tells him is the case about the compatibility of formal law with moral requirements.

Part of the problem here is that deciding between positivism and natural law at the level of legal theory will not affect the claims of officials *within* a society about the moral legitimacy of the laws they enact. Assuming that officials are thorough positivists only means that they deny any necessary connection between law and morality. It does not prevent their claiming a contingent connection and asserting that their own legal order is, happily, a moral one. MacCormick is aware of this problem, but does not seem to realize how it undermines the attempt to put the case for positivism on moral grounds:

> When evil is done in the name of the law, the greatest evil is that whatever is done in the name of the law is also and inevitably done in the name of a public morality.
>
> Hence it seems simply inconceivable that appeals to law – even iniquitous law – can ever shed their moral load. . . . [or] that it will ever be thought other than virtuous, albeit at a modest point on the scale of virtue, for a person to be 'law-abiding' – even when the law by which he or she abides contains much of evil. By the same

token, the law breaker however conscientious, will be stigmatized by the legal officials as a moral wrongdoer and a moral danger.[9]

The fact that law comes "morally loaded" regardless of one's legal theory makes it difficult to see how one might vary the Gandhi/Eichmann example to sustain MacCormick's claim. Here are two possibilities. First, it might be suggested that my example is flawed because it assumes citizens who are already conscientious or not and thus no longer subject to reform through the choice of legal theory. MacCormick's claim might be an educational one: the way to bring up citizens so that they become Gandhis and not Eichmanns is to teach the positivist view from the beginning, instilling in yet-unformed citizens the understanding that no moral tests are part of the criteria for law and urging such citizens to develop for themselves the capacity of sifting formal law through moral filters. But this suggestion highlights the difficulty. It is indeed the case that what we want to do, given my assumption about the correctness of the moral half of MacCormick's argument, is train citizens to be conscientious. (We ought also to put Eichmann back in school and retrain him.) The question is how one's view about the conceptual distinction between law and morality can have any bearing on this educational goal. If we succeed in making citizens conscientious, it will not be because of the legal theory. It will be because of the arguments about why individual autonomy and moral reflection are inescapable and the judgments of others always potentially fallible. Those arguments are not arguments of legal theory, because they are arguments that both positivists and natural law theorists can and do accept. A good positivist knows there is no necessary connection between law and morality. But nothing in that knowledge explains whether he knows what morality is or, more importantly, whether he cares about finding out. Graduates of schools of positivism or of natural law, it seems, must both make their way to some other school to find their moral consciences.

The above response, however, shows only that legal theory, whether natural law or positivist, cannot ensure conscientiousness. It does not yet show us whether one or the other theory might actually interfere with the development of individual moral sovereignty. This claim, that natural law results in the diminution of individual, moral, and political responsibility, has been made by others.[10] The basis for the indictment, as MacCormick's

[9] MacCormick, H. L. A. Hart, at 161. MacCormick makes this point, apparently not to qualify the moral argument for positivism which he accepts, *id.*, at 162, but as a criticism of Hart's failure to recognize that law itself is "in the sense of 'positive morality' a moral order." *Id.*, 160.

[10] See S. I. Shuman, Legal Positivism (1963), at 204–209. For criticism of the claim, see J. Stone, Human Law and Human Justice 253–54 (1965). Professor Stone's discussion of this issue has been valuable to my own thinking and may explain why I share his similarly skeptical conclusions about the attempt to resolve this debate on moral grounds.

argument makes clear, is the assumption that there is some additional power of officials to secure obedience and deter individual moral evaluation of "law," if they can present law as already consistent with morality. Thus, a society that adopts the natural law position will present citizens with the claim that law is not only valid by reference to the required formal tests, but that these laws have already been inspected for moral adequacy because otherwise they could not be claimed to be "laws." Of course, a conscientious citizen should not take this moral endorsement at face value, and citizen Gandhi presumably will not. But ordinary people lie somewhere between the extremes of Gandhi and Eichmann, and many of them will find that the official moral endorsement is just the excuse or reason they need to defer their own judgment and obey the law. To put the argument in constitutional terms, imagine two Supreme Court decisions rejecting, say, a challenge to the draft laws. One decision sustains the state's action on the basis of the Court's interpretation of existing statutes, but the Court explicitly disavows any opinion about the justice or morality of the draft law itself. The other decision reaches the same conclusion about the statute but also explicitly indicates – because of the due process clause in the Constitution – that the statute passes minimum requirements of fairness and, thus, is not too immoral to be enforced. Is not the latter decision more likely to deter citizens from making their own evaluation? If citizen conscientiousness is our goal, would we not sooner achieve that goal by removing any moral filters – even as a contingent matter in connection with our own Constitution – as tests for deciding what is "law"?

This argument, I believe, has some force, but it does not raise a question about the desirability of the natural law position so much as about the desirability of establishing particular, official institutions to pass on the moral merits of official directives. With or without a due process clause, the officials who enact and support the draft law will presumably claim that it is morally justified. Thus, the legislators will purport to have made and will continue to endorse the judgment about the moral validity of the law which the Supreme Court, in the first imagined case, refused to make. It may be true that fewer citizens would defer to the legislature's moral judgment than would defer to the moral judgment of the Court for reasons familiar to those who explain why judicial review is lodged in the Court in the first place. But none of this seems to me to be a consequence of adopting a natural law view about the connection between law and morality. It is a consequence of deciding to filter official directives through institutions which, for whatever reason, enjoy sufficient respect and prestige to give their moral judgments extra weight. If one accepts the empirical premise – that these institutions enjoy more prestige as moral judges – then a positivist society could also happily use the same institution to reenforce its claims about the morality of its laws. (The monarch who also has the Church behind him has more chance of persuading citizens to defer their moral judgments to the official moral judgment.) Of course, doing so involves risks – the risk that the more prestigious judiciary (or other institution) will disagree about the moral merits of legislation; but weighing that risk against the possibility of reducing citizen disobedience can occur independently of the underlying legal theory.

III. THE MORAL CASE FOR NATURAL LAW

In the Hart/Fuller exchange, it was positivism that found itself on the defensive against the charge that it was responsible for the abdication of individual moral responsibility in Nazi Germany. It should be clear from what has been said that this charge seems no more capable of being sustained as an indictment of positivism than of natural law. Indeed, Hart's response to the charge was similar in many respects to the response given above: the fact that law and morality were seen as separate does not explain why individuals in Germany would defer to law rather than to their own assessment of the morality of action.[11] It is easy to imagine ways in which such deference *might* be explained. It might, for example, have something to do with the acceptance of an erroneous political theory about the absolute moral authority of the state, however unjust its laws. Or the explanation might lie in social–psychological theories about the "tendency of most people to submit to actual power, and even to the 'normative tendency of the factual.'"[12] But the suggestion that the legal theory itself had a causal influence is difficult to defend.[13]

Fuller, however, levels another charge against positivism. This charge focuses not on the connection between legal theory and individual moral responsibility, but on the connection between legal theory and the ability of those bent on doing evil within a legal system to achieve their ends. Here is the clearest statement of the indictment.

[11] See Hart, *Positivism*, at 617–618.

[12] See Stone, Human Law, at 255.

[13] Fuller's argument relied in part on the example of the German philosopher Radbruch who appeared to undergo a conversion from positivism to natural law as a result of the Nazi experience. But attempts to understand exactly how Radbruch thought this conversion was connected to legal positivism confront a major problem. Radbruch's most significant conversion seems to have taken place within moral theory. Prior to the conversion, Radbruch's ethical views seemed either highly relativistic (there is no objective way to test the morality of law) or else they gave overwhelming weight to the legal value of certainty over the demands of justice. See generally, Stone, Human Law, at 232–262. It is easy to understand why anyone holding such views might decide such a *moral* theory was inadequate after witnessing the horrors of Nazism. But there is no explanation here for why this change in moral theory is connected to a change in legal theory. Confusion over the significance of Radbruch's conversion may be in part a reflection of the failure to distinguish between natural law as a moral theory and natural law as a legal theory. See Soper, *Legal Theory and the Problem of Definition*, 50 Chi. L. Rev. 1170 (1983).

> [L]et us suppose a judge bent on realizing through his decisions an objective that most ordinary citizens would regard as mistaken or evil. Would such a judge be likely to suspend the letter of the statute by openly invoking a "higher law"? Or would he be more likely to take refuge behind the maxim that "law is law" and explain his decision in such a way that it would appear to be demanded by the law itself?[14]

Fuller's claim is that positivism encourages the kind of buck-passing imagined in one of my previous examples in which the Supreme Court interprets and enforces a draft law, but avoids moral responsibility for the result by disclaiming power to review for fairness. A natural law society, in contrast, would in essence have incorporated a "due process clause" through its legal theory, thus blocking the Court's ability to hide behind its "role."

The validity of this argument partly depends on whether one agrees with Fuller about the inability to "justify" really evil aims. If, after all, it is not only the judges but other officials as well who support the result, the likelihood that a rationale for the result could not be offered may be slim.[15] Note also that the argument relies on empirical assumptions that contrast markedly with those considered in the previous section. The moral argument of the positivist is that if we come to believe that only those official directives are "law" that pass minimum moral tests, then evil will have an easier time: it will reinforce human tendencies to externalize responsibility. Fuller's claim is different. His concern is not with the possibility of preempting independent citizen evaluation, but with the possibility of diffusing evaluation. Concerned citizens, outraged by the evil result, will find they cannot muster what they need in terms of support to overturn the decision because they cannot get a response out of the system. The image is a rather modern one. It is the bureaucratic shell game which avoids citizen complaints by passing them from one agency to another for a response on the merits until the objections diffuse in general frustration.

I have tried to make Fuller's argument as vivid and realistic as possible in order to emphasize that if it fails as an indictment of positivism, it is not because of its empirical assumptions, but because it misses its intended target. The buck-passing scenario is not a consequence of legal positivism, but of a particular societal arrangement for enacting and enforcing laws. To see this, assume *arguendo* that Fuller is right about the restraints entailed by the need to justify. Presumably, then, an evil regime operating in a society that has embraced the natural law view, will also want on occasion to avoid

[14] Fuller, *Positivism*, at 637.

[15] Nazi Germany's reliance on secrecy does, however, provide some empirical support for Fuller's claim.

having to justify its decisions in the way we have just imagined. The critical assumption in Fuller's argument is that a natural law theory will not allow this to be done. But all that natural law requires, in the form that I am considering, is that the regime endorse the view that if official directives are too "unjust," they are not "law." There is nothing in this claim that requires one to institutionalize the process of testing the "justice" of the law in a forum of the sort that Fuller has in mind in talking about the Court. Thus, our imagined regime could simply disempower the Court from considering the merits of the claim. The Court's response could no longer be expressed in the same terms Fuller suggests. It could not claim "This is the law, and we have no power to consider its morality." Instead, its claim would be, "This passes the formal tests for law; whether it passes the substantive tests is a matter we cannot consider, though presumably the legislature has concluded that it does." Thus, the litigant is off on his wildgoose chase after a justification on the merits.

This rejoinder raises critical questions. Is it part of what we mean by a "court" that it must always reach results that it believes accord with "the law." If so, then the above institution is not a court because it has only done half of its job – checked the formal, but not the material status of the statute. Can a society decide not to have courts at all, or not to have some questions decided by courts, and still be a legal system? The answer to that seems to be a qualified yes, at least as respects partial withdrawal of questions from courts, since our own legal system exempts some questions from the competence of courts to decide. Of course, there is a price to pay for thus escaping the need to justify in this way.[16] One must again balance the desire to get away with evil (if that is the motive) against the damage one does to the general institution of the court which even the evil regime will want to use in most cases to underscore its general claim to be ruling justly. But that is a strategic problem that the positivist regime also faces, so again it does not appear that there is a moral advantage here for either theory.

Fuller's argument about natural law constraining evil judges seems to assume an evil judge working within an evil regime. How is the argument affected if we suppose, now, that the regime does not support the wicked ends the judge is trying to impose? The danger of such a judge getting his way is, of course, lessened by the likelihood of legislative response to overturn the decision or remove the judge. But even if some danger remains, it should be clear again that it will exist independently of whether the society believes there are moral tests for law. Thus, a "good" positivist regime might

[16] For further discussion of the connection between the concept of a court and of a legal system, and of the costs involved in dispensing with courts as the primary justificatory organ, see Soper, A Theory of Law, at 113.

also be concerned about "evil" judges who, if they could avoid the need to justify and thus reach decisions inconsistent with the regime's goals, might prove troublesome just because judicial decisions are always to some extent insulated, by time if nothing else, from immediate legislative correction. In that case, the sensible thing for the positivist regime to do is to adopt something like a constitutional due process clause and require judges to enforce "the law." That will cut off a court's ability to hide behind its "role" in refusing to justify a decision, because its role ("find the law") will now require testing official directives for compatibility with minimal moral standards. It has been suggested that a regime that adopted such moral tests for law would no longer be positivist, but as long as the connection with morality remains contingent, it is hard to see why this is so.[17] Indeed, this example illustrates the basic flaw in arguments like Fuller's. If a regime thinks that the empirical claim about evil being constrained by the need to justify is plausible, then – regardless of whether the regime thinks moral tests are *necessarily* part of the test for law – it can take advantage of that empirical fact by requiring any institution – or official – to justify a decision that declares, enacts, or otherwise finds the law. Thus, a positivist regime could even require legislators to write opinions defending the morality of proposed legislation prior to enactment, if it were thought that such a procedure would help ensure better results. All of these strategies seem independent of the prevailing legal theory.

So far I have considered arguments about the effect of legal theory on two kinds of citizens – the conscientious and the unconscientious. I have also considered the potential constraints legal theory might place on one kind of official: the evil judge. What about the opposite kind of judge: the good judge attempting to achieve morally desirable results in a regime that does not support him? Will he have a better chance in a natural law or a positivist regime? Robert Cover's book,[18] analyzing the dilemma faced by antislavery judges who enforced fugitive slave laws, presents a possible test case. Indeed, Ronald Dworkin interprets the dilemma these judges faced as proof that legal theory was partly to blame for judicial failure to move the country more rapidly toward the abolition of slavery.[19] Dworkin's interpretation, however, is not one that will help us in deciding whether there are moral implications in the debate between natural law and positivism as I am using those terms. Dworkin's claim is that if judges had correctly interpreted the available institutional materials, they would have seen that the law supported

[17] Compare Dworkin, Taking Rights Seriously (1977), at 345, with Soper, A Theory of Law, at 181 n. 3.

[18] Cover, Justice Accused (1975).

[19] See Dworkin, *The Law of the Slave-Catchers*, Times Literary Supplement, Dec. 5, 1975, p. 1437 (review of R. Cover, Justice Accused (1975)).

the antislavery result the judge wanted to reach. Thus, there need not have been a dilemma between the judge's role and the morally correct decision. Whether or not Dworkin is correct about what the institutional materials indicated at the time[20] makes no difference, because the "rights thesis" which underlies Dworkin's claim about how judges were supposed to decide cases is independent of the natural law/positivism distinction.[21] A positivist regime, if it thought it made sense to tell judges to seek the best answer even in hard cases, could so instruct judges with the result that the failure here, if it was one, must again be charged not to legal theory but to the particular theory of adjudication judges were using.

The argument that must be made in the case of the antislavery judge goes something like this. Judges in a natural law regime who are morally ahead of the rest of society will be free to express their moral judgments and base their opinions on them without fear of criticism for stepping outside the limits of their role. In doing so, they are more likely to move society ahead in line with their, presumably correct, moral views. This is not possible in a positivist regime which insists on separating "the law" that the judge must enforce from judgments about its morality.

One difficulty with this argument, of course, is that it assumes that the individual judges who are being "freed" to advance society in accordance with their own views do indeed have the correct views. If natural law has the posited freeing effect for those who do not like the accepted rules, it will free in both directions: the proslavery judge after the Civil War, who wants to return, as well as the antislavery judge who wants to "move forward." But there are other problems. Individual judges acting on their own moral lights are not likely to have much chance of reversing the contrary moral judgment of the rest of society. Indeed, if such judges are continually reversed by other judges or replaced by society, at some point the invitation to keep moral tests in view in reaching legal decisions is going to be so obviously futile that a good judge would do better to resign or look for other ways to change opinion. Even in a natural law society, some Court at some point must have the final say about whether the moral tests for law have been met; individual judges who continue to flout that highest court's decisions are not likely to find that they are any more "free" to do so than their positivist analogues.

Yet the argument might still have purchase. Even though individual judges are not likely to immediately effect a change in the rest of society, the fact that they are encouraged to engage in moral evaluation in reaching their decisions might initiate a dialogue that could lead to reevaluation of existing

[20] Serious doubts about this part of Dworkin's claim are raised in Greenawalt, *Policy, Rights, and Judicial Decision*, 11 Ga. L. Rev. 993, 1050–51 (1977).

[21] This claim is defended more fully in Soper, A Theory of Law, at 115–117, 129–30.

doctrine as other courts and society attempt to respond to the moral arguments of the enlightened judges. If judges continue to be reversed, then presumably at some point the prevailing moral judgment should be seen as preventing further argument within the role of judge. But the constant possibility of being allowed to test existing doctrine and force a definitive moral response could well result at least sometimes in greater forward progress.

This argument will be seen to have considerable affinity with Fuller's argument about evil judges. Indeed, it rests on similar assumptions about the relationship between moral dialogue and the direction of moral progress. Where Fuller focused on preventing evil by requiring justification, we are now focusing on undoing evil through the same means: requiring the system to respond to the demand to justify. Because the arguments are so similar, it should not surprise that the same response is available here that we gave above. There is no necessary connection between the society's prevailing legal theory and whether or not it has designed courts to permit this continued possibility of built-in challenge and response. A natural law society, if it preferred not to allow judges to demand justification for settled doctrine, could restrict their role to determining only whether directives passed the required formal tests. In that case, legislators could still claim to have made the judgment that the necessary moral tests had been passed and citizens would have to treat the judicial decision as "law," unless, being conscientious citizens who disagreed with the legislative claim, they decided it was too immoral. Conversely, a positivist society that valued the chance to constantly reevaluate doctrine by responding to moral challenge could empower courts to check doctrine for moral adequacy – though the power could be withdrawn at any time, consistent with the positivist claim that the connection is only contingent.

IV. LEGAL THEORY AND POLITICAL THEORY

So far, I have been considering particular arguments about the moral implications of legal theory. I want now to consider the issues raised by these arguments from a perspective that is more general in two senses. First, I shall consider a general argument that purports to explain why the choice of legal theory could never affect moral deliberations. Second, I shall use this general explanation to suggest a different view about the relationship between legal theory on the one hand, and political or moral theory on the other.

The general reason for doubting that practical consequences hinge on this debate can be seen by noting how odd it sounds to suggest that one can "choose" a legal theory. To suggest that we can "choose" whether to call unjust law "law" sounds as if we are selecting between alternative proposals for a stipulative definition. But stipulative definitions do not normally have practical consequences. They can be criticized by reference to what might be called internal criteria, which ask, for example, whether the proposed definition is convenient or easy to use or consistent with other definitions within a preexisting set to which the new definition is to be added.[22] But the underlying phenomenon will remain unchanged whatever we decide to call it. To suggest that the name we give the phenomenon has practical implications is like suggesting that the impact of the new moons of Uranus on various human interests will depend on the names we give them.

Apply the argument to the present context. We are trying to decide whether anything hinges on whether or not we call "unjust law" "law." The double appearance of the word "law" in this slogan indicates that we have a different potential referent in mind for each use of the term. The "unjust law" whose title is in question is the phenomenon which, like the new moons of Uranus, will remain unchanged whatever we decide to call it. The referent of this phrase is fairly easy to determine: it is the official directive that has passed the formal test of pedigree or source that is determined by the positivist model of law. Thus, we are asking whether to call such official directives "law" without further moral tests, or to call them "law" only if they are not too unjust. But surely, what we call them does not matter. Whether one should obey them or not, and whether one will obey them is determined independently of names. Indeed, that is why some of the arguments considered above failed: If one is worried about the tendency of people to respond to official directives without considering their merits, that tendency is not going to be affected by the name we give to those directives, but only by some more fundamental educational process that brings home the individual's responsibility to evaluate official claims.

I have tried to elaborate this general explanation for the irrelevance of the debate as carefully as possible because, I think, it helps bring out the differences between moral theory, legal theory, and stipulative definitions. The above argument helps explain why debates about law are not likely to affect moral deliberations about what to do. But it would be a mistake to conclude that nothing but names is at stake. This debate is not about how to affect people's behavior, but about how to be consistent when we make claims about law and authority, and moral and legal obligation. The debate may force us to explain how law relates to the obligation to obey, and thus force us to engage in political theory in order to do legal theory. But there remains in this joint enterprise a special role for legal theory. Legal theory explains why the joint enterprise is required in the first place and furnishes plausible pre-analytic candidates (e.g., "official directives") to use as a starting point in conducting the inquiry.

22 See Morris, *Verbal Disputes and the Legal Philosophy of John Austin*, 7 U.C.L.A. L. Rev. 27, 29–31 (1959).

The reason it is a mistake to think that we can simply "choose," in the sense of stipulating, a legal theory is that we *do* have what I called above "internal criteria" that affect our ability to decide what to call official directives. We are not asking whether to call official directives "Arthur" or "Lorien," as if all that mattered were questions of convenience in terms of the string of letters or sounds we should use as interchangeable ways of designating the same phenomenon. We are puzzled about whether to call official directives "law," because we already have some sense of what it means if we say something is "law." Getting at this sense is what legal theory is about. If one wants to say we are stipulating, then we are doing so within a world of preexisting concepts like "obligation" and "duty" that have meanings we cannot ignore. If some of those concepts are connected with what we mean by "law," then we cannot make "law" mean anything we want without affecting the meanings of all of these other terms.

What is, then, this preexisting sense of "law?" One possibility, which underlies some of the arguments considered above, is that the symbol law, simply as a matter of social-psychological fact, has emotive power which tends to induce obedience. This suggestion is like pointing out to someone considering what to name a child that certain names evoke emotional images which may have repercussions on the child's personality or future development. The claim in our context would be that we have to be careful about calling official directives "law," because of the possibility that the name will cause an unjustified obedience response. A natural law theorist might use this possibility to insist that we reserve the name for just those directives that are not too unjust. A positivist, as illustrated in MacCormick's argument, may argue that what is needed is to educate people to get rid of the emotive connotations so that the symbol "law" will not induce obedience. I suggested that both arguments are unpersuasive: The natural law argument ignores the fact that regimes will always claim that their directives are just and hence will always be in a position "to manipulate the symbol."[23] The positivist argument assumes that the emotive force of the symbol can be removed by educating people to see that official directives have no *necessary* claim on their allegiance. But positivist officials will still make a contingent claim on allegiance by insisting that their particular legal system is just and hence its "laws" should be obeyed. As Julius Stone puts it, "How much of the tendency to obey what is 'law' is to be attributed to its power as a symbol, and how much to the tendency of most people to submit to actual power . . . is probably at best rather problematic."[24]

A second explanation for the preexisting sense of law looks for the reason why that symbol might have emotive force. Worrying about the emotive force

[23] See J. Stone, Human Law, at 255.
[24] *Id.*

of "law" is not like worrying about whether to name a child Tristram Shandy and wondering what social-psychological facts would have to be changed to prevent adverse reactions to the name. Law has emotive force because it has already been connected with other concepts of practical reasoning in ways that we cannot alter without altering our existing moral vocabulary.

To see what these existing connections might be, return to the basic problem that confronts attempts to trace moral implications to this debate. The basic problem is that most regimes will claim that their official directives are just. Thus whether or not we limit the term "law" to only those directives that *are* just, officials will not be confronted with an inconsistency in their attempts to connect official directives with practical implications. This conclusion suggests that there are definite practical implications that any regime will want to attach to its official directives. It also suggests that these practical implications are the same ones that give "law" its preexisting sense. What are those implications, and what must be true of official directives if they are in fact to have such implications?

Here are three plausible candidates for the implications we might intend to attach to official directives: Official directives, we might say, are:

(1) Directives courts must enforce (as a matter of the role assigned to them);
(2) Directives citizens ought to obey;
(3) Directives citizens ignore at their peril.

The first statement describes the role of a court in a legal system. The second statement makes a moral claim. The third statement is a reminder of the potential hostile reaction that will attend failure to comply. This last statement would probably be accepted by most people as at least one of the things officials intend people to infer from their directives. (For classical positivists like Austin, it was the only thing one could necessarily infer.) The arguments we considered in the first part of this paper are arguments that focus on the first two possibilities. Fuller's argument seemed to assume that official directives are necessarily things that it is part of a court's role to enforce. Thus, if we require these directives to pass moral tests, courts can do their job only by justifying, which constrains their ability to get away with evil. In response, I suggested that one might require directives to pass moral tests in order to count as "law," while still reserving to the legislature the question whether those tests had been met. Conversely, if having an institution to check the moral status of official directives was thought to be a good thing for the reasons Fuller suggests, a positivist society could also create such an institution. This debate, in short, is independent of arguments about the best institutional way for making and enforcing the judgments about morality which both kinds of societies will implicitly make.

What about the moral claim? If officials intend their directives to be directives that citizens ought to obey (or that courts ought to enforce as a matter of morality, not merely as a description of their assigned role), what must be true of these directives? The answer to that depends on political theory. Here are four possible claims that might be made about the moral implications of official directives:

(1) Citizens are obligated to obey official directives if and only if they are in fact just (in their content);
(2) Citizens have some moral duty to obey official directives regardless of content, but this duty can be overridden by other duties;
(3) Except in very unusual cases (including cases of great injustice) citizens are obligated to obey official directives regardless of content;
(4) Citizens are always obligated to obey official directives.

These four possibilities are listed in order of increasing strength of the claimed moral duty to obey official directives. No legal system that I am aware of makes the first claim: i.e., officials do not claim[25] that citizen compliance is entirely dependent on the correctness of the official claim of justice but, rather, that citizens should obey sometimes even if officials are wrong.[26] Many people probably believe that the fourth claim, demanding absolute submission, is typical of the implicit claim that officials make. If so, officials would be making a claim difficult to justify under any political theory accepted today.[27]

Now we can see why arguments about the moral implications to be attached to official directives are not simply stipulative. Officials hold out their directives as just. Typically, they also hold them out as directives that obligate even if they are wrong about that moral judgment. Thus, officials endorse some version of political theory described in sentences (2)–(4)

[25] I talk about the "claims that officials make," as simply another way of talking about the meaning of "legal obligation" when that phrase is used by persons within a legal system to make demands on others.

[26] When I say that no "legal system" makes such a claim, I am making a statement about the typical, modern legal system. I am not attempting to define "legal system" in a way that would force every society to meet certain tests in order to count as "legal." The goal of legal theory described here is not definition in that sense, but *consistency*. Anyone who claims to be using "law" in a way that entails moral conclusions, must confront the possibility that he is not using "law" and/or "morality" correctly. Officials or societies who do not use "law" in this way – to connect official directives with moral conclusions – will not face this problem of consistency, but that is not, in my view, the typical posture of officials in the modern state. (Again, I put these views in terms of what "officials claim," but that is but another way of getting at the meaning of "legal obligation" from the insider's perspective.)

[27] Whether this *is* the claim that officials implicitly make would be difficult to determine empirically because officials, if they think that their laws are just, probably aren't very self-conscious about what they would expect if their moral judgments prove wrong.

above. Whether these claims are consistent or correct requires one to check political theory to see what connections there might be between official directives and moral obligation.. The positivist who suggests we would do better to keep these ideas totally distinct must persuade not just citizens of that view; he must also persuade officials to stop suggesting that their directives obligate just because (in part) of their status. Officials must make no claim for the practical implications of their directives other than the claim that citizens ignore them at their peril.

Some positivists, of course, have been happy with this last conclusion: that law's only practical meaning is its prudential one. In this respect MacCormick departs from his predecessors. He recognizes that if this is all one meant by "law" one could never explain the persistent view that state coercion is (morally) justified in part just because a legal duty has been breached.[28] But the moral connection that MacCormick establishes cannot account for the claims made in the name of law. MacCormick's view is that law's moral value lies in the fact that it is a formal, rule-like system. By intervening only on the basis of publicized rules, "human beings are treated with some respect for humanity, not like dogs or some other kind of "pets" of the state. . . ."[29] MacCormick acknowledges that this idea traces to Fuller; he also notes that positivists have never been disturbed at conceding this element of value in rule-like structures, because, of course, such rule-like intervention can be consistent with totally immoral aims and purposes.[30] But this concession is fatal to MacCormick's enterprise. Showing only that law meets *necessary* conditions for having moral value does not establish that it has any moral value at all. Gangsters may also order me about by clearly established rules simply because, as a human rather than a dog, that may be the most efficient way to communicate with and use me for their unjust ends. The problem we are considering requires one to show that official directives not only meet necessary but also sufficient conditions for having some moral value – for that is the implicit claim that is made and that must be defended by officials within the state.

V. CONCLUSION

In this paper, I have considered and rejected the recent claim that the best way to promote the sovereignty of individual conscience is to accept the positivist view that what the law requires has no necessary connection with

[28] See MacCormick, *A Case for A-Moralistic Law*, at 23, 39–40. These passages make clear that even MacCormick is determined to retain some conceptual connection between the idea of legal obligation and a practical moral conclusion – a connection that we cannot simply "choose" to give up.

[29] *Id.*, at 26.

[30] This was exactly the criticism levelled by positivists at Fuller.

what morality requires. Two related reasons make one skeptical about such a claim: (1) Moral conscience, if it is inclined to yield to officialdom, is likely to do so regardless of the prevailing legal theory because both positivist and natural law regimes will claim that their directives are just. Whether that claim is a contingent one (as in the case of the positivist), or a matter of the "necessary" meaning of law is too subtle a distinction to affect whether or not individuals defer moral judgment to others. (2) Even if certain institutions, because of their "moral prestige," could preempt individual evaluation of law, the decision whether to include such institutions within a "legal system" is independent of the natural law/positivism distinction.

I have also considered and rejected the claim that it is morally preferable to adopt a natural law view. This claim, in contrast to the claim made on behalf of positivism, focuses on officials rather than on individuals, and suggests that the "moral price" one pays for preserving individual sovereignty of conscience may be an increase in official injustice. I have suggested again that the question whether to restrain officials by forcing them openly to justify their decisions is independent of the natural law/positivism distinction.

In the last part of the paper, I argued that the question of whether legal and moral obligation are connected must be answered on its own terms as a conceptual matter. Officials in modern legal systems implicitly claim such a connection, and even recent positivist theory finds this claimed connection to be sufficiently persistent and in need of justification to warrant some attempt to explain law's perceived moral value. These positivist explanations, however, remain inadequate so long as they show only that law meets necessary conditions for having moral value. The important claim that is typically made and that must be defended is that the breach of a legal duty is a sufficient condition for the act of state coercion. The question for legal theory is not whether it would be a good or a bad thing for such a claim to be accepted as true, but whether it *is* true.[31]

Law, University of Michigan

[31] In deciding whether it is true, one must not make the mistake of thinking that the only task is to check the claims that are made in the name of law with "true" political theory to see if the claims are correct. The persistence of the claim that law (morally) obligates is itself evidence of what we mean by "moral obligation." Thus one who concludes that no plausible account of "law" can be made consistent with both its primary linguistic sense (which tends to identify law by its official source, rather than its content) and with the moral claims made on law's behalf, must stop to consider whether it is the prevailing moral theory that needs revising. The phenomenon in question (the combination of linguistic and moral claims made about "law") serves, in short, as pre-analytic data for both an adequate legal and an adequate political theory.

TAXATION IN A LOCKEAN WORLD*

By Richard A. Epstein

'Tis true governments cannot be supported without great charge, and it is fit everyone who enjoys a share of the protection should pay out of his estate his proportion for the maintenance of it. But still it must be with his own consent, i.e., the consent of the majority giving it either by themselves or their representatives chosen by them. For if any one shall claim a power to lay and levy taxes on the people, by his own authority, and without such consent of the people, he thereby invades the fundamental law of property and subverts the end of government. For what property have I in that which another may by right take when he pleases to himself.[1]

I. LIBERTY AND TAXATION

One constant refrain of political and constitutional history treats taxation as an inherent and indispensable power of the sovereign. In one sense that proposition seems to be a self-evident truth: if the sovereign is without resources, then it cannot carry out any mission, however defined. It must atrophy and die. Taxes are to the state as food is to the body. Yet in another sense the proposition is one that leads to anxiety and disquiet. *Pace* Locke, the institutions of representative government do not work as smoothly as we might hope. Taxation is the power to coerce other individuals to surrender their property *without* their consent. In a world – a Lockean world – in which liberty is regarded as a good and coercion an evil, then taxation authorizes the sovereign to commit acts of aggression against the very citizens it is supposed to protect. The two sides of the dilemma are thus complete. A world without taxation is a world without government; a world with taxation is a world with institutionalized coercion, where the citizen is made the servant instead of the master of the sovereign. Liberty and

* An earlier version of this paper was presented at a conference on "Taxation and Liberty" organized by Alvin Rabushka and held in Santa Fe, New Mexico in September 1985, at the law and economics workshop at the University of Toronto earlier that month, and at the Washington University Business School in January. I should like to thank Walter Blum, James Buchanan, Joseph Isenbergh and William Niskanen for their valuable comments on earlier drafts of this paper.

[1] John Locke, Of Civil Government (Second Treatise) ¶140, 142.

sovereignty are in conflict. With the tension unresolved, we are left only with the unhappy choice between anarchy and totalitarianism.

One central question for any political theory is how to escape the horns of this dilemma. More precisely, the question is how to preserve the power of taxation while curbing its abuse. The most promising line of inquiry, I believe, is to show that taxation, while an inherent power of the sovereign, is a *limited* one as well. This involves applying the general principles of limited government to the program of taxation. This effort to find that middle course invites a set of inquiries that are avoided with both extreme positions. What are the limitations upon the sovereign power to tax? And how do they preserve the liberties of the citizens so taxed? That question itself has two separate parts: first, what is the *substantive content* of the limitations that should be imposed and, second, what are the *institutional arrangements* that give these limitations a fair chance of success?

The failure to answer either of these questions in definitive form has led to the modern consensus that veers too far in the direction of untrammeled state power to tax. The first part of the conventional wisdom is that democratic political institutions are the prime source of protection against abuse of the power of taxation. The risk of exploitation is reduced because no single individual is given the power to tax without being accountable to the public at large, which can voice its collective objection to oppressive taxes at the polls, a check to which all politicians pay homage. Within the American system at least, however, the second part of the consensus answer specifies only weak constitutional restrictions upon the power to tax. Taxes can be struck down if they rely upon a suspect class or limit a preferred individual freedom. An income tax of 10 percent on whites and 20 percent on blacks, or vice versa, is invalid because it relies upon a racial classification. A special onerous tax upon magazines and newspapers is invalid as an infringement of the freedom of speech. These limitations upon the power to tax still leave the legislature enormous discretion with respect to the objects and the level of taxation; and they have done nothing to limit the vast proliferation of special provisions in the Internal Revenue Code that have proved remarkably resistant to intelligent reform nor, in earlier days, to question a steeply progressive tax with top marginal rates that nominally exceeded ninety percent. A clear theory of individual rights and limited government points to more robust constitutional limitations upon the power to tax than the political consensus now accepts.

Both the objects of taxation and the rates are covered by my analysis, which links the modern themes of tax equity to the general theory of political obligation. The paper proceeds as follows. Section II outlines the basic political justification for taxation. Section III explains the basic taxation bargain that this theory calls forth. Section IV then shows how that bargain can be applied to technical questions of both the tax base and the rate structure. Section V gives a brief account of the possible constitutional limitations upon the government's power to tax.

II. THE ORIGINAL POSITION

The American tradition of government has been heavily influenced by Lockean social contract theory. The central question for Locke is how one is to move from a world with a large number of separate and autonomous individuals into a world with a single sovereign able to maintain political order, all the while protecting both liberty and property against government domination. In the Lockean view, all individuals are endowed with rights of personal liberty and rights to acquire property,[2] rights that control against theft, aggression, and fraud. Yet in the absence of any state the only remedy available to these individuals is self-help, whereby force resists or combats force. The weakness in this system lies not in its basic conception of entitlements. Locke himself accepts the set of entitlements that has in fact shaped both the civil and criminal law of virtually all civilized societies. I know, for example, of no one who defends murder, rape, or theft. Similarly, no one thinks that the right of self-defense should be abolished as a matter of first principle, even if they think that the existence of an organized police force calls for pragmatic restrictions upon its use.

The difficulties of the Lockean view lie in the vagaries of its enforcement. It is one thing to believe in the right of self-defense. It is quite another to determine who is the aggressor and who is the victim. To allow every person to make that determination for himself invites in private affairs what is so common in international relations: aggression under the pretext of defense. Similarly, there are limits to the right of self-defense even when the use of force is justified: once the peril has ceased the further use of force is excessive and outside the boundaries of the original justification. But, again, these limits are neither self-defining nor self-enforcing.

[2] There are difficulties in Locke's account of the original position, which treats all external things as being owned in common while each individual has exclusive ownership of his own person. Locke himself thought that his labor theory of value explained why any individual could take land or other property from the original common pool. But his theory is subject to the criticism that the private ownership it creates is subject to a lien for the benefit of the public at large, for otherwise the individual acquirer gets more than his labor has added. Locke's case would have been made more forcefully if he had taken the basic position of both the common and the Roman law – that all external things are unowned in the original position – for then first possession need not defeat any prior claims. The original no-ownership rule has a utilitarian simplicity, for there is little need to worry about a monopoly over natural resources when each person owns his own labor. For a defense of the common law solution, see Richard A. Epstein, Takings: Private Property and the Power of Eminent Domain, Chs. 2 & 20; and *Possession as the Root of Title*, 13 Ga. L. Rev. 1221 (1979).

The state offers a practical way to escape these enforcement difficulties by providing a single umpire whose decisions bind both contestants. Adjudication and public force replace self-help. Difficulties beset the implementation of the plan by the formation of government. Sovereignty sounds like an abstraction, but the power is always in the hands of natural persons ("real people") who may use their monopoly of force as a cloak for aggression against the very persons whose liberty and property they are sworn to protect. *Quis custodiet custodies?*, "Who guards the guardians?" is still the most probing question ever asked in political theory. In light of the manifold disasters of this and every other century, one could almost wish for a world without organized government on the commendable theory that random assaults offer a smaller risk than organized terror. But that solution is simply not in the cards. The void created by the lack of central authority will be filled by some desperado who will then disarm all his rivals. The practical choice therefore is not the choice between government and no government; the consistent anarchist will lose all (hypothetical) wars to the determined statist. The only set of feasible choices therefore are on the second order questions: what kind of state, with what kind of governors, minimizes the abuse of centralized power?

The options are limited and the risks are high, but on balance the best answers seem to come from the cross between the natural rights and the utilitarian tradition that together have inspired contract theories of the state and constitutional theories of limited government. Ideally, one can conceive of a (hypothetical) bargain calling for the universal renunciation of force by all persons, present and future. That agreement promises enormous gains to all the parties to it.[3] The theory of the state fleshes out the terms of that agreement.

The agreement is not real, so how can the argument proceed? Certain individuals might think themselves better off in a world that does tolerate the war of all against all, because they think that this is one war they can win. One person, therefore, might wish to hold out against the multitude. The greater the number of persons, the more likely that one of them will respond in this way. The theory of natural rights is designed to counter just this possibility by noting that the *baseline* against which "being better off" is measured gives to each person only his natural rights to liberty and property, and not the fruits acquired by theft, aggression, or deception.[4] The impulse

[3] The metaphor of bargain has been used to describe other situations in which coercive forced exchanges are designed to overcome common pool problems. Bankruptcy is one such example; see, e.g., Jackson, *Bankruptcy, Non-Bankruptcy Entitlements, and the Creditors' Bargain*, 91 Yale L.J. 857 (1982).

[4] See Frank Michelman, *Ethics, Economics, and The Law of Property*, 24 NOMOS, Ethics, Economics and the Law 3 (1982) for a vision of the world without such a baseline; and the brief rejoinder by Harold Demsetz, *Professor Michelman's Unnecessary And Futile Search For The Philosopher's Touchstone, id.* 41.

behind that intuition comes from two sources: the first is the self-evident belief that individual autonomy is a primary and indisputable good, and the second is that the overall level of human satisfaction and happiness is greater in a world without aggression than in a world with it.

Even if the baseline can be set as Locke would set it, the operation of the state cannot rest on actual or tacit consent. Instead, the justification for the state depends upon the *network of forced hypothetical exchanges* needed to overcome the persistent problems of collective action: holdouts and free-riders flourish in a world of high transaction costs.[5] Armed with that (inchoate) realization, the Lockean solution was simple and correct. It postulated a world in which, as a first approximation, every individual was required to surrender his right to use force to the state in exchange for the like promise of every other individual to so refrain. In such a world, the gains from being free of risk of aggression are worth more than the unqualified rights of self-help they replace. The risk of aggression of course remains, and self-help (now subject to judicial scrutiny and review) remains for emergencies where state intervention cannot be timely. Starting from the original set of entitlements, the formation of the state looks very much like a Pareto-superior move in which some natural rights are surrendered in exchange for the greater protection of the natural rights that are retained. Taxation is the form of surrender, and security is the good received in exchange. In the modern language of welfare theory, one distribution of rights is Pareto-superior to another so long as one person is better off in the first world than in the second, and no one else is worse off.[6] The formation of the state appears to satisfy this social welfare condition. Indeed, one can go further and argue that a more stringent requirement is satisfied as well. The gains of organized society cannot be captured solely by a small few. State protection is general so that each person shares in the social gains, roughly pro rata, in accordance to the value of his original endowments. Insisting that the surplus be divided in this unique way increases the definiteness of legal rights, which in turn reduces the danger of wealth loss from factional struggle.[7] In principle, no person can object to the second world in which the use of sovereign power leaves him better off than he was with his natural endowments. Similarly, no person can be allowed to stand outside the compact, for then the entire arrangement will unravel; for without universal compliance, the monopoly of the state is lost and the regime of self-help,

[5] See, generally, Russell Hardin, Collective Action (1982) for an account of these difficulties.

[6] See, e.g., Coleman, *The Economic Analysis of Law*, 24 NOMOS, Ethics, Economics and Law, Ch. 4 (J. Pennock & J. Chapman eds. 1982).

[7] In contrast, note that a per capita division of the gain from public expenditures may require explicit cash transfers between members of the society. Who is to pay and who is to collect is far from evident. The pro rata position is designed to avoid the social losses that would follow from any effort to redistribute the surplus by direct transfer payments.

with all its deficiencies, will emerge anew. The reconciliation of liberty and coercion is found in the stipulation for a return benefit, unobtainable through voluntary agreement, that exceeds in value the losses of liberty and property entailed by the formation of the state.

III. THE TAXATION BARGAIN

The task of governance does not end with a simple statement of the theory that justifies sovereign power. A Lockean theory leaves the state with functions to discharge – the keeping of order. The state must have the resources to discharge them. These funds could in principle come from voluntary contributions, but that prospect is bleak. Just as voluntary agreements could not form the state, so they cannot fund its continued operations; free riding endures. Everyone has the incentive to let other persons pay the private costs of the public good. The system is then in fundamental disequilibrium, for the state must have the resources it cannot command. Taxation from all is the only viable source of revenue to restore the equilibrium implied by the simple proposition that the state must have a secure revenue base. The question is distribution and incidence of the tax in question. At this point, one might expect that Locke himself would discuss in some detail the nature and the sources of the tax, but apart from his keen sense that taxation should be proportionate to the property protected,[8] he veers away from the issue.

Yet so great is the power of his theory of the state that it does more than account for the existence of the power of taxation. It also provides a blueprint for the closer analysis of the particular rules that limit the exercise of the taxing power. That such limitations are needed seems evident given the constant temptations for self-aggrandisement in politics. Even if all individuals abandon the use of force, they still remain political actors able to resort to influence and intrigue. The modern theory of public choice makes it abundantly clear what everyone who has heard of factions has known intuitively all along. There is a constant pressure for special interest legislation that is fundamentally at odds with the Pareto-superior pattern of forced exchanges appropriate for state initiation. In its place are efforts to achieve implicit transfers of property and wealth from one group to another. In the effort to skew the gains from collective life, taxation can be, and has been, used as a weapon of confiscation.[9] The Lockean theory of government calls for the use of coercion only to create a larger pie with all persons sharing in the gain. In practice, resort to governmental power often leads to a

[8] See note 1, *supra*.
[9] See Epstein, *Taxation, Regulation and Confiscation*, 20 Osgoode Hall L.J. 433 (1982).

smaller pie. Some individuals will obtain larger slices; otherwise nothing will drive the process. But others necessarily will be left with far less than they had before the government program was placed in operation. The standard Pareto measures are systematically violated.[10] There is no possibility that all will be allowed to share pro rata in the social gain. Democratic processes may make it more difficult to form a winning coalition; and they are certainly superior to despotic rule. But they do provide a new arena for abuse that cries out for institutional control. What form should the taxation bargain take?

A. Tax neutrality. A sound tax is designed to interfere as little as possible with the ordinary decisions that individuals would make in the investment and consumption of their capital and labor. On the Lockean theory, the sphere of individual autonomy should be invaded as little as possible in order to secure the maintenance of public order. In the original state of nature no individual can pass judgment on what others decide to do with their liberty or property unless the use of force or fraud is involved. The creation of a system of government should strive not to reduce the scope of permissible individual choice from what it was before. Accordingly, no person or group should be able to use the tax system to change the pattern of preferences of other individuals. If A ranks a set of (noncoercive) alternatives 1 to n before taxation, then A's ranking of those alternatives should remain 1 to n, without alteration, after the tax is imposed. So, too, with all other persons. If subsidies and penalties are generally forbidden, then they are forbidden not only by direct regulation, but by taxation as well.

The postulate of tax neutrality immediately follows.[11] Tax neutrality is a principle that recognizes that before a system of taxation is imposed, individuals order their preferences in a discrete and particular way. The ideal of tax neutrality simply provides that the system of taxation, as far as possible, should preserve the relative priorities that individuals attach to various activities. The function of the state is to protect liberty and property. It is not to aid one group or another in skewing the uses to which individuals put their natural endowments. Observing the principle does more than keep the relations between taxpayer activities constant. It also keeps their relative wealth constant as well, so that an increase for one is matched by a

[10] I explore some of these tensions in Richard A. Epstein, Takings, at Ch. 2, 12, and 18; *Toward a Revitalization of the Contract Clause*, 51 U. Chi. L. Rev. 703 (1984); and *Why Restrain Alienation?*, 85 Colum. L. Rev. 770 (1985).

[11] Here tax neutrality must be kept distinct from the idea of "revenue neutrality" that has been prominent in recent discussions of tax reforms. Revenue neutrality provides that the total revenue collected by the state should not be decreased by any substantive principles of tax reform. But it does not tell us how to decide the soundness of one basic structure against another. As a matter of first principle, once the right structure is worked out, the tax rates should be set so as to provide funds sufficient to discharge the public obligations.

proportionate increase for others. If tax neutrality could be perfectly achieved, the laws would act as a prism which magnified equally all preexisting endowments. The nature of private activities would not change, nor would the relative endowments of private persons.

The desirability of tax neutrality also follows from the more overtly economic view of the subject. In a well functioning economy, every actor should have to face the full opportunity costs of his private decisions. Where private rights in labor and property are well-defined, that normally will be the case. A system of taxation that imposes differential taxes necessarily subsidizes some activities and penalizes others, thereby distorting relative prices and, in consequence, private decisions on consumption and investment. Likewise, if taxation were allowed to make some persons better off and others worse off, struggles would arise between persons who would want to funnel wealth through the tax system and those who would want to keep it out of the system. These resource losses would reduce the likelihood that any tax imposed will be Pareto-superior, for some persons could and would emerge net losers when the tax system incorporated subsidies for a select few and correlative penalties for the rest of us.

Many modern (political) debates on tax reform appear to assume that the level of wealth is independent of the distribution of the tax burden. Too often the question of "fairness" in tax legislation is taken to mean that the distribution of tax burdens has no allocative effects. Nothing could be further from the truth. Taxes can create distortions that reduce wealth. The question is how to minimize these distortions. A sound tax, which funds only needed public goods, will always be subject to some evasive response by private parties. But these are minimized by a system that does not seek to reshape basic preferences and that tries to insure that every public expenditure is worth more to every party taxed than the revenues that are lost. Tax neutrality represents one constraint on government policy that is designed to keep government activity as close as possible to the Pareto ideal.

B. Costs of administration. Any tax system costs money to administer, costs which are incurred both by the state and by private parties. These costs are incurred in order to bring about a simple transfer of wealth between two sides. The smaller their sum, the greater the fraction of the social product that is left for use in either public or private hands. In general, simple rules are far easier to administer when mass transactions are at issue. A tax system that demands extensive information to implement is inferior to one that has greater ease of operation by depending upon reliable and measurable facts on the public record. If the costs of collection are high, it increases the likelihood that the taxation (and its associated expenditure) will not meet the requirements of a proper Pareto-superior forced exchange.

C. Rent-seeking. Taxation should be made as invulnerable to political pressures and manipulation as possible. The dangers of faction and abuse of power tend to unfairly skew the terms of forced exchanges. Again, there is nothing unique about taxation. The general theory of property rights makes it clear that the opportunity for political, rent-seeking behavior is greatest where property rights are ill-defined. Taxation can easily be fitted into the general model of property rights, for any tax creates a *lien* for the benefit of the state upon the assets of all its citizens. Talk of a "tax lien" is no loose or florid analogy. Taxes are "floating liens" (parallel to those obtained by many private lenders) that the state may quickly convert into a fixed lien against particular property when taxes are unpaid. That lien can then be foreclosed and the property sold to satisfy the underlying obligation.[12]

The characteristics of the floating lien influence the operation of the system. The greater the freedom state officials have in specifying the contours of the floating lien, the greater the resource losses the tax system will create. Again, the theory of property rights accounts for this result. Ill-defined rights confer discretion upon public officials. Discretion in turn means that there is greater uncertainty in the income stream of all individuals taxed, which typically implies a welfare loss since most persons are risk averse. Discretion also creates a common-pool problem not dissimilar to that which applies to fisheries or oil and gas. It is one thing for A, B, C, and D each to owe $25; it is quite another thing for A, B, C, and D to owe jointly $100. In the first situation (that of separate debts in equal amounts) the obligations are well-defined, and the persons involved cannot shift by political action the burden of their obligations to others. In the second situation these obligations are ill-defined, and each person is tempted to spend real resources (up to $25) to deflect some or all of the common debt to others. Those strategic expenditures in the aggregate produce dead weight social losses, which threaten the integrity of the taxation bargain: when taxation shrinks the social pie it cannot be a Pareto-superior forced exchange, no matter what the final distribution of rights.

IV. IMPLEMENTING THE BARGAIN

It now remains to consider the extent to which both substantive and institutional rules can implement these primary features of the taxation bargain. I believe that they can. In some cases, the theory points to very clear results, while in others the question of trade-offs (chiefly between adminis-

[12] Hence the demand for the pro rata distribution of the surplus. See Coleman, *The Economic Analysis of Law*.

trative costs and incentive effects) is far more vexatious. What follows is an effort to apply the basic theory to some of the central features of a sound system of taxation.

A. Cash or kind? The first proposition is that taxes should normally be collected in cash, not kind. With virtuous governments and virtuous individuals, the choice in the form of taxation might seem unimportant. The right assets will move from private to public hands but only in ways that surmount the standard public goods problems. But as ever, the choice of institutional form depends critically upon the ability to resist the full panoply abuses, both public and private, that arise when information is imperfect, the costs of monitoring are positive, conflicts of interest are rampant, and the temptation to siphon off public resources for private benefit is pervasive.

In this imperfect world, the monetary tax has major operational advantages. From the side of the individual taxpayer, the imposition of a strict monetary obligation allows him to decide which resources to sell or mortgage in order to pay the tax. In general we can expect that the individual will preserve from the taxing authorities those assets to which he attaches the highest subjective valuation, that is, those in which his value in use is greater than the market value.[13] As all persons are in the same position with respect to the tax obligation, each person is able to appropriate the entire surplus value to himself, which in turn reduces the likelihood that the wrong resources will be taken for public use. The upshot is that it is more likely that the operation of the system will be Pareto-superior, with a pro rata division of the surplus, than will a system that allows the government to select the assets to be taken from each individual.

The constraint that taxes be paid in money also imposes an important limitation upon the discretion of government officials. If the government were allowed to impose taxes in kind (say 25 percent of the goods owned by the taxpayer), individual taxpayers would have powerful incentives to influence the choice of assets taken by the government. Government officials might (improperly?) threaten to take assets with high subjective values in order to increase the opportunities for obtaining bribes.[14] Thus, if one's home is worth $25,000 in the open market, but $35,000 subjectively to the taxpayer, the ability to take the home instead of cash creates the opportunity for bribes between one dollar and $9,999. Side payments in that amount

[13] On the importance of subjective value generally, see Timothy Muris, *Cost of Completion or Diminution in Market Value: The Relevance of Subjective Value*, 12 J. Legal Stud. 379 (1984).

The question of subjective value plays an important role in the law of eminent domain, on which I have written generally; Richard A. Epstein, Takings: Private Property and the Power of Eminent Domain (1985).

[14] On this process generally, see Benson & Baden, *The Political Economy of Governmental Corruption: The Logic of Underground Government*, 14 J. Legal Stud. 391 (1985).

would leave both the official and the private party better off, but would result in large systemic social losses. These opportunities for game playing are not restricted to the immediate relationship of taxpayer and public official, for it is possible to envision deals in which bribes are paid to induce tax collectors to levy against the key assets of a business rival or a political opponent.

The possibilities for abuse do not stop when the specific assets are taken into government hands. The management and sale of unwanted assets must proceed on a gigantic scale, and offer ample opportunities for negligence, corruption, favoritism, and abuse. Even if these forces could be banished from public life, the administrative costs of the system would still be very high. A simple rule that all taxes be paid in cash provides a powerful and workable constraint upon both public and private misbehavior.

It is easy to overlook the importance of these institutional arrangements in dealing with matters of taxation. Robert Nozick has argued, for example, that "Taxation of earnings from labor is on a par with forced labor."[15] His conclusion is true if the only relevant political inquiry is whether or not taxation involves the use of coercion. A pure libertarian could therefore condemn taxation and forced labor with equal vigor.[16] Yet once *any* forced exchanges are admitted into the system, then Nozick has only answered the first question: Is there a taking of private property? He does not begin to answer the question of whether some greater benefit is provided in return. On that question the differences between taxation and forced labor, which are widely understood intuitively, become critical. The problems of private evasion and public abuse just mentioned make it clear that a system of ordinary taxation is more apt to generate Pareto-superior taxes than a system of forced labor. The differences here are as substantial as those between a system of conscription (a tax in kind on some individuals) on the one hand and a volunteer military force paid for by general tax revenues. Nozick's categorical condemnation of all coercion provides no framework for ranking alternative systems of taxation or, indeed, any government action, in any responsible way.

There are, of course, some limits to the principle that the government's sole source of resources should be monetary taxation. While taking labor is generally unwise, taking property may not be. Simple taxation may not work, for example, when holdout problems threaten to block the acquisition of specific land for a public highway. Occasionally, the eminent domain power to take property must be invoked. But as with taxation, the object of the law is to implement Pareto-superior forced exchanges with a pro rata division of

[15] Robert Nozick, Anarchy, State and Utopia 169 (1974).

[16] Nozick has some sense of the point for he notes that he equivocates by the use of the phrase "on a par with," which may mean simply "is" or is "a kind of"; *id.* at 169, note*. Yet he never explores any of the functional reasons that make for the differences.

the surplus. In principle, the eminent domain power should strive to work toward a distribution of benefits and losses identical to that achieved by a well-functioning tax. The compensation requirement operates to insure a return of benefits to the individual equal to the value of the property surrendered, which are then augmented by his pro rata share in the social surplus (if any) generated by the government activity. Eminent domain is far more expensive to operate than ordinary taxation. The in-kind nature of the appropriation calls forth an elaborate network of protections for private parties, not the least of which is the right to a judicial determination of the value of the property taken. Yet here, litigation is so expensive and valuation so controversial that much abuse remains.[17] A well run society subordinates the use of eminent domain to the use of taxation.

B. The Comprehensive Tax Base. The Lockean theory offers guidance on the appropriate base for taxation. The ends of government are to protect a person in all his "life, liberty and estates," so that presumptively everything of value protected by government is subject to taxation. That intuition is captured in the two standard definitions of income, those of Haig and of Simons, which today generally guide theoretical discussions of taxation. Haig's definition of personal income was "the money value of the net accretion to one's economic power between two points in time."[18] Simons' definition made more explicit the place of consumption in the general picture: "Personal income may be defined as the algebraic sum of (1) market value of rights exercised in consumption and (2) the change in value of the store of property rights between the beginning and end of the period in question."[19] Both these comprehensive definitions are required by the Lockean theory, for both advance tax neutrality by preventing distortions in the prior patterns of individual preferences.[20] To be sure, the definition does not answer every question about the proper base for taxation. There is, for example, a debate over whether casualty losses for nonbusiness property

[17] One obvious point is that the government normally need not compensate the owner anything for the legal and business costs incurred when condemnation takes place. See, e.g., Bodcaw v. United States, 440 U.S. 202 (1979). For the complications in setting the right rule, see Ayer, *Allocating the Costs of Determining "Just Compensation,"* 21 Stan. L. Rev. 693 (1969), and Epstein, Takings: Private Property and the Power of Eminent Domain, Ch. 4 (1985).

[18] Haig, The Federal Income Tax 7 (R. Haig ed. 1921).

[19] H. Simons, Personal Income Taxation 50 (1938). Professor Bittker has observed that Simons regarded Haig's definition "as interchangeable with his own." See B. Bittker, *A "Comprehensive Tax Base" As a Goal of Income Tax Reform*, 80 Harv. L. Rev. 925–932 (1967). It is not clear why Simons chose to measure consumption by market value instead of subjective value. For a discussion of the difficulties with subjective variations, see *infra* at section (c).

[20] Simons was no stranger to political theory; see his *Some Reflections on Syndicalism*, 52 J. Pol. Econ. 1 (1944), reprinted in H. Simons, Economic Policy for a Free Society (A. Director ed. 1947).

should provide a deduction to their owner.[21] While it might be thought that the casualty deduction for personal property compromises the rate base, the opposite conclusion seems correct.[22] The destruction of property is a net decrease in wealth, which cannot be regarded as consumption. Hence, by the Haig–Simons definition it reduces income and thus functions as a deduction against income from other sources. Similar but more difficult questions arise with, for example, medical deductions and charitable contributions.[23] But these definitional problems can be given plausible answers, and in any event cannot be allowed to obscure the important agreement over many different kinds of income – wages, interest, royalties, rents, dividends, capital appreciation – now reached by the tax system,[24] and which under any view compromise the huge bulk of any tax revenues.

Finding the appropriate definition of income can be regarded either as an end in itself or as the start of a more complex inquiry into tax policy. In theory, it should clearly be the latter. Once the comprehensive definition of gross income is established, the issue is whether there is any deviation from the original tax base that satisfies dual constraints of Pareto superiority and pro rata division of the gain. A moment's reflection should indicate that further refinement is not only possible, but strictly necessary.[25]

The most vivid illustration is imputed income, that is, income which comes from the productive use of one's talent or property without the interposition of any market transaction, such as a sale or a salary. The consumption of home grown food and the value of services about the home are two common illustrations. In principle, all imputed income falls within the taxation base, as the principle of tax neutrality opposes any differential tax cost on market income that will bias individuals toward nonmarket uses

[21] Internal Revenue Code (I.R.C.), § 165(c)(3).

[22] Epstein, *The Consumption and Loss of Personal Property under the Internal Revenue Code*, 23 Stan. L. Rev. 454 (1971).

[23] See William D. Andrews, *Personal Deductions in an Ideal Income Tax*, 86 Harv. L. Rev. 309 (1972).

[24] See I.R.C. § 61(a), which contains a general reference to gross income and a long list of included items. Cases of the fringes include such matters as the treatment of punitive damages, on which see Glenshaw Glass Co. v. Commissioner, 348 U.S. 426 (1955), covering exemplary damages in fraud cases and the punitive portion of recovery in an antitrust action. The doubts about recovery stemmed from the definition of income used previously by the court in Eisner v. Macomber, 252 U.S. 189 (1920). "'Income may be defined as the gain derived from capital, from labor, or from both combined,' provided it be understood to include profit gained through a sale or conversion of capital assets." Note, this definition excludes the gain received in *Glenshaw Glass* which is, however, taxable under the Haig–Simons definition.

[25] Once the point is grasped, it becomes clear that any attack on the Haig–Simons approach that is content to point out deviations from the system is not sufficient to condemn its usefulness. For an illustration of the error, see Bittker, *A "Comprehensive Tax Base" As A Goal Of Income Tax Reform*, 80 Harv. L. Rev. 925 (1967), effectively criticized in Musgrave, *In Defense of an Income Concept*, 81 Harv. L. Rev. 44 (1967), which, while it does not adopt the explicit framework here, takes much the same approach.

of their own labor. But tax neutrality has to yield something to administrative necessity, for it is simply impossible to value every pleasure or benefit that people routinely enjoy. The intangibles are overwhelming. Do persons with happy home lives get taxed at a higher level than persons who come from broken homes? Should government officials stand over the shoulders of all citizens in order to tax the value of home repairs? The opera fanatic who buys a box seat for $50 may in fact be willing to pay $75, but should $25 in consumer surplus be subject to taxes? Should the worker who loves his job be taxed more heavily than his companion who does not? Should the person who enjoys watching the sunrise or quiet contemplation be taxed for that as well?

It takes little theoretical insight to realize that the problems of monitoring and evaluation doom from the start the enterprise of taxing all imputed income. The conclusion follows a fortiori given that sound rules of taxation are designed to curb both individual and government abuse. Excluding imputed income is a flat violation of tax neutrality in that it biases the tradeoff between market and nonmarket transactions, and between work and leisure. The critical question is whether that violation can be justified. The relevant inquiries are two: first, will the total size of the pie be greater and, second, will the relative *individual* tax burdens remain unaltered?

The answer to the first question seems to be "yes." The administrative savings from excluding imputed income from the tax base are enormous. The need to value nonmarket goods is eliminated, while the discretion vested in the taxing authorities and the size of the government apparatus are both reduced. Revenue neutrality can be preserved, even if tax neutrality is not, by raising the rates on taxable income somewhat to offset the shortfall that might otherwise arise.

The answer to the second question is also "yes." At first blush, the exclusion of imputed income looks mischievous if one assumes, as does Nozick in *Anarchy, State and Utopia*, that one person enjoys going to the movies and the other watching the sunset, so that the first pays taxes on the income earned to pay for the movie ticket, while the other pays no taxes to watch the sunset. Yet the possibility of having the person with the greater total income paying the smaller taxes becomes far less likely given, as seems the case, that everyone has a large market basket of imputed income transactions that are kept out of the tax system. It matters little that the contents of each basket will differ so long as their total value is about the same. Every person has large amounts of imputed income, some from a good job and some from a good homelife. There is no group of individuals that has a monopoly on imputed income, as most people consume *both* some movies and some unpurchased leisure.

Excluding imputed income does not appear, therefore, to create any systematic bias across groups of individuals in the society at large, and is not obviously correlated with race, sex, age, religion, occupation, or even income levels. The rank ordering of individual utility tends to be preserved after the tax base is redefined. Those persons who would pay more in taxes with the comprehensive base continue to pay more even after imputed income is excluded. This diffusion of benefits and burdens also has important political ramifications, for it is hard to see the interest group that would make the inclusion or exclusion of imputed income the target of rent-seeking or factional politics. It is too hard for the players to identify those persons who would win and lose from the shift.

The recognition that imputed income falls outside the tax system thus appears to produce overall gains evenly shared by the population at large, at least with the approximate guesswork that must be made on matters of this scale. The loss of tax neutrality is a serious matter, but the best solution is simply not obtainable. The revenue needs of the state can be met by a higher tax on the smaller base, with no obvious redistributive consequences. To be sure, some items of imputed wealth are of sufficient magnitude that they might be brought back into the rate base – the rental values of private homes is an obvious candidate for the wrinkle upon the wrinkle. Yet suppose the trade-off between administrative costs and tax neutrality here is incorrectly drawn under the current system. Still the question seems close, so that the costs of error are relatively low. A society can easily flourish with such unresolved ambiguities.

C. When to tax: the realization and recognition of income. The second set of qualifications of the rate base have to do with the nature of the receipts and expenditures that trigger collection of the tax. As Simons himself repeatedly stressed, the proper definition of income does not depend upon any prior "receipt" or realization of gain. To illustrate his proposition, if I own 100 shares of IBM stock purchased at $100, but which are now worth $125, then $2,500 in gain is income whether I choose to hold or to sell the stock. Ignoring the transaction cost, holding the stock is no different from a sale and a repurchase of the same securities. The comprehensive definition of income thus includes $2,500 in gain (and would recognize a like amount in losses) whether or not the stock has been sold, and thus minimizes the ability of the strategic maneuvers of private parties to undermine the system.

Yet here, too, the concern with tax neutrality has generally not been strong enough to carry the day in all cases. Every modern tax system works off the concept of receipt of property that is immaterial under the Haig–Simons definition of income. Receipt of wages or the realization of gain, as from the sale of stock, has been generally regarded as a condition for the recognition of gain and for the levying of a tax. The effect in all instances is to delay the *time* for paying the tax until after the increment to wealth or consumption is obtained.

The justifications for the delay are practical in origin but theoretical in their significance. Taxation of unrealized appreciation, for example, can pose real questions of valuation given the absence of market transactions. These are themselves quite insuperable when dealing with real estate or with shares of a closed corporation, when there is no ready market. They are of some modest concern with the shares of public corporations. In both cases, there is also a nagging question of how some taxpayers will raise the cash to pay the tax, for it is quite possible to be cash poor and capital rich. Imposing the tax before realization of the gain can force a taxpayer to go to the market, to mortgage the shares or to sell them at an inopportune time. These transactions can be costly and inconvenient and could disrupt business objectives.

All this is not to say that there are no disadvantages in delaying taxation until the sale of shares or the receipt of cash. Where certain assets appreciate substantially, the clever taxpayer may be able to obtain cash today, without payment of the tax, by the use of a nonrecourse loan, secured by the shares of stock.[26] The system of delayed taxation also tends to discriminate against earned income and in favor of investment income. And it leads to genuine complications of income in periods of inflation or deflation as well. Nonetheless, the administrative burdens of the Haig–Simons definition are too great in a system that must collect taxes from millions of individuals. The deferment of taxation to a later period probably works a smaller shift in wealth between persons than it does between different kinds of income, and it spares everyone the enormous administrative costs that would otherwise be incurred. On balance, deferment looks wealth-enhancing and, hence, Pareto-superior, especially in light of the next feasible alternative. One might want to dispute that point,[27] especially as regards shares of publicly held corporations; but the debate here would not be on the soundness of the

[26] See Woodsam's Associate v. Commissioner, 198 F. 2d 357 (2d Cir. 1952). See, generally, Marvin Chirelstein, Federal Income Taxation §13.02 (1985).

[27] See, e.g., Slawson, *Taxing Ordinary Income the Appreciation of Publicly Held Stock*, 76 Yale L.J. 623 (1967). The opposite side of the coin is the immediate recognition of unrealized losses. Yet the parallel is not precise because even with the realization requirement a taxpayer could always choose to sell in order to recognize the loss. Note too that this strategic power has in more recent times been used by investors in various kinds of options. The basic principle is to invest in a portfolio of options to buy and sell at different prices and dates. As the portfolio is negatively correlated, some items will go up and others down. The losses can then be realized, while the gains are postponed. A forced accounting without realization at the end of the tax year defeats the strategic maneuvers of taxpayers. The problem does not exist in the same degree for stocks because their prices tend to be positively correlated and they have lower volatility.

general criteria, but on their application to a particular case – a second order problem.

The question of realization is at bottom a question of timing: *when* should certain forms of wealth be taxed. Often it is not sufficient to defer taxation until the receipt of wealth. Stated in standard tax language, the realization of gain or loss need not necessarily be the occasion for the "recognition" of the gain. Taxation can be deferred until some later point in the wealth production cycle, usually when the property received is reduced to cash or its equivalent. For example, a shareholder contributes property to his wholly owned corporation in exchange for an issue of its shares; the form of wealth has changed, and gain has been realized from the sale of the thing. But in general, the recognition of the gain for tax purposes will await the sale of the shares for cash by the shareholder, or the sale of the thing by the corporation.[28] Or two pieces of real estate are exchanged and both parties realize a profit, in that the property received is worth more to each party than the cost of the property surrendered. But, again, the deferred recognition of the gain seems appropriate.[29] The practical problems of taxation are evident, and there is a risk that the tax cost might well prevent what would otherwise be a beneficial economic exchange. The gains can still be taxed, either in the form of rental income or upon a subsequent cash sale.

The treatment of unrealized losses raises the same issues in reverse. Normally depreciation of property used in a trade or business precedes its sale; the refusal to make any allowance for depreciation before recognition could result in the bunching of losses in the year property is sold or abandoned. Yet taking these losses into account long after they are sustained produces serious economic distortions. In principle, the proper response is to value real estate at the beginning and end of the tax period, so that losses in depreciation can be combined with appreciation (or depreciation) in property value attributable to market forces to reach a net figure of taxable income or loss. This valuation process is cumbersome and unreliable. One could ignore depreciation over time, as one ignores appreciation (or depreciation) for changes in market value of stocks. But there is a difference: market forces can move value in either direction, while age and obsolescence exert a systematic downward pressure.

It seems, therefore, defensible (and probably correct) to use some simple taxation formula to capture that systematic downward shift in value in order to reduce the anticipated gap between economic and tax definitions of income, all at a tolerable administrative cost. Today, the tax system itself offers a bewildering array of options for depreciation not required by the

[28] See I.R.C. § 351.
[29] See I.R.C. § 1031.

basic theory.[30] The needless discretion they vest in taxpayers should be eliminated because of the strategic game playing (and consequent social losses) it invites. But some simple formula for depreciation over broad categories of property is surely appropriate,[31] even if the present menu of options is not.

The same logic applies to income received today for services to be performed tomorrow. Consider the receipt of the right to future payment from long-term service contracts. The associate who is made a partner at a law firm, the professor who receives tenure at his university, the federal judge appointed for life might be said to have received fair market value of the future income stream that attaches to his employment. Certainly there are chances that he will quit, be fired for cause, or die, but nonetheless the receipt of the contract right from the employer is not a matter of indifference to the taxpayer. There is a clear receipt of a thing of value (the contract right), and the net change in wealth is substantial, even if there can be genuine quarrels on the matter of valuation. But should the income stream, however valued or discounted, be taxed in the year the right is acquired? Here the problems of getting the money to pay taxes on a future and uncertain income stream are acute, for what bank will lend on the strength of the bare contract right that the government is so eager to tax. Nor is it possible at the moment that job rights vest to make an accurate assessment of the future income projection. Partnerships have good and bad years; universities have pay freezes; judges' salaries are tied up in politics. The receipt of the long-term contract right is a poor time to impose the tax. The reduction of the right to the cash is the appropriate instance, as the law now generally provides. Taxation of in-kind benefits (like the collection of taxes in-kind) is perilous and unnecessary business. A little waiting reduces uncertainty and administrative costs. The shift seems to meet the dual requirements of Pareto superiority and pro rata distribution of the gain.

D. Income or consumption taxes. The permutations for the recognition and deferment of gain can be extended one step further, since many people argue that the receipt of income should not be an occasion for taxation; instead, taxation should be further postponed until the moment of consumption. The shift to a consumption tax may appear revolutionary, but a few key structural changes in the tax laws could bring much of it about in a modest way. One change would be to forgive the gain on securities when the

[30] See I.R.C. §§ 167, 168.

[31] In a world without inflation, the proper formula for depreciation would reduce the value of a long term asset (which has uniform value in use) by the present discounted value of the last remaining year's use, not by straight line depreciation, which simply treats the value of each year's use equally. Again, the error, while large in principle, may not shift wealth between individuals, even if it could (by overencouraging investment) result in some allocative losses. See Marvin Chirelstein, Federal Income Taxation ¶6.07 (4th ed. 1985).

proceeds of sale are reinvested in other forms of investment property. Another would be to allow a deduction for savings. These changes would ignore the proper tax treatment of consumer durables,[32] and thus are not complete. Once the choice between the income and consumption tax is seen as one of the timing of gain, there is no obvious need to choose one pure type over another. An intermediate position may prove to be socially preferable. The question of whether the consumption tax is superior to the income tax is vexed indeed,[33] but here, as before, the structure of the inquiry is the same as in all other instances: is the change Pareto-superior with an anticipated pro rata division in the surplus? The proration requirement seems easily satisfied, so that the answer must rest on a detailed examination of the administrative and incentive effects of the two systems and the intermediate position, a task which is largely beyond the scope of this paper.

E. Pathological cases: tax subsidies. Many other deviations from the Haig–Simons definition are not consistent with the dual constraints of the general theory. The Lockean theory places a flat prohibition upon implicit transfers from the state that leave one group better off and another worse off. That prohibition reaches tax subsidies like all other transfers. Any argument that taxation is an efficient mode of implementing subsidies therefore misses the mark, because it presupposes that subsidies themselves are legitimate, a clear violation of the basic political norm.

Within this framework, a large number of special provisions of the Internal Revenue Code are simply improper. The rapid depreciation write-offs for low income housing represent one obvious subsidy that is indefensible on these grounds. The grant of percentage depletion allowances on natural resources in excess of original cost is also indefensible. The decision to keep municipal bond income outside the tax base is similarly suspect. The willingness to allow shareholders who make charitable gifts to deduct the full value of appreciated property without paying any tax on the interim gain is likewise inappropriate.[34] The free stepped-up basis at

[32] See Graetz, *Implementing a Progressive Consumption Tax*, 92 Harv. L. Rev. 1575, 1613–23 (1979). Note, there would be a real disincentive to purchase a home if the full purchase price was regarded as consumption in the year of acquisition. It is possible to defer the collection of the tax over a number of years to reflect the deferred receipt of the benefit. This delayed consumption tax on durables is best understood as the mirror image of the deferred deduction for depreciation now allowed under the income tax.

[33] See, e.g., Andrews, *A Consumption-Type or Cash Flow Personal Income Tax*, 87 Harv. L. Rev. 1113 (1974); Graetz, *Implementing a Progressive Consumption Tax*, 92 Harv. L. Rev. 1575 (1979); Kelman, *Time Preference and Tax Equity*, 35 Stan. L. Rev. 649 (1983). Note, throughout I have ignored the flat value-added tax, even though it is surely a plausible substitute for either income or consumption taxes.

[34] See I.R.C. § 170(e). In its simplest form, the taxpayer contributes shares that cost $100 but which are now worth $1000 to charity. The right calculation imputes the gain of $900 and then allows the deduction of the full $1000. The deduction appears to be $100, but is in reality more if the imputed gain is taxed at capital gains rates and the deduction is permitted against ordinary income.

the time of death is also a source of reproach.[35] Many of these gains are available only to a tiny segment of the population; many violate the principle of tax neutrality while creating additional administrative costs. The existence of a number of close cases should not blind us to the power of the theory in disposing of many easy cases, with enormous importance to the system as a whole.

F. Rate structures. The general theory has important implications for the rates of taxation. In traditional tax parlance, these rates can assume one of three forms. They can be regressive, progressive, or proportionate. All three systems share the basic belief that the amount of taxes owed should increase with the level of income earned. (I ignore here capitation taxes that call for all persons to pay a fixed amount of taxes, regardless of income.) All three systems assume that the rate base can be defined to exclude items of imputed income, and to respond to the demands for the deferred recognition of taxable income. They differ in the way they relate the increase of taxes to the increase in income. Regressive taxes increase more slowly than taxable income; proportionate taxes increase at the same rate; and progressive taxes, today the dominant form, increase more rapidly. From the Lockean perspective, a strong case can be made that the proportionate or flat tax is the only acceptable version, as Locke hints in his own brief account of taxation.

The first point in the argument is to note that within the Lockean world, the redistribution of income through the tax system is an unacceptable function of government, for no exchange can be Pareto-superior if it leaves some persons worse off.[36] Likewise, the requirement of the pro rata division

[35] See I.R.C. § 1014. To explain: if property was bought at $100 and is now worth $1000, the $900 in gain escapes taxation at death, creating the obvious incentive to postpone realization. One solution might be to allow the basis to carry over through death, so that the gain can be obtained on sale. That proves in essence to be quite unworkable if the property is held in trust, because there is no sane formula for the allocation of basis among the beneficial interests. The immediate income tax at death, coupled with the abolition of the estate tax, is the best solution.

[36] Here the learned can debate Locke's own position on the matter. The Second Treatise, his most influential work, contains no hint of any obligation to redistribute wealth that is enforceable by the state. In his criticism of Filmer, he has written passages that indicate the power of charitable obligations to the needy. Yet it is quite clear that even here he regards charity as a different domain from justice, and does not take into account the possibility that imperfect obligations of conscience are different both from legal obligations and pure consumption choices. The relevant passage is Chapter 4, ¶42, which reads as follows:

> 42. But we know God hath not left one man so to the mercy of another that he may starve him if he please. God, the Lord and Father of all, has given no one of His children such a property in his peculiar portion of the things of this world but that he has given his needy brother a right in the surplusage of his goods, so that it cannot justly be denied him when his pressing wants call for it; and, therefore, no man could ever have a just power over the life of another by right of property in land or possessions, since it would always be a sin in any man of estate to let his brother perish for want of affording him relief out of his plenty; for as justice gives every man a title to the product of his honest industry and the fair acquisitions of his ancestors descended to him, so 'charity' gives

of the gain entails that the just tax should not alter the rank ordering by wealth of individuals within the society. All of this is said with the understanding that *if* redistribution were an appropriate social goal, then taxation would be superior to ad hoc forms of direct regulation in bringing it about.[37]

If the questions of income redistribution are put aside, the concerns identified above are surely dominant. The progressive tax scores badly on the ground of tax incentives. One obvious point is that the higher marginal rates encourage individuals to conceal their revenue from the government, thereby increasing the portion of the tax burden that falls on others. Yet even if tax compliance were perfect, distortions would remain, for able high-income individuals will reduce the level of services they offer for sale because of the relatively low after tax return.

The progressive tax also scores very poorly on administration. The question is not one of computation. Instead, it involves the elaborate network of collateral rules that must be developed in order to protect the integrity of the progressive rate structure. Income splitting is of no consequence with the flat tax, for the total amount payable to the government is by definition independent of the number of persons to whom it is paid. But it becomes critical whenever any degree of progressivity is introduced into the system: then, to spread the wealth is to minimize the tax burden. Consider the rules that scrutinize the payment of salary to children, that regulate the taxation of income from family partnerships and multiple trusts and corporations, and that regulate the sale of appreciated property by donees. These, and many more, are all necessary government efforts to counter efforts by taxpayers to avoid taxes. Both private efforts to deflect the progressive tax and government efforts to maintain it are dead weight social losses that can be largely eliminated by the flat tax.

> every man a title to so much of another's plenty as will keep him from extreme want, where he has no means to subsist otherwise. And a man can no more justly make use of another's necessity to force him to become his vassal, by withholding that relief God requires him to afford to the wants of his brother, than he that has more strength can seize upon a weaker, master him to his obedience, and, with a dagger at his throat, offer him death or slavery.

It is far from clear how extensive a system of support for the poor this passage calls for. The duty to supply welfare is limited to cases of "extreme want" and not mere poverty. Locke, moreover, nowhere addresses the question of whether the money received has to be repaid should that become possible, and he does not ask whether "justice" and "charity" require the same modes of enforcement. It is quite possible that claims of justice are enforced through the legal system, and those of charity by a network of imperfect social obligations. I have ignored redistribution questions entirely here, but developed the case against redistributivist government policies in Epstein, *The Uncertain Quest for Welfare Rights* [1985] B.Y.U.L. Rev. 201 (1985).

[37] See A. Mitchell Polinsky, An Introduction to Law and Economics, 9–10, 105–113 (1983). The one great unanswered question is whether it is possible to have any effective scheme of income redistribution with a flat tax.

The progressive rate structure also introduces other complications. The constant, unhappy debate over joint returns for married couples arises because the progressive tax collides with the definition of the unit of taxation, be it individual, household, or family. With a flat tax, there is only one table, no matter what the taxable unit. There need be no question of a "marriage tax" when the income of husband and wife are treated as earned by a single person. Income averaging raises similar problems. The bulges in one year are not a reflection of permanent income. The taxpayer who earns $100,000 in each of two years is treated differently from one who earns $200,000 in one year and $0.00 in the other. A flat tax removes the need for further sets of costly provisions. At every point, the progressive structure of the taxes invites thrust and counterthrust. The effort to shift tax burdens is another illustration of the negative-sum games that a flat tax would largely forestall.

Last, there is the problem of rent-seeking through the tax system. Today, the requirement that all individuals in the same tax bracket pay the same tax provides an important brake against factional intrigue. It would be quite intolerable for the government to set individual tax rates for individual taxpayers: general tax brackets check that manifest form of abuse. But progressive taxation still leaves open a degree of freedom that can be exploited by political action. The flat tax gives the government only one degree of freedom: what is the level of the revenues and, hence, of taxation? That discretion it needs. The progressive tax leaves it a second degree of freedom: what is the level of the tilt for which there is no unique answer. It offers the government a discretion that has no social benefit, but the usual social costs. As persons know their anticipated income with some degree of reliability, they can seek to impose the costs of government upon others while keeping the benefits for themselves. Forestalling those struggles (while giving a tolerable match between the benefits and costs of government services) is one virtue of the flat tax. A rule that says you must pay a dollar for the dollar that you wish to exact from your neighbor is not a perfect safeguard against political intrigue, but it acts as an effective constraint. The flat tax has the necessary effect of reducing the total level of expenditures that are funneled through the government and, in consequence, reduces the tax gap between imputed and taxable income. It is an indispensable part of the Lockean program of taxation.

V. THE CONSTITUTIONAL DIMENSION

The last part of the inquiry is what set of institutions are needed in order to stabilize the power of the government to tax. Initially the question is, do we need any kind of constitutional constraint at all? The answer to that question depends (at least in part) on the dominant political mores of the time. A system (like England of the nineteenth century) may witness the simultaneous growth of two doctrines: the absolute sovereign power of Parliament and a strong social commitment to the principles of laissez-faire. But the question is whether that will endure or, as has been the case in England, whether the opportunities for gain through political markets will in the end undermine the position of voluntary markets. Here there is reason for pessimism: a political victory for voluntary markets does not preclude a future attack, as the opportunity for gains is still present. Yet a victory for government markets sets up entrenched groups whom it is very hard to root out after the fact. As rent-seeking and faction are the major sources of abuse, there is no obvious presumption that the form and objects of taxation should be left to legislative whim, and some strong reason to believe that in the long run the power to tax will be used to increase the size of government.

As a practical matter, however, it is not enough to identify a major source of abuse. The question is whether it is possible to construct at reasonable costs institutional arrangements that will control it. In this instance, constitutional restraints on the power to tax are the only available tool known to political theory. Whether these are obtainable politically or by judicial action is beyond the scope of this paper. What I do address briefly is the question of whether it is possible or desirable to frame constitutional limitations that address each of the six points raised in the proceeding section. The task is one that is undertaken only briefly, and with great trepidation. It seems clear that our own original constitutional structure did purport to impose explicit limitations upon the power to tax,[38] and contains other general provisions (such as the due process clauses and the eminent domain clause) that could be applied to the legislative power to tax.[39] Yet as noted earlier, where suspect classes and fundamental rights (as defined by the current jurisprudence) are not at issue, these limitations have all eroded with time; so today, over vast spheres of economic activity, the power to tax is plenary.[40]

But what kind of strategy could do better? Here it seems best to trace the possible constitutional responses to each of the six issues raised to see what could be done.

[38] See, e.g., Art. I, § 8, cl. 1: "The Congress shall have Power to lay and collect Taxes, Duties, Imposts and Excises, to pay the Debts and provide for the common Defense and general Welfare of the United States; but all Duties, Imposts and Excises shall be Uniform throughout the United States." The provision appears to limit the proper objects of taxation to the provision of various types of public goods, and was tied to the enumerated powers elsewhere in Art. I. Transfer payments, which consume an ever larger fraction of the government, were not part of the business of the federal government under the original scheme.

[39] I have discussed these issues at length in Richard A. Epstein, Takings: Private Property and the Power of Eminent Domain, Ch. 18 (1985).

[40] See, e.g., A. Magnano Co. v. Hamilton, 292 U.S. 40 (1934); Alaska Fish Salting & By-Products Co. v. Smith, 255 U.S. 44 (1921).

A. Cash or kind. In a fundamental sense, this limitation is already contained in the present constitution which, with its implicit distinction between the taxing and the eminent domain power, recognizes that far greater institutional safeguards are required when specific assets are taken from private individuals. One can quarrel with the present law for its inability to subject the full range of takings (e.g. through regulation) to the appropriate level of scrutiny, but those criticisms do not reach the fundamental decision to raise government resources by taxation.

B. The Comprehensive Tax Base. It seems very hard to define by constitutional means the appropriate base for taxation. In general, the federal statutes have taken the very broad base that the Lockean theory requires. Yet that theory is only the first approximation, given the administrative problems, for example, with imputed income. To draft a provision that speaks both to the original base and the permissible transformations of it seems a very hard task indeed. As the level of abuse from this quarter at least seems quite small, the current position is probably an acceptable one. Certainly the constitutionalization of the tax base would, even if on balance desirable, rate very low on the ladder of pressing constitutional reforms.

C. The realization and recognition of gain. There is no plausible reason to enshrine the timing of income in either direction. Thus, there are occasions in which recognition of gain and loss should proceed its realization, and others in which it should follow it. The key limitation is equal treatment across taxpayers, which is by and large observed in the major provisions concerned with the recognition of income and the allowance of deductions.

D. Income or consumption taxes. The choice between these two categories of taxes is simply a special case of the debate over realization and recognition. There is no reason for a constitutional provision to commit us to one form or the other.

E. Pathological cases. Here the case for some constitutional limitation seems more attractive, but nonetheless not clearly compelling. As noted above, there seems little reason for constitutional provisions that regulate the *timing* of income and deduction, above and apart from one that requires equal treatment across taxpayers. Yet there are many types of tax shelter which work not only to *defer* income from taxation, but to exclude it all together: percentage depletion beyond cost recovery, the exclusion of municipal bond income, and the tax free stepped-up basis at death. In principle, it should be possible to draft a provision that requires that each item of income be recognized at some point during the life of a transaction (i.e., from the time that all relevant players start and end with cash). Identifying a tax loophole is not all that difficult, at least in the easy cases.[41] But it is apt to be a fertile

[41] "While theorists may argue about what constitutes preferential treatment, sophisticated taxpayers have not experienced a similar difficulty." Blum, *The Effects of Special Provisions of the Income Tax on Taxpayer Morale*, 1955 Compendium 251.

source of litigation, and may not be an effective restraint upon the behavior of Congress, especially if there is some legislative power to exclude economic income from the tax base altogether. On balance, I think that the inquiry is at least worth pursuing further.

F. Rate structures. It is here that one sees the greatest opportunity for constitutional reform. At the general level, there is much to be said for a simple provision that says that "all income currently taxable shall be taxed at a uniform, flat rate," with no exclusions of any sort. Yet at the very least, it is problematic whether any system of welfare (or, indeed, any other) transfers could survive under this limitation, as the progressive tax is at least one important source of income redistribution. (How important it is depends at least in part on the way in which expenditures are skewed by government.) In any event, whatever the desirability of this provision as a general matter – and I believe it is great and consistent with the structure of the eminent domain clause – it would be a major revolution in taxation and political economy. Whatever doubts might exist about this provision, they do not carry over to the various special taxes (such as the windfall profits tax) which have begun to proliferate in recent years. Throughout the nineteenth century there was an active constitutional tradition that opposed special taxes for general revenues, and that position should be reaffirmed again today.[42] Special taxes offer greater opportunity for faction and present virtually no opportunity for Pareto-superior exchanges. Any income redistribution can be well done without them via the progressive tax. To enforce a constitutional prohibition against these taxes does not in my judgment require any new constitutional provisions, but only a renewed awareness of the importance of the uniformity and eminent domain provisions of the present constitution and the disproportionate impact tests that are explicit in the uniformity provisions and the "just compensation" requirement of the eminent domain clause.[43]

There is, I think, an important lesson that emerges from the foregoing analysis. In a world that operated without frictions of any sort, no individuals should be allowed to take property under the mantle of public authority. If transaction costs were zero, there would be no case for the state. Nozick would have made his case. But the existence of major frictions of all sorts calls for government. Within this environment, it becomes almost indefensible to argue that private property carries with it the absolute right under all circumstances to exclude others from its use. Yet as forced exchanges are allowed, someone must monitor their terms. As the direct measurements of

[42] See Diamond, *The Death and Transfiguration of Benefit Taxation: Special Assessments in Nineteenth-Century America*, 12 J. Legal Stud. 201 (1983).

[43] "The Fifth Amendment's guarantee that private property shall not be taken for a public use without just compensation was designed to bar Government from forcing some people alone to bear public burdens which, in all fairness and justice, should be borne by the public at large." Armstrong v. United States, 364 U.S. 40, 49 (1960).

benefits and costs are hard to make, a test of equal treatment across taxpayers becomes the next best alternative. In large measure, our current system of taxation, notwithstanding its impersonal and impenetrable character, provides much of the protection that is needed against government abuse. There are some changes, such as those which relate to flat and special taxes, that are important and obtainable. And there is a pressing need to get rid of the conscious subsidies built into the tax system. But most fine points of tax theory (on such matters as realization and recognition) are now construed in a way that is quite consistent with sensible Lockean principles. On these further constitutional control would be inadvisable.

CONCLUSION

In closing, it might be useful to summarize the article. Systems of taxation are needed to supply the public goods that are necessary to protect the lives, liberties, and estates of citizens from aggression by their fellow men. In principle, if one could measure perfectly the benefit that each person obtained from government, then the tax should be levied in proportion to the benefit so provided. Yet insuperable obstacles lay in the path of any system of direct measurement, not the least of which is the massive expansion of government that this scheme requires. To avoid these pitfalls, it is necessary to simplify the tax system to make it workable. Taxes are levied largely upon cash and cash equivalents, usually at the time of their receipt in monetizable form. Rates are kept flat and special exemptions and subsidies are rooted systematically from the tax system. The tax system is designed to minimize the inevitable distortions from the tax free world. These simple rules have some very durable properties, in that they guard against the abuses of faction and reduce the administrative power and discretion that is vested in the state. Controlling taxation is, of course, only one side of the problem. A comprehensive system of social control recognizes the need to impose parallel restrictions on the expenditure side of the budget and on the direct regulation of the economy. In one sense, it is easy to identify the most fundamental problem of all: too many resources today are channeled through government. Sensible constraints on the powers of taxation are not a conclusive remedy to all our ills. But they are a step in the right direction.

Law, University of Chicago

CONSTITUTIONAL INTERPRETATION AND ORIGINAL MEANING*

By David Lyons

I. Constitutional Originalism

> By "originalism" I mean the familiar approach to constitutional adjudication that accords binding authority to the text of the Constitution or the intentions of its adopters. At least since *Marbury*, in which Chief Justice Marshall emphasized the significance of our Constitution's being a written document, originalism in one form or another has been a major theme in the American constitutional tradition.[1]

Indeed, originalism can seem to be the only plausible approach to judicial review. One might reason as follows: "A court cannot decide whether an official decision conforms to the Constitution without applying its rules. The Constitution was written down to fix its content, and its rules remain unchanged until it is amended. Courts have not been authorized to change the rules. So courts deciding cases under the Constitution should follow the rules there laid down. By what right would courts decide constitutional cases on any other grounds?"

That challenge is conveyed by writings on judicial review that are regarded as originalist. But it is misleading. Most of the positions that are condemned by contemporary originalists accept the authority of the Constitution.[2] Although originalists present the issue as fidelity to the Constitution, it primarily concerns, I shall argue, how the Constitution is to be interpreted.

* This is a revised version of a paper presented on March 14, 1986 to the conference on philosophy and law sponsored by the Social Philosophy and Policy Center and held at the University of Michigan Law School. Earlier drafts of all or part were presented at the State of Washington Annual Judicial Conference, the University of Utah, the University of Saskatchewan, and the Cornell Law School. I am grateful for comments offered on those occasions as well as comments from Gary Simson, Sterling Harwood, and the editors of *Social Philosophy & Policy*. Research for this paper was supported in part by a Constitutional Fellowship from the National Endowment for the Humanities and a summer research stipend from the Cornell Law School, for which I am also grateful.

[1] Brest, *The Misconceived Quest for the Original Understanding*, 60 B.U. L. Rev. 204 (1980).

[2] At the same time, it seems that most if not all theorists hold that constitutional cases may sometimes be decided by rules that cannot be attributed to the Constitution. We shall touch on "nonoriginalism" in section III.

A distinctively originalist mode of interpretation assumes that the doctrinal content of the Constitution was completely determined when it was adopted and that constitutional doctrines can be identified by a value-free factual study of the text or of "original intent." It is part of my purpose to show that this type of theory is not only less plausible than its severest critics have suggested,[3] but that significant alternatives to it are available (sections II and III).

An approach to judicial review includes not only a theory of interpretation, which tells us how to understand the Constitution, but also a theory of adjudication, which tells us how to apply the Constitution so interpreted – how it should be used in constitutional cases. Originalist theory is not usually analyzed in this way, but we shall find that the distinction is needed when considering contemporary originalism.

One would expect a distinctively originalist approach to adjudication to hold that constitutional cases should be decided on the basis of doctrines in the "original" Constitution (that is, the Constitution interpreted in an originalist way), and on no other basis whatsoever. I shall show that contemporary theorists who present themselves as strict originalists accept rules for judicial review that cannot be found in or otherwise attributed to the "original" Constitution (sections IV–VI).

A third point I wish to make is that doctrines drawn from general philosophy – ideas about meaning and morals, for example – play a significant role in contemporary originalist theorizing. This point is important because these philosophical notions are dubious and controversial. It must be emphasized, however, that some of the same philosophical ideas have wide currency in legal theory generally.

Although originalism has relatively few defenders, its most prominent champions are highly placed within the federal government. These include Robert H. Bork,[4] Judge on the United States Court of Appeals for the District of Columbia Circuit, Edwin Meese III,[5] Attorney General of the United States, and William H. Rehnquist,[6] Associate Justice of the United States Supreme Court. It is important for us to recognize the quality of the constitutional theories that are embraced by these responsible officials.

This paper is, then, a critique of constitutional originalism. We need a

[3] See, e.g., John Ely, Democracy and Distrust, ch. 2 (1980); Brest, *The Misconceived Quest*; Dworkin, *The Forum of Principle*, 56 N.Y.U. L. Rev. 469–500 (1981); and Schauer, *An Essay on Constitutional Language*, 29 UCLA L. Rev. 797 (1982). MacCallum, *Legislative Intent*, 75 Yale L.J. 754 (1966) applies here too.

[4] Bork, *Neutral Principles and Some First Amendment Problems*, 47 Indiana L.J. 1 (1971).

[5] Meese, *Construing the Constitution*, 19 U.C. Davis L. Rev. 22 (1985).

[6] Rehnquist, *The Notion of a Living Constitution*, 54 Texas L. Rev. 693 (1976).

better theory. Although I shall not offer one here, I shall suggest some requirements for an adequate theory of constitutional adjudication.

II. ORIGINAL INTENT

Paul Brest's definition of "originalism" mentions two variants – "textualism" and "intentionalism."[7] The difference between them is significant. This section deals with constitutional intentionalism, especially its need for justification and the difficulties of finding any.

An originalist mode of interpretation holds that the doctrinal content of the Constitution was fixed when (or by the time that) the Constitution was adopted,[8] and that constitutional doctrines can be identified by a value-free factual inquiry. An intentionalist version of originalism holds that we must understand the Constitution in terms of the "intentions" of its framers, adopters, or ratifiers,[9] such as the specific applications that they had in mind, those they would have been prepared to accept, or their larger purposes.[10]

Champions of "original intent" seem to regard that approach to constitutional interpretation as so obviously correct that it requires no justification; for none seems to be offered. So it will be useful to begin by noting some aspects of intentionalism that imply its need for justification.

Reference to "original intent" is inherently ambiguous. The following questions indicate some (but not all) of that ambiguity. Whose intentions count? The intentions of, for example, one who drafts a text or one who votes for it? Which intentions count? To establish as authoritative some particular text, or some text understood in a certain way, or to serve some identifiable larger purposes? Reference to original intent is problematic in other ways

[7] Brest also draws a distinction between "strict" and "moderate" originalism, which I take up below.

[8] On this view, the meaning of an amendment would presumably be fixed when (or by the time) it was ratified, and its incorporation into the Constitution would presumably modify (and in that sense fix anew) the doctrinal content of the Constitution as a whole.

[9] I shall occasionally use "author" to refer to such an exclusive subclass of the population.

[10] This covers both species of intentionalism in Brest's typology. "Strict intentionalism requires the interpreter to determine how the adopters would have applied a provision to a given situation, and to apply it accordingly." (Brest, *The Misconceived Quest*, p. 222) This permits "intentions" to include general principles, as most original intent theorists appear to accept. "A moderate intentionalist applies a provision *consistent with* the adopters' intent at a relatively high level of generality, consistent with what is sometimes called 'the purpose of the provision.'" (*ibid.*, p. 223) The words I have emphasized suggest the view that "intentions" are relatively concrete or specific whereas "purposes" are relatively abstract or general, so that an appeal to original intent, strictly speaking, should be limited to the former. Brest does not defend this view, which does not square with his definition of "strict intentionalism" and is not required by the concept of intent. On the relevance of abstract intentions, see Dworkin, *The Forum of Principle*.

too. While two or more individuals can share an intention, it is by no means clear how (or whether it is always possible) to aggregate the relevant attitudes of the members of a group so as to determine their collective intentions.[11]

The answer that one gives to such questions should affect originalist interpretation, so the selection of any particular criterion of original intent as the basis for interpreting the Constitution requires specific justification. In the absence of a satisfactory rationale, we should regard any particular criterion of original intent as theoretically arbitrary. Sad to say, original intent theorists generally ignore these fundamental problems, despite their having systematically been surveyed in law reviews for at least two decades.[12]

But the differences among the various versions of originalist intentionalism do not chiefly concern us now. The point I would like to emphasize is that *any* intentionalist approach requires substantial justification. Intentionalism is a special theory of constitutional interpretation, not a platitude.

Early in our constitutional career, the Supreme Court refused to apply the Bill of Rights to the several states, holding that the first ten amendments restricted only the federal government, although their language does not explicitly limit most of those amendments in that way.[13] In so deciding, the Court made some reference to the intentions of "the framers." Although the Court's grounds for its decision went far beyond original intent, its reference to framers' intent might suggest that the Court followed that criterion of constitutional meaning instead of the apparent meaning of the authoritative text. If that were so, the Court would have followed a special theory of constitutional interpretation, and one that requires substantial justification.

In general, we recognize that we do not always mean what we say or write; *we* may mean something different from the meaning *of the language* that we use. This is reflected in our reading of legal instruments such as wills and contracts. It has also been observed, by advocates as well as critics of intentionalism, that the surest guide to authors' intent is the authoritative constitutional text itself. This is possible only because the text is understood

[11] The most plausible criterion in such cases – which are, of course, most directly relevant here – would refer to the meaning of a text that has been adopted as authoritative. But that criterion would subordinate intentionalism to textualism and would make authors' intent a derivative rather than a basic determinant of meaning. I am here considering intentionalism as a basic general theory of constitutional interpretation. I am not considering, for example, the idea that considerations of original intent may for one reason or another properly play a secondary, subordinate, or supplementary role in constitutional interpretation.

[12] See Ely, Democracy and Distrust; Brest, *The Misconceived Quest*; Dworkin, *The Forum of Principle*; Schauer, *An Essay on Constitutional Language*; and MacCallum, *Legislative Intent*.

[13] Barron v. The Mayor and City Council of Baltimore, 7 Pet. 243, 8 L. Ed. 672 (1833).

to carry a meaning that stands on its own – that is independent of its authors' intentions.[14]

It follows that intentionalism is a special theory of constitutional interpretation, not a platitude. Either it derives from a failure to appreciate the distinction between the meaning of a text and what its authors meant to convey; or else it presupposes some reason for holding that the meaning of the constitutional text, unlike that of texts generally, is a matter of authors' intent. So intentionalism is either confused or else requires substantial justification.

What might justify intentionalist constitutional interpretation? Originalists might appeal to (1) the idea (not limited to law) that interpretation should generally be governed by authors' intentions; (2) a specifically legal canon of construction; or (3) some theory of political morality that implies that we are under an obligation to respect the intentions of the framers, adopters, or ratifiers.

(1) *Intentionalism as a general approach to interpretation*. The notion that textual interpretation seeks generally to determine authors' intentions is plausible when our primary concern is what some individual had in mind, as in the case of personal communications, studies of literary figures and, in law, wills and contracts. The question is whether our proper concern when interpreting an authoritative public text such as a constitution is to determine what its authors had in mind. The suggestion seems to me implausible.

I do not wish to deny that, just as a poem can be a political statement, law can be read as literature. But law's distinctive functions are significantly different from those of literature and personal communications. Law tells us what we must or must not do, threatening punishment for disobedience. It places the coercive power of the state behind some individuals' decisions. It quite literally regulates death and taxes, war and peace, debts and compensation, imprisonment, conscription and confiscation, and innumerable other matters of direct, vital interest to individuals, communities, and often all humanity. That is the explicit, normal business of the law, including the U.S. Constitution.

An important feature of law's normal business is that it requires justification. The same applies, of course, to judicial decisions, including those that turn upon legal interpretation. They require justification, too. The justification of judicial decisions, like the justification of the normal business of the law generally, cannot be understood in narrowly legalistic terms.

[14] This point does not presuppose a general theory of text meaning. The argument of section III would seem to imply, however, that the meaning of a text is not determined solely by linguistic conventions.

Adequate justification concerns not merely whether something is required or allowed by law but, also, whether what the law does is what I have elsewhere called "defensible."[15] All of this suggests that the need for justification may properly regulate matters of legal and specifically constitutional interpretation and, thus, that these matters turn on political morality.

(2) *Intentionalism as a theory of legal interpretation.* Could intentionalism be based on a general canon of construction for legal instruments? The possibility is suggested by the fact that statutory construction is said to seek out "legislative intent." But there are several difficulties here. Insofar as constitutional intentionalism relies upon a canon of construction that derives from precedent or common law, there will be some difficulty incorporating such a theory of interpretation into originalism, as I shall explain later.

Another problem is this. Conventions regulate the identification of "legislative intent," such as the authority given to official reports from legislative committees. Such conventions have only problematic application to the U.S. Constitution. The existence of such conventions suggests something else that seems important, namely, that the search for "legislative intent" is not a purely factual inquiry about a consensus that obtained at a particular historical moment. This is suggested also by the fact that statutory construction characteristically seeks to interpret legislation in as favorable a light as possible; for example, as a reasonable and legislatively legitimate means to a reasonable and legislatively legitimate end. Such a normative bias can be explained by the fact that statutory construction seeks to provide, if possible, a grounding for judicial decisions that are justified. If what counts as "legislative intent" is in fact shaped by normative considerations, it could not serve as a model for "original intent," for those who endorse the latter as the criterion of constitutional meaning regard it as a plain matter of historical fact, accessible to a value-free inquiry.

Originalists assume that the Constitution is a morally adequate basis for judicial decisions (as well as for our political arrangements generally). The normative bias within interpretation to which I refer requires that we interpret the Constitution in such a way that it is, if possible, capable of performing that function.

If statutory construction is no help to constitutional intentionalism, what about the interpretation of other legal instruments, such as wills and contracts? The first point made about "legislative intent" applies here, too: insofar as constitutional intentionalism relies upon a canon of construction that derives from precedent or common law, there will be some difficulty incorporating such a theory of interpretation into originalism.

[15] See my *Derivability, Defensibility, and the Justification of Judicial Decisions*, 68 The Monist 325 (1985).

It might nonetheless be thought that an intentionalist interpretation of contracts[16] could serve as a model for constitutional intentionalism. That is because political rhetoric often refers to the Constitution as the upshot of a "social contract." Now, the idea of a "social contract" is invoked to argue for obedience to law, however objectionable on other grounds it might be, so long as it does not violate constitutional restrictions. This means that a "social contract" basis for intentionalism is dependent on a theory of political morality. To accept intentionalism on this basis, we must establish the legitimacy of a "social contract" argument and its valid application to this case.

(3) *Intentionalism as a theorem of political morality*. Our discussion suggests that we should seek a rationale for constitutional intentionalism in the political morality of constitutional creation and application, that is, in principles that explain why the Constitution is worthy of respect and morally binding. Two ideas are provided by political rhetoric. One, already noted, refers to a "social contract." Another, asserted within as well as outside the Constitution, holds that it comes from "the people."

The latter idea is promising because contemporary originalists, like most constitutional theorists, emphasize the predominantly "democratic" character of our constitutional arrangements. Representative government nicely complements popular sovereignty. Political rhetoric suggests that "the people" knowingly and freely agreed to respect government so long as it conforms to the Constitution, and that "the people" are accordingly bound by that agreement. But this does not yet yield the constitutional theory of original intent, which requires that the Constitution be understood in terms of the "intentions" of a special subclass of "the people," namely, the framers, adopters, or ratifiers, as opposed to (say) the understanding that one might have of the Constitution based on text meaning.

The present line of reasoning requires us to suppose, then, (a) that "the people" *contracted to accept the intentions of the authors*, by reference to which the Constitution must therefore be understood, and (b) that *this* makes the Constitution binding on us now. The theory seems fatally flawed.

(a) In the first place, only a small minority of the people of that time and place were permitted to participate in the original adoption process. We lack precise figures, but it should suffice for present purposes to observe that the process excluded not only many adult white males (and, of course, children) but also women, chattel slaves, and Native Americans. It could not have included more than a small fraction of the total population, and willing contractors would have amounted to a smaller fraction still.

[16] Insofar as such interpretation is, in fact, intentionalist. It seems relevant that contractual interpretation is not purely a matter of actual intent, but is also regulated by legal norms.

In the second place, it is doubtful whether any such contractors would have been morally competent to create obligations to respect political arrangements that continued chattel slavery, second-class citizenship for women, and the subjugation of Native Americans. At the very least, those subject to such arrangements could not be bound by a constitution simply because it was agreeable to others.

(b) In the third place, it is unclear how contracts made by members of earlier generations can bind succeeding generations. This is not to suggest that law can bind only those who have given their consent. But the mere fact that some people some time in the past have accepted a political arrangement cannot by itself automatically bind others. More is required than that to show that later generations are bound.

But the rhetoric of popular sovereignty is nonetheless illuminating. It suggests a commitment to popular government, however narrowly that was at first conceived.[17] Furthermore, the Constitution is a piece of public, not private law. Our proper concern in interpreting it is not to implement the understanding of parties to a limited, private agreement or the personal wishes of a testator, but to establish the basis for political arrangements and justified judicial decisions that legitimately concern the community as a whole. Whatever else is needed for a theory of constitutional adjudication, the legitimate interest of the entire population strongly suggests that the primary criterion of constitutional meaning should be popular understanding, the basic index of which must be text meaning.

Consider the alternative. Interpretation in terms of the intentions of constitutional framers or ratifiers would seem to assume a conception of law like that of the classical legal positivists Bentham and Austin, according to which an exclusive subgroup of the population makes law for others to follow.[18] That is objectionable because of our interest in justification. Interpretation based on anything like that conception of the law will present formidable obstacles to justifying the Constitution, justifying compliance with morally deficient laws so long as they conform to the Constitution, and justifying judicial decisions that those laws require.

The upshot is that constitutional intentionalism is profoundly problematic. There is no obvious linguistic or moral basis for interpreting the Constitution by reference to the intentions of an exclusive political group, as opposed to the meaning of the text. When these considerations are combined with other substantial objections to intentionalism, the theory seems unpromising indeed.

[17] The idea of popular sovereignty was reflected in constitutional *rhetoric* from early on. It became increasingly reflected in the constitutional *system* as time passed, as major changes occurred in the Republic, including of course major constitutional amendments.

[18] This aspect of that theory is discussed by H. L. A. Hart, The Concept of Law 41–43 (1961).

III. ALTERNATIVES TO INTENTIONALISM

In this section, I argue that intentionalism does not win out by default, despite its deficiencies. According to Brest's typology, the originalist alternative to intentionalism is textualism, which comes in two varieties. "A strict textualist purports to construe words and phrases very narrowly and precisely."[19] Brest appears to argue that this is untenable both as textual interpretation and as originalism: "An originalist would hold that, because interpretation is designed to capture the original understanding, the text must be understood in the contexts of the society that adopted it."[20] This means that textualism must be "moderate" to be plausible. "A moderate textualist takes account of the open-textured quality of language and reads the language of provisions in their social and linguistic contexts."[21]

In other words, Brest judges the only legitimate originalist alternative to intentionalism[22] to be a reading of constitutional language as "open textured."[23] Unfortunately, Brest does not explain what he takes this to mean. But his reference to the spurious precision of "strict" textualism suggests that we might understand "moderate textualism" by reference to Hart's use of "open-textured" when he introduced that technical term into legal theory.[24]

Following the received wisdom of the time, Hart held that all terms in "natural" languages (which include the language of the law) are "open-textured." An "open-textured" word has a core of determinate meaning, encompassing fact situations to which it uncontroversially applies, and a "penumbra" encompassing fact situations to which the term neither clearly applies nor clearly does not apply. The idea of "open texture" assumes that the meaning of a word is indeterminate whenever there are reasons both for and against applying the word. This aspect of the theory of "open texture" provides a theoretical rationale for a view that is widely accepted by legal theorists, namely, that legal language has indeterminate meaning insofar as its proper application is unclear.

On this understanding, to characterize constitutional language as "open textured" is to imply that the doctrines given by that language are incompletely formed. Provisions that many theorists seem to believe fit this description to an extreme degree include the so-called "vague clauses" guaranteeing "free speech," "due process," "just compensation," "equal

[19] Brest, *The Misconceived Quest*, p. 204.
[20] *ibid.*, p. 208.
[21] *ibid.*, p. 223.
[22] Actually, Brest seems to believe that moderate *textualism* amounts to the only plausible originalist alternative to "strict" *intentionalism*, as he says that "moderate textualism and intentionalism closely resemble each other in methodology and results." *ibid.*
[23] *ibid.*, pp. 205, 223.
[24] Hart, The Concept of Law, pp. 121–132.

protection," and the like. On the "open texture" model, these provisions are seen as having tiny cores of clear (and therefore determinate) meaning and relatively wide unclear (and therefore indeterminate) penumbras.

This is a politically significant idea. For it implies that, insofar as the judicial process of "interpreting" the Constitution makes its proper application clearer, the process really *changes* the Constitution by making its meaning more determinate. The clearer doctrines resulting from such "interpretations" could not then be attributed to the "original" Constitution. That is the view of constitutional language that Brest seems to regard as the ("moderate") originalist alternative to "strict" textualism.

Given this conception of the alternatives, we can better understand why originalists regard as most significant the dividing line between "strict" and "moderate" originalism. That is because moderate originalism appears to collapse into nonoriginalism.

Originalism regards the authority of the "original" Constitution as axiomatic, whereas nonoriginalism holds that adherence to the Constitution requires justification and that principles of political morality that are capable of providing such justification might also justify deviation from it.[25] To clarify this difference, we can distinguish two categories of doctrines that might be used in constitutional cases. Those that can and those that cannot truly be attributed to the Constitution may be called "constitutional" and "extra-constitutional," respectively. Nonoriginalism is prepared to consider using extra-constitutional doctrines in constitutional cases, whereas a distinctively originalist theory of adjudication would presumably reject any such use of them.

"Moderate" originalism regards unclear constitutional language as "open-textured," or inherently somewhat vague. It also accepts the judicial practice of deciding cases under unclear aspects of the Constitution. But it seems to regard the constitutional "interpretations" that are used as creating, and the resulting decisions as applying, doctrines that are extra-constitutional – judicial amendments to the "original" Constitution. On this view, "moderate" originalism's approach to deciding cases under unclear aspects of the Constitution *is equivalent to nonoriginalism*. Such decisions would be condemned by a "strict" originalist who holds that, as courts have no authority to amend the Constitution, they should refrain from doing so.[26]

It must be emphasized that the line of reasoning sketched in the last few paragraphs assumes that "moderate" textualism regards the Constitution as indeterminate insofar as its proper application is unclear. But we need not

[25] Compare Brest, *The Misconceived Quest*, p. 225. For a work that might be considered "nonoriginalist," see M. J. Perry, The Constitution, The Courts, and Human Rights (1982).

[26] We shall consider the originalist approach to this issue in section V.

assume this; we need not accept the dubious assumption that the meaning of a text is indeterminate whenever it is unclear, or whenever interpretation of it would be controversial, so that the discovery of text meaning is impossible precisely when it is needed.

Instead of discussing these issues in the abstract, it will be useful to consider an approach which agrees that such language in the "original" Constitution does *not* provide *complete* doctrines of just compensation, free speech, and the like. This approach nevertheless provides grounds for attributing the doctrines resulting from sound interpretations to the Constitution. This will provide us with all that we require for present purposes, namely, an alternative to "strict" intentionalism that might justifiably assign meaning to the Constitution and enable courts to decide cases on constitutional grounds.

It has been suggested[27] that the so-called "vague clauses" incorporate "contested concepts." It is the nature of such a concept to admit of competing "conceptions" and thus routinely to *require* interpretation. Contested concepts do not have built-in criteria of application; they are more abstract than that. As a result, different people can use the same (contested) concept while accepting and employing different standards for its application. It would seem, for example, that general normative concepts, such as "right" and "wrong," "good" and "bad," "right" and "obligation," as well as more specific normative concepts, such as particular virtues and vices, are "contested" in this way. When people agree about the "facts" but disagree in their evaluations, their disagreement concerns the principles that determine the proper application of those concepts to particular cases.

The notion of a "contested concept" is explicitly used, for example, in Rawls's theory of social justice, the relevant part of which can be explained as follows. Imagine that you and I disagree about the substantive requirements of social justice. We then differ as to how the concept of justice applies; we differ, that is, about the principles of justice. This is possible if the concept of justice admits of different interpretations, or competing conceptions. That seems to be the case.

Rawls maintains that the mere concept of justice determines no detailed, substantive criteria of justice, only the skeletal requirement that there be no "arbitrary distinctions" between persons but, rather, "a proper balance between competing claims."[28] The task of a theory of justice is to show (not merely to claim) the superiority of one conception (one principle or set of principles) over competing conceptions as an interpretation of this require-

[27] R. Dworkin, Taking Rights Seriously 132–137 (1977). This suggestion is independent of other aspects of Dworkin's legal theory.

[28] J. Rawls, A Theory Of Justice 5, 10 (1971).

ment. The possibility of a uniquely correct interpretation of a provision incorporating the contested concept of justice, then, depends on the superior justifiability of a particular conception of justice.

Now consider a constitutional example. Past judicial interpretations aside,[29] a court applying the just compensation clause would not necessarily decide a case as the original authors would have done, nor would it automatically follow a more popular consensus of the time (even if either were possible). Instead, a court would understand the Constitution to mean precisely what it says and thus to require *just compensation*. A court would need to defend a particular conception of just compensation (that is, it would need to defend principles of justice appropriate to compensation) against the most plausible alternatives. It would then apply that conception to decide the case at bar.

Someone might be skeptical about the possibility of justifying such an interpretation. Someone might believe it is impossible to provide a rational defense of, say, principles of just compensation and might therefore claim that a court adopting this approach would inevitably impose its own arbitrary conception of just compensation instead of the conception embraced by the authors of the Constitution or by a broader "original" consensus. (It should be emphasized that, on this view, an "original" conception of just compensation is completely arbitrary and indefensible.) Someone might hold, in other words, that all such principles are inherently arbitrary, so that courts cannot possibly do what is required to implement this approach to the interpretation of "vague" constitutional language.[30] I shall not offer a general critique of such skepticism,[31] but I shall suggest below why it is reasonable to believe that there can be a best conception among competing conceptions of some contested concepts. I shall later show how philosophical skepticism about values is, in this context, incoherent.[32]

Contested concepts do not seem confined to morality and law. Their properties are at any rate similar to those of concepts referring to natural

[29] If a court works under a doctrine of precedent, then the criterion of a justifiable interpretation cannot simply be fidelity to the "original" Constitution. In that case, past judicial interpretations can presumably affect the content of a justifiable interpretation, even when those past interpretations were mistaken. I ignore that complication here.

[30] We should distinguish such philosophical skepticism about values from concern about the difficulty a court might have trying to identify the best conception of a contested political concept (even when the alternatives are severely limited in number) and from an appreciation of the fact that any attempt to identify the best conception is likely to be controversial. We may also assume that reasonable judges can differ in their interpretations. It should be emphasized, however, that approaches to judicial review that seek to avoid controversial interpretations of the Constitution cannot be assumed to be justifiable by reference to the "original" Constitution. That is precisely one of the points at issue here.

[31] I address some aspects of this issue in Ethics and the Rule of Law, ch. 1 (1984).

[32] Section VI.

substances or phenomena, such as water and heat. On a plausible understanding of the development of science, for example, the caloric and kinetic theories of heat are (or at one time were) competing conceptions of the concept heat. This is suggested by the fact that "heat" refers to a physical phenomenon that is but partially and imperfectly identified by any prescientific verbal definition of the word, and that something very much like the idea of a contested concept is required to explain how there can be two theories of heat, that is, two different conceptions of the single concept heat.

If, as most people would agree, "heat" refers to a determinate physical phenomenon, there can be, in principle, a best theory of heat. This implies that there can be a best conception of a contested concept, at least in some cases. This suggests, in turn, that contested concepts in the Constitution might have best interpretations.

The kinetic theory of heat has displaced the caloric conception and is currently our best conception of heat. As this example implies, we may be justified in using *our* best conception even if it is not in fact *the* best. Similarly, just as our best conception of heat is liable to change, so we may expect change from time to time in our best conception of, say, just compensation. This involves no moral relativism.

Now if the idea that the Constitution includes contested concepts is correct, then to apply the Constitution in terms of their best interpretation is, in effect, to apply doctrines whose application is called for by the original Constitution. But, just as interpretation of the concept heat requires more than mere reflection, any interpretation of this type inevitably draws upon resources that are neither implicit in the text nor purely linguistic. It makes essential use of political argument, though at a relatively general or abstract level. So this alternative approach implies that a sound interpretation – one faithful to the meaning of the text – can include substantive doctrines that are not derivable from the text (even supplemented by its original social and linguistic context) but that are identifiable only by reasoning about political principles in the context of the federal system.

It is important to emphasize that this approach to constitutional interpretation, where applicable, requires that an interpreter go outside the "four corners" of the text, its strict linguistic implications, and the relatively specific intentions of its authors,[33] for interpretations and arguments supporting them. But, as this is done because it is understood to be required by the very nature of contested concepts found within the Constitution, both the strategy of argument and its results can claim fidelity to the Constitution. For this reason, the interpretive approach just sketched might reasonably be regarded as "originalist."

[33] Interpretation by reference to "original intent" also, of course, draws upon information outside the "four corners" of the text.

As usually understood, however, "originalism" assumes that constitutional doctrines must be identified by a value-free factual study of the text or of original intent and that doctrines that are not implicit in the "original" text or "understanding" cannot truly be attributed to the Constitution. It accordingly rejects without a hearing the possibility of attributing to the Constitution interpretations of those contested concepts that are in the Constitution. That possibility gives reason to withhold assent from the more familiar originalist theories.

IV. ORIGINALIST ADJUDICATION

The Fourteenth Amendment says that no state "shall deny to any person within its jurisdiction the equal protection of the laws." The meaning of this provision is unclear. If (as some suggest) the provision does not have any determinate meaning, how should courts deal with cases under it? The Constitution does not tell us what we should then do.

As I have suggested, a comprehensive theory of judicial review can be understood as having two parts. A theory of interpretation purports to determine constitutional meaning. If well grounded, such a theory should be welcome when the text is unclear. Furthermore, anyone who holds the text to be misleading needs a good theory to justify such a claim.

But theories about judicial review go beyond straightforward interpretation; they include theories of adjudication, which purport to determine how the Constitution should be applied.[34] Such a theory is required if cases are decided when the meaning of the Constitution is undetermined, or to justify departure from the Constitution's implications.

To illustrate the latter possibility, consider Thayer's famous deferential doctrine.[35] Thayer argued that federal legislation should never be nullified by federal courts unless it cannot reasonably be doubted that the legislation violates the Constitution. He held that this judicial policy was needed to promote respect for federal law and to protect the courts from legislative interference.[36] Thayer did not assume that the Constitution has no determinate meaning when there is reasonable disagreement about its meaning. On the contrary, he insisted that the judiciary should not apply its best interpretation of the Constitution but should defer whenever it is possible to regard the legislature's actions as constitutional.

[34] A theory of adjudication would seem to presuppose an independently determined interpretation of the Constitution, to fix whatever is (or is not) to be applied.

[35] Thayer, *The Origin and Scope of the American Doctrine of Constitutional Law*, 7 Harv. L. Rev. 129 (1893).

[36] These are Thayer's chief arguments for judicial deference. Although he nods in the direction of democratic sentiments, he expresses little respect for the virtue, sense, or competence of legislators, but he fears their collective power.

> [W]hen the ultimate question is . . . whether certain acts of another department, officer, or individual are legal or permissible, . . . *the ultimate question is not what is the true meaning of the constitution, but whether legislation is sustainable or not.*[37]

Thayer recommends, in effect, that the courts should sometimes refrain from enforcing the Constitution, even when they have a good, justifiable, and perhaps sound idea of what it means. That amounts to a special theory of adjudication (and, incidentally, one that seems decidedly extra-constitutional).

The distinctively originalist approach to adjudicating constitutional cases would seem to hold that they should be decided exclusively by doctrines that can be found in the "original" Constitution, that is, interpreted in an originalist way. There is a problem here. It is by no means clear that originalist theory can be found within the "original" Constitution. If originalism itself includes extra-constitutional doctrines, then insofar as a court applied and was guided by this theory of adjudication, it would decide cases in a nonoriginalist way!

It may accordingly seem reasonable to revise the originalist theory of adjudication so that originalism does not prohibit its own application. It would be modified to say that a doctrine may be applied within judicial review if, but only if, the doctrine either is attributable to the Constitution (in the sense required by an appropriate originalist theory of interpretation) or else is a doctrine of originalism itself.

That problem seemed easily solved. But it may suggest how difficult it is to embrace originalism unqualifiedly. Take another example. Raoul Berger's attack upon judicial decisions that fail to respect "framers' intent" leads him to suggest that courts should repudiate all decisions that cannot be grounded upon the Constitution so construed, regardless of "undesirable consequences."[38] But Berger hastily retreats from this proposal, saying:

> It would, however, be utterly unrealistic and probably impossible to undo the past in the face of the expectations that the segregation decisions, for example, have aroused in our black citizenry – expectations confirmed by every decent instinct. That is more than the courts should undertake and more, I believe, than the American people would desire.[39]

Berger's retreat appears unprincipled. At best, he invokes an undefined and undefended extra-constitutional principle of constitutional adjudication, which clashes with his originalist pretensions.

[37] Thayer, *The Origin*, p. 150 (emphasis in the original).
[38] R. Berger, Government By Judiciary 112 (1977).
[39] *ibid.*, pp. 412–413.

Henry Monaghan appears sensitive to Berger's problem. He too says that the school desegregation decisions should not be undone. Unlike Berger, however, Monaghan suggests a judicial principle that would permit leaving those decisions undisturbed, even though he questions their constitutional warrant. His solution is to advocate a doctrine of judicial precedent.[40]

The question now is whether a doctrine of judicial precedent can be attributed to the "original" Constitution. Monaghan appears not to think so. But he believes that such a doctrine can be justified because it serves "the long-run values of stability and predictability for ordering our most fundamental affairs."[41]

Monaghan does not seem to appreciate the awkwardness of his position. In offering a justification for a doctrine of precedent based on its desirable consequences, he commits himself to holding that judicial review may be regulated by *any* principles whose use would serve the same "long-run values." That would permit the use in judicial review of an indeterminate class of useful extra-constitutional principles.[42]

One might, alternatively, suggest that a doctrine of precedent was in fact provided by the "original" Constitution. For the Constitution was grafted upon a system whose common law heritage includes, of course, a doctrine requiring courts to respect judicial precedent.[43] The trouble with this way of reasoning, from an originalist perspective, is that it would render the Constitution much less limited doctrinally than originalists tend to view it. It would imply that the Constitution contains a multitude of common law principles.

Monaghan's predicament suggests the instability of originalism. If an originalist believes that there is justification for respecting a judicial principle

[40] Monaghan, *Our Perfect Constitution*, 56 N.Y.U. L. Rev. 387–391 (1981); and *Taking Supreme Court Decisions Seriously*, 39 Maryland L. Rev. 1–12 (1979).

We are presumably concerned here with precedents on the same court level, as distinct from precedents that are binding due to the hierarchical structure of a layered court system.

[41] Monaghan, *Our Perfect Constitution*, p. 389; compare *Taking Supreme Court Decisions Seriously*, p. 7.

Lawyers seem to favor consequentialist arguments for precedent over the notion that precedent is grounded upon the fairness of treating like cases alike. For a discussion of this alternative, see Lyons, *Formal Justice and Judicial Precedent*, 38 Vanderbilt L. Rev. 495 (1985).

[42] Perhaps Monaghan would like to limit the use of consequentialist argument in some unexplained way. It will be difficult to show, however, that such limitations are not ad hoc. Indeed, Monaghan's consequentialist strategy of argument threatens to get completely out of hand. For his argument commits him to approving all principles whose use would serve *any* values that are as desirable as "stability and predictability." It may also be noted that insofar as originalist doctrine, such as strict intentionalism, appeals to past judicial practice, its originalist credentials must be as problematic as those of a doctrine of precedent.

[43] Monaghan distinguishes the doctrine of precedent that is needed for constitutional cases from "common law analogies" because of differences in details, and he may infer from these differences that the constitutional doctrine could not be based on common law traditions; *Taking Supreme Court Decisions Seriously*, p. 12. But that reasoning is dubious.

that is no more controversial than precedent, he not only runs the risk of agreeing that constitutional cases may properly be decided by doctrines that cannot be attributed to the Constitution; he may become committed to accepting a relatively indeterminate theory of judicial review, incorporating all the principles of constitutional adjudication that can be justified by the criteria that are needed to justify a doctrine of precedent.

This point is generalizable. Contemporary originalists are often preoccupied with "restraining" the federal judiciary in constitutional cases and tend to embrace theories of adjudication that are designed in part to limit judicial nullification of decisions made by elected officials. The relevant judicial principles require justification. If such principles cannot be found in the "original" Constitution, they require justification by reference to some principles of political morality. The considerations that are adduced or required to justify such doctrines are capable of justifying an indefinite class of other doctrines that are relevant to constitutional adjudication. To endorse an extra-constitutional principle is to commit oneself to endorsing any other principle that is justifiable on the same grounds that justify the one endorsed. Such an approach to constitutional adjudication is hardly consistent with the spirit of originalism.

V. DEMOCRATIC SENSIBILITIES

Constitutional theorizing nowadays puts an emphasis upon "democracy" that we have so far neglected. It arises in contexts like the following. Intentionalists believe that our knowledge of constitutional meaning extends only so far as our knowledge of original intent. What remains unclear can be assigned no determinate meaning. If it is assumed that the "interpretation" and application of unclear aspects of the Constitution involves extra-constitutional doctrines, it would be natural for originalists to prefer that courts refrain from deciding such cases.

One who wishes to justify such a policy of "judicial restraint" might suggest that the defendant should win whenever law is unclear and therefore indeterminate, because then the burden of proof cannot effectively be shouldered by a plaintiff or appellant.[44] This reasoning seems warranted by the notion that courts should decide cases by reference to existing law. Not requiring extra-constitutional doctrines, it seems compatible with originalism.

But extensive use of the burden-of-proof rule would be problematic in our system. Suppose, for example, that district courts in different circuits,

[44] See, e.g., Van Alstyne, *Interpreting This Constitution: The Unhelpful Contributions of Special Theories of Judicial Review*, 35 U. Fla. L. Rev. 229 (1983).

believing they had adequate constitutional grounds for doing so, decided similar cases, but did so differently. Suppose, further, that their decisions involved aspects of the Constitution that their respective circuit courts regarded as indeterminate because unclear. If the circuit courts invoked the burden-of-proof rule, the result would in effect establish conflicting constitutional doctrines in different circuits. The federal courts would seem to require some extra-constitutional doctrine to extricate us from that predicament.

The alternative basis for a policy of "judicial restraint" is an argument from "democracy," which concludes that nonelected judges should not nullify decisions made by "electorally accountable" officials. The reasoning may be understood as follows. Insofar as political arrangements are subject to popular control through elections, they are regarded by many constitutional theorists as respecting democratic values. In addition, our system involves a division of political power under which popularly elected legislatures are authorized to make law and the judiciary is conventionally understood as authorized to interpret and apply, but not to make law.

One who assumes that unclear law is indeterminate will also believe that judges must "legislate" whenever they decide "hard cases." This practice is tolerable, or even desirable, when kept to a minimum, judges are elected and, most importantly, elected legislatures are able, if they wish, to modify the results by means of subsequent legislation. This would normally be the case except when courts must rule on limits to the legislature's authority.

From that perspective, judicial review by the federal courts of decisions made by elected officials is most problematic. In the first place, federal judges are not elected, but are appointed with indefinite tenure. Popular control is more limited over the federal judiciary than over elected officials (or, more generally, over those who are considered "electorally accountable" – those who, for example, are appointed but serve at the pleasure of elected officials). In the second place, such review concerns the constitutionality of nonjudicial decisions. Decisions made by electorally accountable officials are liable to be nullified by nonelected federal judges, and electorally accountable officials will be unable to override those judicial decisions. It is accordingly held by many constitutional theorists that such judicial review severely strains democratic principles.

These same democratic sensibilities are most seriously offended when judicial review is thought to be combined with "judicial legislation." Therefore, when constitutional cases turn upon the testing of nonjudicial decisions against unclear constitutional provisions, legal theorists tend to suppose that any substantive decision involves judicial revision of the Constitution itself. On the basis of such reasoning, contemporary originalists sometimes hold that decisions made by officials who are answerable to the electorate should not be nullified by nonelected judges unless it is clear that those decisions violate the Constitution.[45]

Some constitutional theorists are thought to lack such scruples. They are accused of claiming that courts may take it upon themselves to change the supreme law of the land. An example of such thinking is discussed by Justice Rehnquist, who quotes from a brief filed in federal court on behalf of state prisoners as follows:

> We are asking a great deal of the Court because other branches of government have abdicated their responsibility. . . . Prisoners are like other 'discrete and insular' minorities for whom the Court must spread its protective umbrella because no other branch of government will do so. . . . This Court, as the voice and conscience of contemporary society, as the measure of the modern conception of human dignity, must declare that the [named prison] and all it represents offends the Constitution of the United States and will not be tolerated.[46]

Rehnquist understands this to imply that "nonelected members of the federal judiciary may address themselves to a social problem simply because other branches of government have failed or refused to do so."[47] Federal judges would then have "a roving commission to second-guess Congress, state legislatures, and state and federal administrative officers concerning what is best for the country."[48] Rehnquist accordingly describes such a view as "a formula for an end run around popular government, genuinely corrosive of the fundamental values of our democratic society."[49]

Rehnquist's rhetoric is fired by "democratic" flames, so let us look more closely at this argument from democracy. It challenges the legitimacy of judicial review. If we were to formulate the argument rigorously, its conclusion would amount to the following proposition:

> Judicial review of a non-judicial decision violates democratic principles to the extent that the reviewing judiciary is less directly accountable to a popular electorate than is the non-judicial decision maker.

[45] This assumes, of course, that judicial review can be justified despite the argument from democracy. We shall return to that point presently.

[46] Rehnquist, *The Notion of a Living Constitution*, 54 Texas L. Rev. 695 (1976).

[47] *ibid.*

[48] *ibid.*, p. 698.

[49] *ibid.*, p. 706.

To reach this conclusion, a premise like the following is needed:

> Democratic principles imply that the more directly accountable an official decision maker is to a popular electorate, the greater the priority that should be given her official decisions.

This claim is dubious. It assumes that democratic standards apply directly to the several branches of a political structure, although the several branches are supposed to complement each other so as to yield a structure that is democratic overall. On the contrary, just as various amendments to the Constitution can be understood as promoting the system's respect for democratic values, rather than compromising that commitment, judicial review may be instrumental in securing that respect.

The sort of premise that seems to be needed by the standard argument against judicial review invokes "democracy" in a problematic way. It seems to invoke a theory of the Constitution. But no attempt is made to explain what relation such a view must have to the Constitution if the former is to qualify as a theory of the latter, no less how a particular theory might be defended. This is especially important because it is uncertain whether any view can both qualify as a theory of the Constitution, to be used in constitutional interpretation, and be reconciled with "strict" originalism.

More generally, the premise of the standard argument from democracy fails to reflect any appreciation of the values that might explain the importance of accountability to a popular electorate. It is implausible to suppose that "electoral accountability" is a fundamental value. That it is not is suggested, for example, by the qualifications that one would reasonably place on electoral accountability before it could serve in such a role; for example, that elections be free and fair. This strongly suggests that electoral accountability derives its importance from some more fundamental value, such as the right to participate in shaping the rules that may be enforced against oneself or, perhaps, political equality. These values and their relation to electoral accountability require clarification. Until we understand the basic values at stake, we can hardly determine the relation between judicial review and a commitment to democracy. And yet the literature on judicial review is silent on such matters.

Now, a federal judge might find it awkward to endorse the argument from democracy. For it suggests that the constitutional system is "democratic" in such a way as to make judicial review illegitimate. One who endorses such an argument might find it difficult to function honestly in the federal judiciary, where judicial review is firmly established.

It turns out, however, that the argument from democracy is used not to block judicial review but, rather, to establish a presumption against it. It is thought to counsel "restraint." This is illustrated by Rehnquist's response to the argument from democracy. He does not reject judicial review. He endorses it on the ground that the constitutional arrangements including judicial review are given by "the people."[50] Unfortunately, Rehnquist's version of this claim is no more plausible than the one we considered in section II. A specious argument receives a glib reply.

It should be observed, finally, that Rehnquist charges those he criticizes as favoring "the substitution of some other set of values for those which may be derived from the language and intent of the framers."[51] As this formulation suggests, his argument really turns on how the Constitution is to be understood. The quoted brief claimed, after all, that courts have a special responsibility to protect "discrete and insular minorities." This is a proposition with which some constitutional scholars agree.[52] They hold this responsibility to be based on the Constitution, not created by judicial fiat. Rehnquist disagrees with this interpretation and treats its proponents as if they recommend infidelity to the Constitution.

VI. THE WAGES OF SKEPTICISM

An initially more promising argument regarding judicial review is presented by Professor (now Judge) Bork, who begins by rejecting the crude argument from democracy and by describing our constitutional system as "Madisonian":

> A Madisonian system is not completely democratic, if by "democratic" we mean completely majoritarian. It assumes that in wide areas of life majorities are entitled to rule for no better reason than they are majorities. We need not pause here to examine the philosophical underpinnings of that assumption since it is a "given" in our society. . . .[53]

Bork refrains from reflecting on the values that are at stake. This may be deliberate, for reasons that will emerge presently. But it is unfortunate because Bork, too, appears to offer us a theory of the Constitution.

Bork claims that "the Madisonian model" has two "premises." One is "majoritarian," the other "counter-majoritarian."

> The model . . . assumes there are some areas of life a majority should not control. There are some things a majority should not do to us no matter how democratically it decides to do them.[54]

[50] *ibid.*, p. 696.
[51] *ibid.*, p. 695.
[52] See, e.g., Ely, Democracy and Distrust.
[53] Bork, *Neutral Principles*, pp. 2–3.
[54] *ibid.*, p. 3.

To reconcile these "premises," we charge the Supreme Court to "define both majority and minority freedom through the interpretation of the Constitution."[55] Thus Bork accepts the legitimacy of judicial review. But, he says,

> the Court's power is legitimate only if it has, and can demonstrate in reasoned opinions that it has, a valid theory, derived from the Constitution, of the respective spheres of majority and minority freedom. If it does not have such a theory but merely imposes its own value choices, or worse if it pretends to have a theory but actually follows its own predilections, the Court violates the postulates of the Madisonian model that alone justifies its power.[56]

This passage suggests Bork's concern that the Court not impose its own "value choices."

He explains that concern in the course of an argument that appears more promising than Rehnquist's because it deals with the issues at a more fundamental level. Bork's argument may be summarized as follows:

1. Judicial decisions *should be* "principled."
2. Judicial decisions either *make* or *implement* "value choices."
3. Judicial decisions that *implement* "value choices" *can* be "principled."
4. There is *no* "principled" way to *make* a "value choice."
5. Judicial decisions *should implement*, rather than make, "value choices."
6. Law-creation, such as legislation or the framing of a constitution, involves *making* "value choices."
7. "Courts [reviewing legislation] must accept any value choice the legislature makes unless it clearly runs contrary to a choice made in the framing of the Constitution."[57]

This argument is originalist in spirit, if not entirely in content. An originalist theory of interpretation is suggested by the notion that certain "value choices" were made by the framers and are now available to be implemented by the courts. This corresponds to the idea that Constitutional doctrines are fixed when the document is framed. An originalist theory of adjudication is suggested too, as Bork comes near to claiming that only those doctrines embodying the "framers' value choices" should be applied by the Court.

Note that the last step in the argument appears to presuppose a nonoriginalist principle:

[55] *ibid.*
[56] *ibid.*
[57] *ibid.*, pp. 10–11.

> Whenever the Constitution is unclear, the Court should defer to the legislature.

What basis could there be for such a doctrine of "restraint"? Bork has no grounds for suggesting, for example, that the practice of judicial review should be confined because it suffers under a cloud of illegitimacy. For, as we have seen, he has rejected the dubious argument from democracy, endorsed the practice of judicial review, and assigned it an indispensable constitutional function.

Here is one possible explanation of that last step in Bork's reasoning. As we have observed, many legal theorists embrace assumptions about meaning which lead them to believe that law is indeterminate when it is unclear. As we shall presently see, Bork explicitly endorses an even more radical type of philosophical skepticism – about value judgments generally. It would therefore not be out of keeping for Bork to indulge in the semantical skepticism that leaps from "unclear" to "indeterminate." This would lead him to reason that, when (a) the Constitution does not *clearly* contain a doctrine that is violated by a piece of legislation, then (b) the Constitution contains *no* such doctrine, (c) the legislation does not violate the Constitution, and (d) the legislation should accordingly be accepted by the Court.[58]

But the most serious difficulty with Bork's reasoning derives from his value skepticism. To see this, we might begin by asking what is meant by a "value choice." This expression is so commonplace in constitutional theory that we may need to remind ourselves that it is an artifact of theory. Compare the expression with "value judgment." "Value choice" omits any reference to judgment, and so encourages the suggestion of arbitrariness and discourages any contrary suggestion of rational defensibility. The difference fits nicely into Bork's strategy of argument, which explicitly invokes a general philosophical doctrine of skepticism about the rational defensibility of value judgments.

As we have seen, Bork defines the central problem of "Madisonian democracy" as the need to strike a balance between "majority and minority freedom."[59] It is precisely in this context that he says, for example:

> Every clash between a minority claiming freedom and a majority claiming power to regulate involves a choice between gratifications of the two groups. When the Constitution has not spoken, the Court will be able to find no scale, other than its own value preferences, upon which to weigh the respective claims to pleasure.[60]

[58] This assumes the use of a burden-of-proof rule discussed in section V.
[59] Bork, *Neutral Principles*, p. 3.
[60] *ibid.*, p. 9.

Bork has two examples. One is *Griswold*, which he views as a judicial choice between two "claims to pleasure" and their respective "gratifications." Another is "a hypothetical suit by an electric company and one of its customers to void a smoke pollution ordinance as unconstitutional. The cases are identical."[61]

To make Bork's position perfectly clear, we should consider a different example. Prior to the Fourteenth Amendment, Bork would presumably respond to a suit seeking invalidation of a law banning Jews and Catholics from certain occupations, as follows:

> There is no way of deciding these matters other than by reference to some system of moral or ethical values that has no objective or intrinsic validity of its own and about which men can and do differ. Where the Constitution does not embody the moral or ethical choice, the judge has no basis other than his own values upon which to set aside the community judgment embodied in the statute.[62]

My point is not that a refusal to invalidate the statute would have been unfaithful to the law, for the contrary interpretation is, unfortunately, plausible. My point is that Bork's express reason for a judicial policy of "restraint" is that all opposing positions, including the rejection of bigotry, are rationally indefensible, so that, lacking constitutional warrant, a judicial decision favoring one would be "unprincipled" *just because* any "preference" for one side or the other *could not be* "principled." Value "choices" are required to adjudicate between any two opposing views, because moral and political positions are in Bork's view equivalent to preferences. The judicial vindication of a morally motivated claim is likewise equivalent, in his eyes, to favoring one person's gratification over another's. But:

> There is no principled way to decide that one man's gratifications are more deserving of respect than another's or that one form of gratification is more worthy than another.[63]

Such "value choices" might be made by judges or derived from the Constitution. If made by judges, Bork maintains, the judicial decisions in which

[61] *ibid.*

[62] *ibid.*, p. 10.

[63] *ibid.* Bork's note explains: "The impossibility is related to that of making interpersonal comparisons of utilities." He apparently assumes that if there is any morally defensible criterion for making decisions (including those adjudicating interpersonal conflicts of interest), it is that they should maximize (in Bork's terms) "gratifications." The alleged impossibility to which he refers would make that criterion impossible to satisfy. Normative welfare economics avoids the problem by giving up the maximizing requirement and replacing it with a conception of economic efficiency, such as Pareto's, that requires no interpersonal comparisons of utility. Bork's note suggests that he is unaware of or refuses to consider either economic or deontological alternatives to classical utilitarianism.

they are embodied are "unprincipled," because value judgments are in general "unprincipled."

> Where constitutional materials do not clearly specify the value to be preferred, there is no principled way to prefer any claimed human value to any other.[64]

But if the "value choices" are derived from the Constitution, then the judicial decisions implementing them are "principled."

It is important to emphasize that in these passages Bork is *not* simply asserting the standard originalist claim that judges reviewing legislation should not impose their own values, but should apply doctrines derived from the Constitution. For that is what he is trying to prove. He is arguing, in effect, that *when the Constitution is unclear and interpretation of it may seem to require moral reasoning*, judges should defer to the legislature. His philosophical skepticism is deployed to show that judges should make no value judgments when deciding constitutional cases.

That is relevant to an earlier argument of this paper. The alternative to "strict" originalism that was sketched in section III requires that courts applying "vague clauses" of the Constitution interpret "contested concepts," which requires reasoning about moral or political principles. Bork's view that judges should not make "value choices" seems to mean that courts should not engage in any such reasoning. Bork reasons: judicial review should be neutral, principled, and nonarbitrary; it is impossible to make value judgments that are neutral, principled, or nonarbitrary; so judges should not incorporate value judgments into their constitutional decisions.

Bork's value skepticism is assumed and applied without justification.[65] Needless to say, value skepticism cannot be found within the Constitution. Indeed, the two are clearly incompatible. Thus Bork invokes an *anti*-constitutional doctrine to significant effect.

It is worth noting that Bork's skepticism renders his overall position incoherent. Consider his claim that judges *should* decide constitutional cases in a certain way – that (as he seems to argue) they are *under an obligation* to do so. Bork writes as if he is providing a rational defense for that sort of conclusion about the responsible, legitimate use of judicial power. He appears to believe that his reasoning excludes contrary conceptions of judicial obligation. In his terminology, however, to embrace such a doctrine is to make a "value choice," which according to his value skepticism is irremediably "unprincipled," or rationally indefensible.

The result is a dilemma for Bork. If it is possible to provide good reasons

[64] *ibid.*, p. 8.

[65] But see note 63.

(as Bork purports to do) for his conception of the legitimate (justified, responsible) exercise of judicial power – reasons designed to show that his conception is superior to contrary conceptions – then "value choices" can be principled. On the one hand, the success of any argument for the attribution of an obligation to judges would refute his value skepticism and undermine his argument that value judgments have no legitimate place in constitutional adjudication. On the other hand, his wholesale value skepticism excludes the possibility that any conception of the legitimate exercise of judicial power might be rationally defensible; so his skepticism undermines his own argument for and resulting judgment about responsible adjudication.

Consider now Bork's notion that judges must rely upon the value judgments that are embedded in the Constitution if their decisions are to be "principled." Bork assumes that decisions involving the exercise of judicial review can be "principled" insofar as they are grounded upon constitutional doctrines. This apparently means that the decisions can be justified relative to, or conditional upon, those doctrines.

But conditional justification is only as good as its condition. Recall that one piece of Bork's argument goes as follows:

> Law-creation, such as legislation or the framing of a constitution, involves making "value choices."

Another piece says:

> There is no principled way to make a "value choice."

Put together, these pieces yield the conclusion that the "value choices" embodied in the Constitution and the corresponding doctrines are themselves "unprincipled" or, in other words, unjustifiable. But if the doctrines on which the justification of judicial decisions depends are themselves unjustifiable, then the same applies to those decisions.

This means that Bork is faced with another dilemma. On the one hand, if "value choices" are unjustifiable, then so are the "value choices" reflected in the Constitution, and the same applies to all that relies on them for justification. On the other hand, if some value judgments can be justified (such as the idea that the Constitution merits respect), then Bork's general value skepticism is unsound, and his main argument collapses.

Bork might seem to avoid this particular incoherence when he remarks that his value skepticism "is not applicable to legislation. Legislation requires value choice and cannot be principled in the sense under discussion."[66] Bork might seem to suggest that there is another sense of "principled" in which

[66] Bork, *Neutral Principles*, p. 8.

the "value choices" embodied in legislation (and thus the legislation itself) can be "principled." Bork might mean, for example, that, rationally defensible or not, legislation by popularly elected officials is *permissible* under both democratic principles and our constitutional system. He might also wish to infer from this that those subject to such laws are under an obligation to respect them.

But this interpretation would not enable Bork to avoid the dilemma. Either he accepts the idea that democratic standards *justify* political arrangements that satisfy them, or he rejects it, presumably because of his value skepticism. If he rejects the idea, then there is no apparent sense within Bork's skeptical system in which legislation or indeed our constitutional system can be justifiable; there is no apparent sense in which the Constitution can *truly* be said to merit respect, in which judges can *truly* be said to be under an obligation to respect it. If Bork believes that any of these value judgments can *truly* be justified, then he must forsake his objection based on value skepticism to the exercise of moral judgment within judicial review.

VII. CONCLUSION

Originalism seems to derive its initial plausibility from a simplified conception of how written constitutions work. Interpretation in terms of original intent promises a stable, uncontroversial version of the Constitution. But intentionalism faces overwhelming difficulties and appears to lack compensating justification, either in political or linguistic terms. Seeing no promising alternatives, opponents of strict originalism have accepted the need for extra-constitutional doctrines in constitutional adjudication. Originalists appear to reject such heterodoxy, but they unselfconsciously embrace a variety of extra-constitutional doctrines. Their theorizing about the Constitution tends toward the superficially descriptive and has yet to face the substantive value commitments implicit even in ritualistic appeals to democracy. Just as the Constitution cannot be value-free, so our understanding of it must be informed by reflection on the principles it serves.

Philosophy and Law, Cornell University

JUSTICE IN SETTLEMENTS*

By Jules Coleman and Charles Silver

INTRODUCTION

In any society relatively few disputes are brought to judges for resolution. Most are handled informally or forgotten. Fewer still are cases that go to trial. Most are settled. Compromises are reached even in cases where issues are hotly contested and where millions or billions of dollars in damages are claimed. Recently, for example, one of the most controversial lawsuits of our time, the *Agent Orange* case, was settled.[1] In that case, veterans of the Vietnam War, their spouses, and their children alleged that a defoliant — Agent Orange – used in Southeast Asia contained dioxin and was responsible for deaths, debilities, miscarriages, and birth defects suffered by members of the plaintiff class. Class members argued that the manufacturers of the defoliant, seven major chemical companies, knew that it was tainted and should be made to compensate them for their injuries, claiming billions of dollars in damages. The case received national exposure and became a rallying point for veterans, a means they hoped to use to publicize their plight and to spur Congress to come to their aid. On the eve of trial, the case was settled. The defendants, who denied liability throughout the pretrial period, agreed to pay the veterans $180 million. In turn, the plaintiff class agreed to drop the suit. Thus ended a controversy which not only presented novel legal issues and tested the ability of the federal courts to handle complex lawsuits, but concerned the well-being of a large number of veterans, their spouses, and their handicapped children as well.[2]

Most lawyers, judges, and law professors think it is good that so few cases are tried.[3] Many want to reduce the amount of litigation even further.[4] To

* Earlier versions of this paper were presented to the Law and Economics Workshop at the University of Chicago and at a Conference on Law and Philosophy at the University of Michigan. We would like to thank the participants on both occasions for their helpful comments. We especially appreciated the comments of Al Alschuler, Richard Epstein, Daniel Fischel, Victor Goldberg, William Landes, Geoffrey Miller, Donald Regan, and Cass Sunstein. We would also like to thank Steven Fasman, Owen Fiss, Leo Katz, Steve Neuwirth, and David Schlecker for comments and assistance given at various stages of this paper's development. A longer look at possible defenses of the uses that are made of class action settlement funds is taken in Charles Silver, "Using Class Action Settlement Funds Justly and Wisely," Working Paper #XX, Program in Civil Liability, Yale Law School, March 1986. We thank George Priest for making the support of the Program in Civil Liability available to us. Finally, we participated equally in this project and take equal responsibility for it. We list our names alphabetically only for the sake of convenience.

this end, they have invented and incorporated into the legal system a variety of devices that encourage parties to settle. For example, the *Manual for Complex Litigation*[5] and the *Federal Rules of Civil Procedure*[6] encourage judges to hold pretrial conferences at which they are to invite the parties to come to terms. And a proposed amendment to Federal Rule of Civil Procedure 68 would require "a party who rejects a settlement offer and then receives a judgment less favorable than that offer [to] pay the [postoffer] attorney's fees of the other party."[7] The reasons most commonly given for discouraging trials are that settlements conserve resources and enable parties to resolve their differences amicably. Settlements are said to reduce attorneys' fees and court costs, free space on crowded dockets, speed relief to injured plaintiffs, and avoid the need for judges to decide difficult legal questions.[8] These beliefs are so widely accepted that even legal encyclopedias – the most conservative of authorities – recite them.[9]

[1] See "In re Agent Orange Product Liability Litigation," *Federal Supplement*, vol. 597 (Eastern District of New York, 1984), p. 740; and "In re Agent Orange Product Liability Litigation," *Federal Supplement*, vol. 611 (Eastern District of New York, 1985), p. 1396.

[2] The history of the Agent Orange case is chronicled in detail in Peter H. Schuck, *Agent Orange on Trial: Mass Toxic Disasters in the Courts* (Cambridge, Mass.: Harvard University Press, 1987). See also Schuck, "The Role of Judges in Settling Cases: The Agent Orange Example," Working Paper #36, Program in Civil Liability, Yale Law School, Sept. 1985.

[3] Even Abraham Lincoln favored settlements. He addressed the following remarks to a group of young attorneys: "Discourage litigation. Persuade your neighbors to compromise whenever you can. Point out to them how the nominal winner is often a real loser — in fees, expenses and waste of time. As a peacemaker, the lawyer has a superior opportunity for good. There will still be business enough." Quoted in an editorial by Gary T. Johnson, *Chicago Tribune*, August 9, 1985. The source for Lincoln's remarks is *Fragment: Notes from a Law Lecture*, July 1, 1850.

[4] See, for example, Derek Bok, "A Flawed System," *Harv. Mag.* (May–June 1983); Warren E. Burger, "Isn't There a Better Way?" *American Bar Association Journal*, vol. 68 (1982), p. 274, and "Agenda for 2000 A.D. — A Need for Systematic Anticipation," *Federal Rules Decisions*, vol. 70 (1976), pp. 93–96; and Richard A. Epstein, "Settlement and Litigation: Of Vices Individual and Institutional," *University of Chicago Law School Record*, vol. 30 (Spring 1984), p. 2.

[5] "In order to produce a climate in which counsel may explore the possibility of early settlement, the judge should ask the views of counsel on the possibility of settlement at the first principal pretrial conference . . . [S]ettlement should always be encouraged. . . ." *Manual for Complex Litigation*, sec. 1.21.

[6] "In any action, the court may in its discretion direct the attorneys for the parties and any unrepresented parties to appear before it for a conference or conferences before trial for such purposes as . . . facilitating the settlement of the case." *Federal Rules of Civil Procedure*, Rule 16(a)(5).

[7] Owen Fiss, "Against Settlement," *Yale Law Journal*, vol. 93 (1984), p. 1074. For the text of the proposed amendment to Rule 68, see Committee on Rules of Practice and Procedure of the Judicial Conference of the United States, "Preliminary Draft of Proposed Amendments to the Federal Rules of Civil Procedure," *Federal Rules Decisions*, vol. 98 (1983), pp. 361–363.

[8] See, e.g., Burger, "Isn't There a Better Way?" p. 275ff.

[9] "The resolution of controversies and uncertainties by means of compromise and settlement is generally faster and less expensive than litigation; it results in a saving of time for the parties, the lawyers, and the courts, and it is thus advantageous to judicial administration, and, in turn, to government as a whole. Moreover, the use of compromise and settlement is conducive to amicable and peaceful relations between the parties to a controversy." "Compromise and Settlement," *American Jurisprudence* 2d, vol. 15A (Supp. 1985), sec. 5.

The consensus within the legal community notwithstanding, settlements are by no means unproblematic. Whenever cases settle, plaintiffs get less than they want and either more or less than they would receive at trial. Defendants give more than they want and, again, either more or less than they could be required to pay. Plaintiffs therefore either get more or less than they deserve, and almost never just what they deserve. Defendants pay more or less than they ought to, and almost never just what they owe. If justice requires giving each party his or her due, that is, his or her desert, then settlements almost never satisfy this principle of justice. One concern, then, is the extent to which parties can legitimately or justifiably negotiate around the requirements of justice, and the extent to which legal institutions that encourage their doing so, i.e., institutions that encourage and facilitate settlements, are desirable and defensible.

In a recent article, Owen Fiss raises several further objections to the institutions that foster settlements and to settlements themselves. In general, he argues that settlements are inferior to judgments and, therefore, ought not to supplant them.[10] For Fiss, settlement is "a highly problematic technique for streamlining dockets," "the civil analogue of plea bargaining," and "a capitulation to the conditions of mass society [that] should be neither encouraged nor praised."[11] In this paper, we propose to introduce philosophers to the terms of the debate over the morality of compromises and settlements and to contribute to the literature in this important field. We will begin by setting out some of our reasons for thinking that settlements may sometimes be morally objectionable. This discussion will familiarize philosophers with some of the procedures and principles settlements involve. We will then show that a particular practice now standard in the federal courts – that of dividing settlement funds among the members of a plaintiff class – cannot be defended on the ground usually given for it, which is that justice, the principle that people ought to be compensated for wrongfully inflicted losses, entitles class members to payments.

Before moving to the arguments, however, we wish to emphasize the conditional nature of the claims that follow. Our view is that trials offer advantages that are often overlooked and that cannot be procured by means of settlements, not that all disputes should be tried or that all means of resolving disputes informally should be abolished. We realize that the advantages adjudication provides come at a price, and very often the price

[10] Fiss, "Against Settlement." See also the response to Fiss by Andrew W. McThemia and Thomas L. Shaffer, "For Reconciliation," *Yale Law Journal*, vol. 94 (1985), p. 1660, and Fiss's rejoinder, "Out of Eden," *Yale Law Journal*, vol. 94 (1985), p. 1669. Federal District Court Judge Jack Weinstein also grapples with one of Fiss's arguments in "In re Agent Orange Product Liability Litigation," *Federal Supplement*, vol. 597, p. 760.

[11] Fiss, "Against Settlement," p. 1075.

may not be worth paying. But, as we endeavor to show in the pages that follow, settlements also exact a price, one that may sometimes be sufficiently high to call into question the advisability of institutions that encourage settlements.

I. WHY SHOULD WE WORRY ABOUT SETTLEMENTS?

Although procedures vary from jurisdiction to jurisdiction, and even from courtroom to courtroom, a lawsuit is settled in roughly the following way.[12] Some time after a suit is initiated, the judge assigned to it will call the attorneys into chambers for the purpose of exploring the prospects for settlement.[13] The conference will be informal. Only the judge's sense of propriety and the attorneys' desire to play their cards close to the vest will act as constraints. The attorneys will describe the case to the judge, highlighting its strengths and weaknesses. The judge will then ask counsel for the plaintiff whether the case can be settled and, if so, at what price.[14] At this point, negotiations will begin. Usually, plaintiff's counsel will suggest a figure well above the amount the defendant is willing to pay. Opposing counsel will then make a counteroffer, and it will be up to the judge to narrow the distance between the parties.[15] Of course, the judge can bridge the gap either by encouraging the defendant to come up or the plaintiff to come down, or both. The choice of strategy will depend on the judge's views of the merits of the case, the ability of the defendant to make a larger payment, the extent of the plaintiff's need, and perhaps other factors. Moreover, the judge will always be conscious of the need to clear the docket. Primarily by playing on counsels' hopes and fears – for example, by suggesting that close calls may be decided for or against a particular party, by praising the quality of counsels' efforts, and by emphasizing the common

[12] We thank David Schlecker of the law firm of Anderson, Russell, Kill & Olick for giving us the benefit of his experience litigating and settling personal injury lawsuits.

[13] The judge may do so *sua sponte* or at the request of counsel for either party.

[14] Although the word "price" calls the idea of money to mind, defendants often agree to provide services in lieu of, or in addition to, cash. In-kind relief is especially likely to be offered or requested in cases alleging civil rights violations. For example, in "Women's Committee for Equal Employment Opportunity v. National Broadcasting Co.," *Federal Rules Decisions*, vol. 76 (Southern District of New York 1977), p. 173, a case brought under Title VII of the Civil Rights Act of 1964, the defendant agreed to revamp its policies concerning the employment and promotion of women and to award back pay. When in-kind relief is agreed to, the parties ask the judge to enter a consent decree in which their rights and obligations are spelled out in detail.

[15] Judges use a variety of tactics to bring parties together. In the Agent Orange case, for example, Judge Weinstein appointed a special master for settlement, told counsel how he was likely to decide close issues, arbitrated disputes, set limits on the settlement price, and required counsel to attend a marathon bargaining session immediately before the trial was to begin. See Schuck, *Agent Orange on Trial*.

interest the judge and counsel have in settling the case and moving on to other matters – the judge will broker the settlement. When the parties agree on a price, everyone will reenter the courtroom and, assuming counsel have their clients' consent, the case will be dismissed. The plaintiff's attorney will then prepare a release which states that the plaintiff agrees to renounce the suit in return for a payment from the defendant. When the release is executed and the payment made, the case will be at an end.

A settlement, then, is a contractual exchange.[16] Parties settle because they expect settlements to make them better off than they would be if they continued to litigate. A plaintiff may prefer settling at a particular price now to the risk of losing at trial or to the prospect of waiting years to recover. A defendant may want to avoid the risk of liability or to be free of the burdens of litigation. And both parties want to keep legal fees and court costs to a minimum. Since there is room for mutual gain, and since there may be strong pressure from the judge to settle, the parties negotiate an exchange in which the plaintiff gives up the right to sue and the defendant makes a payment to, or performs a service for, the plaintiff. Because aspects of the exchange extend into the future, the exchange is regulated by a contract – a release or a consent decree. A defendant may be required to make a series of payments, to reform its employment policies, or to refrain from monopolistic practices. A plaintiff may want to renew a suit, for example, because alleged injuries have worsened or because newly acquired evidence strengthens the case against a defendant. Each party will therefore want a means of binding its counterpart to the settlement. Moreover, each will want to commit itself to an agreement as a means of convincing its opponent to do the same. Finally, if after compromising the lawsuit the parties disagree about their rights and duties under the settlement, a judge will look at the contract and interpret it according to standard contractual principles when resolving that and any related subsequent dispute.[17]

(*1*) *Justice versus efficiency*

It is worth noting that settlement agreements bind parites irrespective of the legal validity of a plaintiff's claim, that is, regardless of the outcome that would have been reached or ought to have been reached at trial. Although the parties' and the judge's perceptions of the merits of a case may affect the price at which it settles, the validity of the underlying claim is never

[16] See Richard A. Posner, *Economic Analysis of Law*, 2nd ed. (Boston: Little, Brown & Co., 1977), pp. 434–441.

[17] See, for example, "Beecher v. Able," *Federal Reporter* 2d, vol. 575 (Second Circuit 1978), p. 1010, a securities fraud case in which the parties disagreed over their rights to an unused portion of a settlement fund.

adjudicated.[18] No facts are found, no conclusions of law are drawn, no judgment is entered, and no opinion is written. The agreement binds as long as the claim it settles was disputed in good faith, "[e]ven if [the] claim . . . is actually invalid and its invalidity is not even doubtful in legal contemplation."[19] The law reaches this result because, in general, contracts bind whenever one person confers a benefit on another who knowingly receives it. And since defendants gain whenever suits against them are withdrawn – if only because they are allowed to live in peace – settlements bind in virtually all cases.[20]

It should come as no surprise that settlements preclude adjudication. First, settlement would be a poor means of economizing resources and preserving relationships if plaintiffs were required to demonstrate even the prima facie validity of their claims at trial. If a minihearing on the merits were held, for example, evidence would have to be gathered, documents read, depositions taken, witnesses prepared, arguments and strategies mapped, a hearing held, and an opinion entered. This would raise the cost of settling a case substantially, and could further impair the parties' relationship. Moreover, the hearing would likely be a sham. Given the parties' mutual interest in settling a case, an adversarial presentation of views could not reasonably be expected.

Second, there is a sense in which everyone knows that "[t]o settle for something means to accept less than some ideal."[21] Plaintiffs and defendants often emerge from settlement conferences with mixed emotions. On the one hand, they may be relieved to set aside a lawsuit and to avoid the worst possible outcomes. On the other hand, they may be upset at being denied justice. A defendant may think that a plaintiff's claim is groundless, that a trial would have proved its invalidity, and that the legal system enables plaintiffs to extort settlement payments by threatening defendants with litigation costs. A plaintiff may think that victory at trial is likely, that settlement is a bargain for the defendant, and that the legal system disadvantages plaintiffs by using costs and delays to hamper their pursuit of justice. In short, both sides may believe that for all practical purposes the private and social costs of adjudicating the validity of an allegation prevent them from

[18] "[A] claim need not be valid or well founded to support a compromise, and as long as there has been good faith, the courts will not inquire into the merits of a claim or the actual rights of the parties . . . [T]he courts will not inquire into the validity of a claim which was compromised in good faith . . ." "Compromise and Settlement," sec. 17. See also Fiss, "Against Settlement," p. 1082.

[19] "Compromise and Settlement," sec. 16.

[20] The grounds for invalidating a compromise or settlement are illegality, fraud, duress, undue influence, and mistake. See *ibid.*, secs. 27–34.

[21] Fiss, "Against Settlement," p. 1086.

pursuing the justice of the matter, and that justice is sacrificed for efficiency.[22]

Another way to put the matter is to note that in a world with zero litigation costs, we would want the validity of all complaints to be adjudicated. This is so because what we would really like to see is the payment of full compensation to persons whose allegations are valid and the payment of no compensation to those whose charges are false. Equally, we would like to see all and only defendants who commit wrongs brought to justice. In a world where lawsuits could be maintained without expense, we would come as close as possible to achieving these goals by trying every complaint. However, since we live in a world where costs cannot be ignored, and where litigation severely strains relationships, we tolerate a state of affairs in which most plaintiffs get more or less than they deserve, and most defendants pay more or less than they ought. In other words, we sacrifice justice for the sake of efficiency and peace.[23]

By saying that we would come as close as possible to achieving justice in a costless world by trying every complaint, we mean to suggest only that there is a high correlation between vindication at trial and the actual validity of a claim, and that the strength of that correlation would reach its highest point if trials were conducted in light of all potentially relevant information about a claim. Even then, however, we do not think that adjudication would be an infallible means of identifying valid claims. Our ability to gather and process information may be limited even in a costless world. Still, in the real world we are a long way from reaching the limits of our ability to gather and process information. Because settlements are encouraged, far less money is spent investigating issues than would be spent if more cases went to trial. Since we could better achieve justice in this world by investing more heavily in information, the policy of encouraging parties to settle, that is, of conserving resources at the expense of doing justice, stands in need of a defense.[24]

[22] Epstein writes that "Early in teaching I received this advice from a shrewd and experienced lawyer. 'You can tell the sign of a good deal — everyone leaves the room happy. You can also tell the sign of a good settlement — everyone leaves the room unhappy.'" "Settlement and Litigation: Of Vices Individual and Institutional," p. 3.

[23] We thank Leo Katz of the law firm of Mayer, Brown & Platt for suggesting this formulation of the matter. Also, see Fiss, "Against Settlement," pp. 1085–1087.

[24] Since settlements may occur at any time prior to final judgment, the amount of information available to parties who settle may also vary considerably. For example, there may be more reason to think that a plaintiff who settles to avoid an appeal after winning at trial is entitled to compensation than there is to think that a plaintiff who settles before trial is so entitled because more information may be available about the former's claim than about the latter's. Even so, since many cases settle before trial, and since additional resources could be invested in gathering and processing information whenever a case settles, it is plausible that we could promote compensatory justice more fully by trying every complaint to finality. Moreover, settlements and trials differ procedurally in relevant ways. For example, trials, but not settle-

(2) Unfair bargaining

Institutions may be defensible on balance even though they trade off justice against efficiency. It could be argued that the policy of permitting and encouraging settlements is justified because settlements make people better off (even though they sacrifice justice for efficiency), and, moreover, because people consent to them. In other words, the sacrifice of justice for efficiency may be justified on both consensual and Paretian grounds.

Not every bargain that is voluntarily entered into is beyond reproach, however. The literature on the law of contract tells us that people are forbidden from carrying out some exchanges on certain terms and from entering into others entirely. It is well known, for example, that courts will invalidate contracts by which people would sell themselves into slavery or bind themselves to perform immoral acts, and that courts will release minors and incompetents from the agreements they sign. It is less well known that courts will refuse to enforce agreements by which people would waive the right to marry, to divorce, to sue for relief under the bankruptcy laws, to alienate labor freely, or to require a landlord to provide an apartment that meets minimum standards of habitability.[25] Moreover, even contracts that regulate permissible transactions may be unenforceable if their terms or the circumstances in which they are negotiated are objectionable. Courts routinely ignore "boilerplate" provisions in contracts and void contracts that result from fraud, deceit, or duress.

Many reasons can be given for finding fault with contracts or even for invalidating them. Of particular interest for our purposes is the possibility that the parties to an agreement may not be in a position to bargain with one another on fair terms. A landlord, for example, will often know much more than a prospective tenant about the condition of a rental unit, and the prospective tenant may not easily be able to redress the imbalance. Consumers usually have far less experience than automobile dealers and department store managers with credit agreements, and may suffer an unfair bargaining disadvantage as a result. Contracts that are negotiated against a background of unequal bargaining power are said to be "adhesive," and

---

ments, are held in public, are conducted in accordance with rules of evidence, involve the formal presentation and argument of issues of law and fact, are subject to appeal, and are often decided by judges who rationalize their rulings in written opinions. If, as we have assumed, these procedures tend to increase the reliability of trials as means of discerning the validity of claims, our confidence that claims that are vindicated at trial are in fact valid may greatly exceed our confidence that people who settle deserve the payments they receive.

[25] See Anthony Kronman, "Paternalism and the Law of Contracts," *Yale Law Journal*, vol. 92 (1983), p. 763, for a discussion of nondisclaimable rights. See Joel Feinberg, "Legal Paternalism," *Canadian Journal of Philosophy*, vol. 1 (1971), p. 105, for a discussion of related philosophical issues.

judges often feel bound to alter their terms or, in extreme cases, to nullify them entirely.[26]

There is reason to think that parties to settlement agreements sometimes possess unequal bargaining power. In some respects, this may not be a bad thing. An inequality that reflects the objective merits of the parties' claims may be unobjectionable. In other respects, however, disparities call into question the moral acceptability of a settlement. Although the bargain struck in any given case will reflect in part the parties' predictions of the likely outcome of a trial, it will also reflect the parties' relative abilities to finance a lawsuit, to tolerate delays, to withstand adverse publicity, to spread losses among others, to tolerate risk, and many other extralegal factors.[27] For example, a personal injury case may pit an unemployed plaintiff who faces mounting medical and personal expenses against an insurance company.[28] Or a class action alleging antitrust violations may threaten a corporation with treble damages – a potentially staggering loss even in cases where the harms suffered by individual class members are small.[29] When one party has a significant resource or threat advantage over the other, it is reasonable to question the acceptability of the terms on which they agree to settle their dispute.[30]

(3) Agreements contrary to public policy

It would be a mistake, however, to focus attention solely on the circumstances in which bargaining takes place. In some cases the fact that a bargain

[26] Kronman, "Paternalism and the Law of Contracts," pp. 770–774.

[27] See Fiss, "Against Settlement," pp. 1076–1078.

[28] See Note, "The Availability of Excess Damages for Wrongful Refusal to Honor First Party Insurance Claims — An Emerging Trend," *Fordham Law Review*, vol. 45 (1976), pp. 164–166.

[29] See, for example, "In re Cuisinart Food Processor Antitrust Litigation," *Trade Cases* (Commerce Clearing House), vol. 1983–2 (District of Connecticut, 1983), ¶ 65,680, p. 69,472, in which the damages alleged ranged from $32 to $75 per class member and the class contained in excess of 1.5 million members, so that Cuisinart's total possible liability after trebling was between $144 million and $337.5 million. See also "Phillips Petroleum Co. v. Shutts," *Supreme Court Reports*, vol. 105 (1985), p. 2965, a suit for failure to pay royalties on oil leases, in which claims averaged $100 per member for a class of 28,100 people. The use of the class action device to threaten defendants with extraordinary litigation expenses and liabilities prompted one author to write of the "*in terrorem*" effect of class antitrust actions, and to describe them as "legalized blackmail." Handler, "The Shift from Substantive to Procedural Innovations in Antitrust Suits — The Twenty-Third Annual Antitrust Review," *Columbia Law Review*, vol. 71 (1971), p. 9.

[30] See Jules Coleman, "Liberalism, Unfair Advantage, and the Volunteer Armed Forces," Robert K. Fullinwider, ed., *Conscripts and Volunteers: Military Requirements, Social Justice, and the All-Volunteer Force* (Totowa, NJ: Rowman & Allanheld, 1983). It is worth noting that power imbalances may obtain at trials, too. Wealthy parties may be able to hire better lawyers and to maneuver more freely than poor ones. However, trial procedures are designed to reduce the impact of such imbalances in ways that settlement procedures are not. For example, a trial judge can ask questions, suggest motions, and take other steps to ensure that a proceeding is fair, and the appeals process provides a measure of security that obvious imbalances will be redressed.

is struck at all should cause concern. This is so, for example, when parties use settlements to do things they are otherwise legally forbidden to do by means of contracts. When this occurs, a settlement provides for a result that is contrary to public policy, even if it is in keeping with the parties' wishes.

To take an example with far-reaching implications for corporate behavior, consider the case of *Globus v. Law Research Service, Inc.*[31] In *Globus* a jury convicted the name defendant, Law Research, and its underwriter, Blair & Co., of securities fraud. The convictions reflected the jury's belief that officers of both companies knew that an offering circular misrepresented the value of securities issued by Law Research. Both companies were therefore required to compensate the purchasers of the securities for losses they incurred as a result of the fraud. After paying the judgment against it, Blair & Co. sued Law Research, claiming that the underwriting agreement obligated Law Research to make good any loss Blair & Co. suffered as a result of the fraud. The trial judge disagreed, holding that the indemnification provision of the underwriting agreement violated public policy and was unenforceable. He argued that if Law Research reimbursed Blair & Co., the latter "would have less of an incentive to conduct a thorough investigation and to be truthful in the prospectus distributed under its name . . ."[32] The Court of Appeals concurred, noting that "[i]t is well established that one cannot insure himself against his own reckless, wilful or criminal misconduct."[33]

Indemnification agreements are a mainstay of corporate life. Not only underwriters, but officers and directors of corporations, investment bankers, brokers, and accountants try to insulate themselves from liability for material misstatements made in connection with the purchase or sale of securities.[34] Possibly all of these arrangements are contrary to public policy.[35] However, they are unenforceable only when fraud is proved. That is, if a case alleging

[31] "Globus v. Law Research, Inc.," *Federal Supplement*, vol. 287 (Southern District of New York 1968), p. 188, *affirmed in part and reversed in part, Federal Reporter* 2d, vol. 418 (Second Circuit 1969), p. 1276, *certiorari denied, United States Reports*, vol. 397 (1970), p. 913.

[32] *Federal Supplement*, vol. 278, p. 199.

[33] *Federal Reporter* 2d, vol. 418, p. 1288.

[34] For discussions of indemnification, see Dale A. Oesterle, "Limits on a Corporation's Protection of Its Directors and Officers from Personal Liability," *Wisconsin Law Review*, vol. 1983 (1983), p. 513; Joseph W. Bishop, Jr., "New Problems in Indemnifying and Insuring Directors: Protection against Liability under the Federal Securities Laws," *Duke Law Journal*, vol. 1972 (1972), p. 1153; and Bishop, "Sitting Ducks and Decoy Ducks: New Trends in the Indemnification of Corporate Directors and Officers," *Yale Law Journal*, vol. 77 (1968), p. 1078.

[35] In the opinion affirming "Globus" the Court of Appeals noted that the Securities and Exchange Commission "has announced its view that indemnification of directors, officers and controlling persons for liabilities arising under" the securities laws is against public policy. *Federal Reporter* 2d, vol. 418, p. 1288.

securities fraud is settled, a defendant can collect an indemnity.[36] After all, the defendant will not have been convicted of fraud. This almost certainly means that many people who commit frauds go unpunished, that many plaintiffs receive settlement payments even though their allegations would fail at trial, and that the incentives in the securities market are not what they might be.

An even more surprising possibility is that indemnities can be paid even in cases where fraud is proved. In *Globus*, for example, it would not have been abnormal for Law Research and Blair & Co. to have settled their dispute instead of exhausting the appeals process.[37] In this event, Law Research would have paid an indemnity smaller than that requested by Blair & Co., but larger than that permitted by public policy. In other words, the defendants would have achieved by settlement a result they were prevented from achieving by contract.[38] Thus, whenever a securities fraud case involving multiple defendants is settled, the public policy behind the securities laws may be impaired.[39]

In fairness, it must be said that judges can refuse to permit settlements that violate public policy, and they can invalidate existing settlements for the

[36] For example, had Law Research and Blair & Co. settled *Globus*, Blair & Co. would have been entitled to an indemnity per the underwriting agreement. See, for example, "Cambridge Fund, Inc. v. Abella," *Federal Supplement*, vol. 501 (Southern District of New York, 1980), pp. 598, 618 (distinguishing *Globus* on the ground that "unlike the situation in ["Globus," here] there has been no adjudication of willfullness — only the entry of a consent order with such findings").

[37] Indeed, in view of the size of the judgment after the first appeal — approximately $32,500 — it is startling that they continued to press their claims at all.

[38] It is worth noting that after losing on the indemnification issue Blair & Co. sued Law Research for contribution — allocation of responsibility for a judgment among defendants each of whom is liable for it in its entirety — and won. "Globus, Inc. v. Law Research Service, Inc.," *Federal Supplement*, vol. 318 (Southern District of New York 1970), p. 955, *affirmed sub nom* "Globus v. Law Research Service, Inc.," *Federal Reporter* 2d, vol. 442 (Second Circuit), p. 1346, *certiorari denied sub nom* "Law Research Service, Inc. v. Blair & Co.," *United States Reports*, vol. 404 (1971), p. 941. Even so, since indemnification and contribution are distinct claims, settlement of the indemnification issue would have been against public policy. It would have further reduced Blair & Co.'s liability.

[39] Throughout this section we have assumed that the policy of preventing people from insulating themselves from the legal consequences of securities fraud is correct. This assumption is questionable, that is, it is possible that *Globus* was wrongly decided and that indemnification agreements are unobjectionable. An argument to this effect could be made on the ground that issuers who can monitor underwriters efficiently should be permitted to offer insurance as a means of enticing underwriters to handle their securities. Even if *Globus* was wrongly decided, however, the analytical point that people may use settlement agreements to accomplish ends they are legally forbidden to achieve by means of contracts would remain intact. Only the example we have used would be impeached. In other words, the general point that settlements may undermine sound public policy goals would survive a showing that the policy of forbidding indemnification in securities fraud cases is unwarranted. It is the general point, not the example suggested by *Globus*, to which we are committed.

same reason. Nonetheless, many objectionable agreements may go unnoticed. First, judges cannot expect parties to call attention to questionable aspects of settlements. Once parties form an agreement, their interest is to get a judge to approve it, not to invite an inspection of its terms. After a settlement is approved, the parties to it will raise the issue of its acceptability only if one of them thinks it is worthwhile to begin the trial of the dispute anew. Even in this event, however, it may be difficult for a judge to decide whether a settlement is contrary to public policy because the issues presented by the underlying dispute will not have been aired. Second, institutional pressures discourage judges from acting *sua sponte* to invalidate settlements. As the amount of civil litigation grows, judges must process cases more quickly. Consequently, they have less time to familiarize themselves with the facts and issues cases present and must rely more heavily on counsels' opinions and recommendations. As a result, judges are more likely to miss objectionable elements of settlements. Third, parties can sometimes appeal a judge's decision to refuse to dismiss a case, which means that a judge who interferes with settlements sometimes risks being reversed by a superior court.[40] Thus, although judges can take steps to insure that settlements accord with public policy, there is no cause for optimism that they will do so as often as needed nor reason to think that the efforts they make will succeed.[41]

(4) Third party effects

Settlements may also be of concern for reasons other than that parties may use them to do things they are forbidden to do by contracts. For example, if a complaint alleges that the process of selecting books for classroom and library use at a public school discriminates against minority students, a settlement will affect all students at the school, not merely those involved in the lawsuit. This is so because the settlement agreement will determine how limited funds are allocated among competing goals and needs. The same problem would exist in a case in which it was alleged that a welfare agency may not lawfully cancel a recipient's payments without first providing the recipient an opportunity to be heard. Money spent holding hearings for some people cannot be used to provide benefits for others. In many cases,

[40] This is the case, for example, when judges perform their Tunney Act duty to determine that a proposed settlement of a government antitrust suit is in the public interest. *United States Code*, title 15 (1980), sec. 16(e). It is also the case when judges perform their duty to assess the fairness, reasonableness, and adequacy of proposed settlements to class actions. See footnote 75.

[41] It must be noted that settlement agreements contrary to public policy could be negotiated even if all complaints were tried. Parties would simply need to conspire with each other to achieve this result. Our suggestion is only that the frequency of such agreements may decline as the rate of trials increases. We thank Don Regan for helping us clarify this point.

then, settlements affect third parties, and there is reason to worry that third parties' interests may be neglected.[42]

Thus, settlements may be open to the same objections that have been leveled at contracts. Indeed, the range of possible objections is larger than we have suggested here. For example, we have said nothing about the problem of generating consent to settlements in cases that involve classes of litigants, a matter Fiss discusses at length.[43] Nor have we raised the issue of paternalism: Is it ever appropriate to prevent a person from settling a claim, against his or her wishes, but for his or her own good? Although we lack space to discuss these issues in this paper, it would be silly to pretend that they do not exist. It would be equally foolish to give an unqualified endorsement to policies that discourage trials, for example, policies like the proposed amendment to Rule 68, until all of these issues are raised and settled.

(5) *Underproduction of public goods*

To this point we have argued that the practice of permitting settlements may involve a sacrifice of justice for efficiency, and that the sacrifice may not be adequately defended on the ground that settlements serve parties' interests or that parties consent to them. A rational bargain is not necessarily a voluntary one, and even when the voluntariness of a contract is not at issue, settlement agreements may permit individuals to do what they otherwise would be legally prohibited from doing, or they may have objectionable third party effects.

We now want to ask whether the policy of encouraging settlements promotes efficiency as fully as its advocates suggest. Even if it is admitted that justice can sometimes be traded off against efficiency, it hardly follows that policies that promote neither justice nor efficiency should be adopted. And there is at least one reason to think that institutions that encourage settlements may be inefficient. The reason is that trials often produce opinions and precedents – public goods – that benefit not only the parties to a lawsuit, but third parties as well. Public goods are positive externalities. Opinions and precedents are public goods because they are sources of information about the things that can and cannot lawfully be done in a

[42] This paragraph draws heavily on examples and arguments discussed by Owen Fiss. In addition to "Against Settlement," we direct the reader to the following articles by Fiss: "The Supreme Court 1978 Term — Forward: The Forms of Justice," *Harvard Law Review*, vol. 93 (1978); "The Social and Political Foundations of Adjudication," *Law & Human Behavior*, vol. 6 (1982); and "Objectivity and Interpretation," *Stanford Law Review*, vol. 34 (1982). To avoid misleading the reader, we should also note that trials can affect the interests of nonparties in much the same way that settlements can. However, third parties can sometimes intervene in trials in ways that they cannot intervene in settlements, as when a dispute is resolved before a complaint is filed.

[43] Fiss, "Against Settlement," pp. 1078–1082.

society. Lawyers and others whose lives are affected by law use them when planning their affairs and when advising others. When cases settle, judges have no opportunity "to explicate and give force to the values embodied in authoritative texts such as the Constitution and statutes. . . ."[44] For this reason, settlements do not increase the amount of information or the number and variety of legal precedents available to the public, and policies that encourage settlements decrease the rate at which these public goods are produced. Had the codefendants in *Globus* settled the claim for indemnification, for example, the opinions that case produced would never have been written.

That settlements reduce the number and variety of legal opinions has two implications. First, it means that the public subsidizes litigants. Even cases that settle consume public resources. Although litigants are required to pay court costs, taxpayers defray the fixed costs of keeping the judiciary running.[45] The net result is that forums for dispute resolution are made available to settling parties at prices that fail to reflect their full social cost.[46]

There may be nothing wrong with subsidizing people who settle civil cases, but the practice requires a defense. An argument that has been made for using tax monies to support the judiciary is that since lawsuits produce positive externalities – information in the form of opinions and precedents – the public should encourage litigation by making forums for the resolution of civil disputes available at subsidized rates.[47] One could also argue that, in fairness, taxpayers should bear part of the expense of producing public goods simply because taxpayers consume them.[48] Obviously, neither argument justifies the practice of subsidizing litigants who settle their claims. When cases settle, the public gets little or nothing in return for its investments in the court system because in general settlements produce neither

[44] *ibid.*, p. 1085.

[45] It is estimated that public funds were used to support the federal courts (excluding the Supreme Court) in the following amounts in 1985: judges' salaries, $74,540,000; salaries of supporting personnel, $370,228,000; fees of jurors and commissioners, $42,000,000; expenses of operation and maintenance of the courts, $101,500,000; space and facilities, $140,000,000; and court security, $25,500,000. *Annual Report of the Director of the Administrative Office of the U.S. Courts (1984)* (Wash., D.C.: Government Printing Office, 1985), pp. 78–80. Although these fixed costs apply to both civil and criminal matters, the former far outnumber the latter. In 1984, 261,485 civil cases and only 36,845 criminal cases were filed in the U.S. District Courts; *ibid.*, pp. 4–6.

[46] This may come as a surprise to readers who think that litigation costs are already prohibitively high.

[47] See Posner, *Economic Analysis of Law*, pp. 400–401, 419–427.

[48] For a discussion of the conditions under which it may be fair to require people to defray the costs of public goods they consume, see Richard J. Arneson, "The Principle of Fairness and Free-Rider Problems," *Ethics*, vol. 92 (1982), p. 616.

opinions nor precedents.[49] And since the vast majority of cases settle, subsidies may be better thought of as wealth transfers than as investments in public goods. It is therefore reasonable to ask why public funds are used to provide forums for the settlement of private disputes.[50] In other words, it may be reasonable to require people who settle their cases to reimburse the public for the full social cost of supporting the courts while permitting people who take their cases to trial to pay only a fraction of that cost.

The second implication of the fact that settlements produce neither opinions nor precedents is that institutions that encourage settlements may cause too few public goods to be produced.[51] For example, the proposed amendment to Rule 68 would require a plaintiff who refused a settlement offer and who then received a judgment smaller than the offer to compensate a defendant for attorney's fees incurred after the offer was made. For example, under the new rule a plaintiff who refused a settlement offer of $500,000 and was then awarded only $400,000 in damages would have to pay the defendant's postoffer attorney's fees. Obviously, if the amendment is adopted, plaintiffs will become more receptive to settlement offers and settlement prices will decline. Less obviously, if the new rule reduces the frequency of trials, as the authors hope it will our society's capital stock of information will be affected because precedents will be produced at a slower rate. The need for precedents, however, will remain unchanged at best. Uncertainty will continue to exist, precedents will continue to become obsolete, and disputes will continue to arise. A new increase in litigation may therefore occur. This is so because, as circumstances change and precedents obsolesce, litigants will become less sure of the outcomes of lawsuits and will file more complaints as a result. As Posner notes, "litigation would seldom occur were there no uncertainty concerning the outcome. . . . [O]nly if each disputant expects to do much better in the litigation than the other disputant expects him to do are the parties likely to fail to agree on [a] settlement . . . ; and uncertainty is a necessary condition of such a divergence of estimates."[52] In other words, a possible explanation of the increase in litigation that so many writers find so deplorable is that the policy of encouraging settlements results in the underproduction of opinions and

[49] Class action settlements are an exception to this rule. And, of course, we realize that precedents concerning the enforcement of settlements arise from settled cases. However, even these precedents emerge only because claims are taken to trial.

[50] Even Richard Posner, a proponent of settlements, writes that "[i]f the function of the legal system were solely to settle disputes, it would be appropriate to impose the entire costs of the system on the disputants." *Economic Analysis of Law*, p. 401.

[51] "[T]he settlement rate is an important determinant of the direct costs of resolving legal disputes. Beyond a certain point, however, a further increase in the settlement rate would increase the total costs of dispute resolution by reducing the production of precedents below the optimal level." *ibid.*, p. 434.

[52] *ibid.*, p. 422.

precedents. If this explanation is valid, institutions that foster even higher rates of settlement will only make matters worse.

The problem with devices like the proposed amendment to Rule 68 is that they discourage litigation by increasing its cost, not by attacking its cause – controversy. Those who would raise the price of using the courts do not see that precedents help people figure out their legal rights and obligations, plan for the future, and interact with others smoothly. In other words, precedents reduce transaction costs by reducing the amount of time people have to spend planning their affairs and by reducing the amount of uncertainty that sets in when unanticipated events occur. For example, precedents that clarify the meaning of words and phrases enable lawyers, contractors, testators, lessees, legislators, underwriters – everyone who uses legal language – to carry out their aims cheaply and effectively. When language is standardized, forms can replace tailor-made documents, people can spend more time performing their obligations and less time hammering them out, and disputes are both less likely to arise and more easily managed.

It is easy to forget the value of precedents as public goods. The gains they provide are spread across millions of interactions. We are so accustomed to dealing with others without a lot of fuss that we fail to notice the ways in which the common law smooths out the wrinkles in our affairs. By contrast, litigation costs are easily remembered. They provide a rude and unwelcome shock to everyone who brings a case to court. This is the reason so many people think that lawsuits ought to be discouraged, and in a sense, we agree. We think it would be nice if people spent more time being productive and getting along, and less time arguing. It's just that we think it is more appropriate to seek this end by enabling people to avoid disputes than by denying them access to the means of justice when disputes arise. We are therefore skeptical of devices that would reduce the litigation rate, especially when they increase the amount of uncertainty that attends human affairs.

One could reply to our claim that the number and variety of precedents may fall to a suboptimal level in two ways. First, one could argue that the relationship between uncertainty and litigation is self-equilibrating. As uncertainty grows, more lawsuits go to trial, more precedents are produced, and more information is made available. After the tide of litigation rises, then, uncertainty will diminish and the flow of new lawsuits will ebb. On this view, uncertainty and litigation feed back upon each other and, as a result, a suboptimal level of precedent production cannot persist for very long.[53] Second, one could argue that too much information is as bad as too little. Beyond a certain point, information may be of little, no, or even negative value. For example, a precedent that obscures a "bright line" rule may create

[53] See *ibid.* for a presentation of this view.

uncertainty where none previously existed, and the information value of a precedent that simply reaffirms a well-entrenched legal doctrine may be too low to justify the cost of its production. Thus, too much information may be a problem, and it is wrong to assume that the production of precedents is always a good thing.[54]

Although both theses have merit, neither of them fully allays the fear that institutions that encourage settlements may cause too few public goods to be produced. The view that uncertainty and litigation maintain an optimal supply of information assumes that relevant features of the legal system remain unchanged over time. It assumes, for example, that judges who are appointed by Republican presidents and judges who are appointed by Democratic presidents exert roughly the same amount of pressure on parties to settle. Otherwise, changes in administration would alter the rate at which precedents are produced. However, as the proposed amendment to Federal Rule of Civil Procedure 68 makes abundantly clear, legal institutions may change in relevant ways over time. The amendment to Rule 68 was offered because of concern over rising rates of litigation.[55] If the amendment is adopted, and if it discourages trials as its authors hope it will, the balance between uncertainty and litigation will be altered. Specifically, fewer precedents will be produced at a given level of uncertainty than was the case before the amendment was proposed. On the other hand, if the amendment is rejected, or if it fails to reduce the rate of litigation,[56] the same people who proposed the amendment can be expected to invent other means of discouraging trials. Thus, even if uncertainty and litigation feed back upon one another, the possibility remains that too few precedents will be produced.

In response to the thesis that too much information is as bad as too little, we note only that we have not claimed that too few precedents are in fact produced. We advance the weaker thesis that institutions that encourage settlements *may* cause too few public goods to be produced. Whether legal institutions currently produce a supraoptimal, optimal, or suboptimal flow of information is an empirical matter we are not in a position to resolve. It is, however, a matter of importance that ought to be studied before unconditional approval is given to devices that increase the settlement rate. If, as seems plausible to us, the recent surge in litigation that has so alarmed scholars and judges is a result of the historic underproduction of legal

[54] See Epstein, "Settlement and Litigation: Of Vices Individual and Institutional," for a discussion of the trend away from "bright line" rules.

[55] The number of civil cases filed annually increased by more than 100% between 1977 and 1984. *Annual Report of the Director of the Administrative Office of the U.S. Courts (1984)*, p. 4.

[56] See Geoffrey P. Miller, "An Economic Analysis of Rule 68," *Journal of Legal Studies*, vol. 15 (1986), p. 93; and George L. Priest, "Regulating the Content and Volume of Litigation: An Economic Analysis," *Supreme Court Economic Review*, vol. 1 (1982), p. 163.

precedents, we would be ill-advised to place additional burdens on parties who are inclined to take their cases to trial. Alternatively, if more lawsuits are being brought because too much information is available, it may be reasonable to alter existing rules as a means of encouraging settlements. In either event, the factual issue cannot be resolved from the armchair and, until it is resolved by investigation, there is no reason to dismiss the possiblity that precedents are in fact or are likely to be underproduced.

Moreover, even if precedents are currently overproduced, it would not necessarily follow that trials ought to be discouraged. Although trials often produce precedents, they need not and do not always do so. Cases are sometimes decided without opinion, and opinions are not always published. If trials are advantageous for reasons other than that they are sources of public goods, for example, because they achieve justice more fully than settlements do, we may want to encourage trials even though we also may want to reduce the flow of information to the public. In this event, the appropriate course of action would be to regulate the number and variety of precedents, not to encourage settlements.

II. MAKING JUST USE OF CLASS ACTION SETTLEMENT FUNDS

In the preceding section we argued that institutions that encourage settlements may sacrifice justice for efficiency. We also argued that this trade-off may be inadequately defended on certain grounds. In this section we will suggest that even if the trade-off can be defended, that is, even if it is reasonable to encourage settlements, considerations of justice continue to play a role in the settlement process. Once a case is settled and a gain in efficiency is achieved, questions of justice may arise in a new form.

Some lawsuits, for example, simple contract and tort cases, pit a single plaintiff against a single defendant. Others have a far more complex party structure. As we mentioned above, in the *Agent Orange* case a plaintiff class containing hundreds of thousands of members opposed seven corporate defendants. When a simple two party case is settled, money flows from one person (the defendant) to another (the plaintiff). When a case involving a plaintiff class settles, something entirely different occurs: money is paid to a group of people the vast majority of whom never appeared in court and were probably unidentified at the time of the settlement. Whenever a class action settles, then, a question of justice not presented by a simple two party case may arise. The question is: what, in justice, should be done with the money paid to settle the case?

Judges have answered this question by saying that since justice requires that people who are injured wrongfully be compensated, settlement funds should be used to reimburse class members for their losses.[57] On the basis of this reasoning, judges have required that monies paid in settlement of class actions be divided among class members in proportion to the size and strength of their underlying claims.

We think that justice does not require this use of class action settlement funds, even if it does require that people be compensated for losses that are wrongfully inflicted upon them. Since our arguments presuppose a bit of familiarity with the law, we will take a moment to describe class actions before setting out our reasons for thinking that the principle of compensation does not warrant the practice of dividing settlement funds among class members.

(1). *Class action procedures*

The class action is a procedural device for adjudicating in a single lawsuit similar claims that are held by many different individuals.[58] For example, the residents of Bhopal, India who were injured or killed during the recent disaster there have similar claims against the Union Carbide Company. Although the nature and extent of their injuries may vary enormously, each resident would have to prove that the chemical leak caused an injury and that Union Carbide should be held liable. If each resident initiated a separate lawsuit, then, the same issues of fact and law would have to be decided thousands of times, at considerable expense to both the plaintiffs and the defendants. To economize on litigation costs, Federal Rule of Civil Procedure 23 permits a single, representative plaintiff to sue on behalf of all other persons who are similarly situated. Any injured Bhopal resident could hire an attorney and file a suit on behalf of all potential claimants. If the suit was successful, the costs of bringing it would be assessed against the fund recovered by the class. In other words, litigation costs would be distributed pro rata among all class members.

The preceding discussion is misleading in one respect. Although all class actions involve persons whose claims are similar, class actions may differ in a variety of respects. For example, class members are permitted to opt out of some classes but not others.[59] For our purposes, the size of members' claims is an important dimension along which class actions vary. In some cases, class members would sue on their own even if the class action device was

[57] "A tort settlement, conceptually and in practice, is intended to compensate an individual for injuries to his or her person." "In re Agent Orange Product Liability Litigation," *Federal Supplement*, vol. 611, pp. 1424–1425.

[58] Classes can be both plaintiffs and defendants. In this paper, however, we will be concerned with only plaintiff classes.

[59] Class members are not permitted to exclude themselves when, for all intents and purposes, the trial of a class action would be dispositive of their interests. For example, the trial of a school desegregation class action would adjudicate the rights of all minority students, even those who wished to exempt themselves from the lawsuit.

unavailable. In others, members' claims are so small that it makes sense to press them only as a group.[60] In *Phillips Petroleum Co. v. Shutts*,[61] for example, members' claims averaged only $100 per plaintiff. As Justice Rehnquist noted in the majority opinion in that case, when claims are this small, "most of the plaintiffs would have no realistic day in court if a class action were not available."[62]

As the law now stands, monies defendants pay to settle class action lawsuits must be divided among class members. Ordinarily, the amount each member receives is determined by the putative size and strength of that member's claim. For example, if members *A* and *B* allege injuries worth $10,000 and $50,000, respectively, and both claims stand an equal chance of success on the merits, *B* would receive five times the amount *A* receives from a settlement fund. Likewise, if *A* and *B* assert equal claims, but *A*'s stands only a 10% chance of success while *B*'s stands a 50% chance of success, again *B* would receive five times as much as *A*.

The reader may want to know how legally similar claims could stand unequal chances of success on the merits. This possibility arises because claims need not be identical to be grouped in a class – they need only raise common issues of fact and law. For example, in a class antitrust action, some claims may be older than others and may have to surmount a statute of limitations barrier that newer claims do not confront,[63] and some purchasers may have better records than others.[64] In a class tort action like *Agent Orange*, some class members' injuries may be direct and others' indirect. In that case, veterans claimed to have been harmed by being exposed to dioxin, while their spouses and children alleged that the primary exposure of veterans had adversely affected them, too. The claims of spouses and children were therefore more difficult to prove than those of veterans themselves.[65] Thus, even though class members' claims must be similar, they may differ in size and strength.

(2). *Does the principle of compensation require that class members receive settlement payments?*

What grounds are usually given for dividing settlement funds among class members in amounts that reflect the putative size and strength of their

[60] A rational person will refuse to sue on a claim when the opportunity cost of a lawsuit exceeds its expected return (the payoff given that the lawsuit may be won, lost, or settled times the probability of each outcome).

[61] "Phillips Petroleum Co. v. Shutts," *Supreme Court Reports*, vol. 105 (1985), p. 2965.

[62] *ibid.*, p. 2974.

[63] See "In re Cuisinart Food Processor Antitrust Litigation," and "In re Corrugated Container Antitrust Litigation," *Federal Reporter* 2d, vol. 643 (Fifth Circuit 1981), p. 195.

[64] See "Ohio Public Interest Campaign v. Fisher Foods," *Federal Supplement*, vol. 546 (Northern District of Ohio 1982), p. 1.

[65] *Federal Supplement*, vol. 611, p. 1411.

claims? Oddly, no one has offered a comprehensive defense of the practice. Even judges have advanced few arguments for it.[66] However, when judges do give reasons, they usually argue that justice requires the payment of compensation to class members. Compensation is said to be warranted either because settlements partially validate members' claims[67] or because members are stripped of the right to sue when a class action is settled.[68] In the following two subsections we will show that neither of these arguments supports the practice of dividing settlement funds among class members in paradigm class actions. Paradigm class actions possess the following trait: class members' claims are too small to litigate individually, but sufficiently numerous to be worth litigating as a group. We call these cases "paradigm class actions" because no one would bring them if the class action device was unavailable. This would entail a failure of both compensation and deterrence.[69] By contrast, cases in which members' claims are large would be brought in the absence of Rule 23. They would be styled as individual actions, and, of course, they would be more expensive for plaintiffs and defendants to deal with. Thus, in what follows we will argue against a practice that is a part of the core of Rule 23.

A. Do settlements validate class members' substantive claims?

The argument that settlements confer partial validity on class members' claims has never been fleshed out fully. We are therefore called upon to reinvent the rationale used by judges who take this view. A plausible argument for their position runs as follows: defendants settle to limit their liability; that defendants face any liability at all indicates that class members' claims have some merit; indeed, if their claims wholly lacked merit, a judge would have a

[66] In "In re Corrugated Container Antitrust Litigation," p. 220, for example, Judge Tjoflat wrote, "It is *self-evident* that . . . [a] distribution should be weighed heavily in favor of plaintiffs whose claims" (emphasis added) are most likely to succeed at trial.

[67] "Whether or not the defendants have formally admitted some responsibility for defects in their products and for possible injuries to some plaintiffs, the public can justifiably assume, for perhaps the first time, that there is some merit to the claims of those exposed to Agent Orange that they are suffering because of their war and post-war experiences." "In re Agent Orange Product Liability Litigation," *Federal Supplement*, vol. 597, p. 749.

[68] "All the settlements release the claims of all class members for the entire eighteen-year period of the alleged conspiracy. Thus it is appropriate that some compensation be given for purchases made in the pre-statute of limitations period." "In re Corrugated Container Antitrust Litigation," *Trade Cases* (Commerce Clearing House), vol. 1981–1 (Southern District of Texas 1981), ¶ 64,114, p. 76,717, *affirmed*, *Federal Reporter* 2d, vol. 659 (Fifth Circuit 1981), p. 1329.

[69] "Where it is not economically feasible to obtain relief within the traditional framework of a multiplicity of small individual suits for damages, aggrieved persons may be without any effective redress unless they may employ the class action device." "Deposit Guaranty National Bank v. Roper," *United States Reports*, vol. 445, p. 339, *rehearing denied*, *United States Reports*, vol. 446 U.S. (1980), p. 947. See also "State of West Virginia v. Chas. Pfizer & Co.," *Federal Reporter* 2d, vol. 440 (Second Circuit 1970), p. 1090.

duty to dismiss the lawsuit; therefore, the fact of settlement indicates that plaintiffs' claims have some merit; therefore, each class member is entitled to a settlement payment by virtue of the partial validity of his or her claim.

This argument fails for three reasons. First, defendants often settle cases for reasons that have nothing to do with the validity of the charges against them. Defendants settle to limit attorneys' fees, court costs, unfavorable publicity, uncertainty in financial markets, lost managerial time, discovery costs (including invasions of privacy), and other expenses. In the *Agent Orange* case, for example, one observer estimated the defendants' litigation expenses at approximately $1 million per week during the period immediately prior to the settlement,[70] and another observer set their costs at $75 million overall.[71] It is also worth noting that the *Agent Orange* defendants managed to settle for far less than the damages claimed and consistently denied being at fault. In view of Judge Weinstein's subsequent dismissal of the suits brought by veterans who opted out of the *Agent Orange* class, the chemical companies' plea of innocence has considerable plausibility.[72]

Second, even if settlements confer informal recognition on class members' claims, they do not legally validate those claims.[73] As indicated above, settlements bind even in cases where plaintiffs' claims are legally invalid.[74] Moreover, settlements preclude adjudication, the ordinary means of establishing the validity of allegations. This is stated explicitly in the cases, where it is held that when approving a class settlement neither a trial court nor an appellate court has "the right or the duty to reach any ultimate conclusions on the issues of fact and law which underlie the merits of [a] dispute."[75]

The relevance of the fact that settlements preclude adjudication stems from the assumption we made above that winning at trial and having a valid claim to compensation are highly correlated. If this assumption is correct, the fact that a person wins at trial gives us good reason to think that the person is actually entitled to compensation. All we are claiming in this section is that settlements are less probative of the validity of claims than are trials. In other

[70] See Schuck, *Agent Orange on Trial.*

[71] Stephen Sugarman, "Doing Away with Tort Law," *California Law Review*, vol. 73 (1985), p. 598.

[72] Preliminary results of a 20-year study of people who worked with Agent Orange suggest that it neither decreased the subjects' longevity nor caused their deaths. *Miami Herald*, Dec. 28, 1985, p. 7A.

[73] Except when the parties explicitly recognize their validity, as discussed further below. See the text immediately preceding and accompanying footnote 80.

[74] See the text accompanying footnotes 18–22.

[75] "Cotton v. Hinton," *Federal Reporter* 2d, vol. 559 (Fifth Circuit 1977), p. 1330. Settlements of class actions must be approved by judges because Rule 23, which empowers plaintiffs to bring class actions, also provides that "[a] class action shall not be dismissed or compromised without the approval of the court. . . ." *Federal Rules of Civil Procedure*, Rule 23(e).

words, we think that the evidence for the validity of settled claims is in general less compelling than the evidence for the validity of claims that prevail at trial, not that settled claims are necessarily invalid claims. When a case settles, neither the facts surrounding an alleged injury nor the theories in light of which its wrongfulness is to be assessed are developed. For this reason, our confidence that plaintiffs who receive settlement payments deserve to be compensated should in general be weaker than our confidence that justice is served when plaintiffs who prevail at trial are awarded damages.

Third, and finally, even if it is admitted that settlements partially validate class members' claims, when cases settle judges are poorly placed to estimate the relative size and strength of those claims. This is so because judges often learn little about a case before trial. The discovery process that plaintiffs and defendants use to build their cases is ordinarily self-executing, and in complex cases disputes that arise during the course of discovery may be resolved by a special master rather than a judge. Also, different judges may preside over a case as it moves toward trial. Moreover, as we mentioned above,[76] the adversarial presentation of views that sharpens a judge's understanding of a case is strikingly absent from the process that produces plans for dividing settlement funds among class members. Given the small size of their claims, absent class members cannot be expected to show up and defend their interests. And neither class representatives nor class counsel have an incentive to oppose plans that are unfair to absent members.[77] Thus, even if settlements partially validate class members' allegations, judges' ignorance of the merits and the absence of the adversarial process all but guarantee that they will gauge the relative size and strength of members' claims inaccurately and that no one will know how far wide of the mark their guesses really are.

At this point, it might be argued that if class members were not compensated for their losses when cases settle, they would take their claims to trial, at considerably greater expense to the parties. Even if this is admitted, all that follows is that class members should receive payments sufficient to discourage them from continuing to press a lawsuit. At best, this amount is only contingently related to the size and strength of members' claims. It is

[76] See Part I, sec. (.1).

[77] Several cases attest to the fact that class counsel may attempt to "buy off" named plaintiffs, and that named plaintiffs may be receptive to such overtures. See, e.g., "Plummer v. Chemical Bank," *Federal Rules Decisions*, vol. 91 (Southern District of New York 1981), p. 434 (disapproving a proposed settlement in which named plaintiffs were to receive "substantially more benefits" than other members of the class); and "Holmes v. Continental Can Co.," *Federal Reporter* 2d, vol. 706 (Eleventh Circuit 1983), p. 1144 (reversing and remanding lower court decision approving settlement under which the eight named plaintiffs would have received half of the settlement fund).

also a function of the benefits members hope to gain by opting out of classes and by objecting to proposed settlements. In other words, on the assumption that class members are rational, they will settle if they are paid just a bit more than they can expect to receive if they don't settle. But in paradigm cases, refusal to settle has a negative expected value. To begin with, class members' claims are small, so that even a class member who would achieve a complete recovery by refusing to settle has a weak incentive to put up a struggle. Moreover, it is expensive to oppose a proposed settlement or plan of distribution. Members who would lodge objections must sift through discovered documents, read depositions, construct arguments, file briefs and appear in court. Those who would opt out carry an even heavier burden. They must exclude themselves from a class and, if they are to receive anything at all, they must file a separate lawsuit. Since the expected returns from objecting and opting out are negative, we doubt that the failure to make settlement payments to individual members on the basis of the relative size and strength of their claims would move class members to refuse to settle.

Further evidence for this view can be found in the literature on attorneys' fees. By and large, paradigm class actions are conceived and initiated by the plaintiffs' bar, not by class members themselves. This should come as no surprise. After all, class members' claims are too small for them to litigate individually. Lawyers therefore bear the primary responsibility for ferreting out instances in which small losses are wrongfully imposed on large numbers of people. That lawyers are also the main force behind the settlement of class actions may come as more of a surprise but is no less true. Counsel may get nothing if they lose a case at trial, and the amount they get if they win may not be sufficiently larger than the fee they receive if they settle to offset the risk of coming away empty-handed.[78] Since we do not propose to do away with attorneys' fees or to change the way they are awarded, we doubt that the failure to make settlement payments to individual class members would increase the rate at which class actions go to trial.

In response, one might say, "Look, even if settlements don't validate members' claims, and even if payments to members don't facilitate settlements, surely class members, like plaintiffs in ordinary cases, must have contractual rights to payments by virtue of settlement agreements." Strictly speaking, this claim is false. Although members have rights to payments when plans for dispensing benefits are written into agreements, very often such plans are formulated after settlements are negotiated and controversies concluded. And it is no answer to this to say that the solution is to require attorneys to incorporate such plans into all settlement agreements. To

[78] For an excellent discussion of the effect of attorneys' fees on settlement rates see Geoffrey P. Miller, *Agency Problems in Settlement* (unpublished typescript, University of Chicago, 1986).

propose this solution is to argue that we should insist on contractual provisions because otherwise class members will lack rights to settlement payments. This, of course, merely assumes what must be proved, namely, that settlement funds *ought* to be divided among class members.

Another way to approach this matter is to ask why counsel have any control whatsoever over this aspect of settlements. Although counsel are permitted (and even encouraged) to formulate utilization plans, to the best of our knowledge the only argument given for this practice is that it relieves the court of "the almost impossible task of determining the distribution of the settlement fund among the myriad claimants' and can be desirable if . . . representatives have information sufficient to allow them to formulate a reasonable division."[79] Obviously, this is a weak argument. For one thing, it concedes that judges are unable to supervise settlements effectively and that the risk that arbitrary utilization plans will be chosen is great. For another, it fails to tell us why either judges or lawyers are busying themselves with this task. In response to the question "Why should settlement funds be divided among class members?" the answer "Because lawyers do a better job of apportioning payments than judges" is no answer at all.

Finally, the reader may want to respond to our argument that settlements preclude the legal validation of claims by pointing out that plaintiffs can legitimate their allegations simply by insisting that appropriate stipulations be written into settlement agreements. In other words, one might say that, even if class counsel should be forbidden to formulate utilization plans, they should certainly be permitted to convince defendants to concede the validity of class members' charges, and when they succeed in doing so class members ought to be compensated.

The obvious deficiency of this argument is that settlement agreements rarely stipulate the validity of plaintiffs' claims. To the contrary, defendants usually disclaim fault and liability. Moreover, courts typically treat settlements as "effort[s] to obtain peace rather than as admission[s] of the validity of another party's claim. . . ."[80] Thus, even if settlement agreements can validate the claims of a settling class, most often they do not, and the problem of justifying the division of funds among class members remains.

A less obvious weakness is that "validation by adjudication" and "validation by agreement" differ in a relevant respect. A claim is validated at trial when a judge applies laws to a set of facts. A claim is validated by agreement when parties bargain for this result. This difference is important because arguments for compensating people whose claims are valid undoubtedly turn

[79] "In re Corrugated Container Antitrust Litigation," *Federal Reporter* 2d, vol. 643, p. 219 [quoting "In re Equity Funding Corp. of America Securities Litigation," *Federal Reporter* 2d, vol. 603 (Ninth Circuit 1979), p. 1465].

[80] "Compromise and Settlement," sec. 4.

on the means by which the validity of those claims is established. For example, assume that compensation may reasonably be paid to plaintiffs who win in courts that operate within the confines of significant procedural, evidentiary, and precedential safeguards. Does it follow that compensation ought also to be paid to plaintiffs who win in courts where judges decide cases by tossing dice? No. Nor does it follow from the fact that we compensate plaintiffs who succeed at trial that we must also compensate those who prevail at the bargaining table. The institutional framework within which settlements are negotiated differs markedly from that which regulates class action adjudications. Arbitrary, extralegal factors like litigation costs, need, and degree of risk averseness of the parties figure far more prominently in settlement negotiations than they do at trial. Thus, although class members who win at trial may deserve compensation, those whose claims are validated by agreement may not.

For the same reason, it would also be wrong to argue, as Judge Flaum did in the *Folding Carton* antitrust case, that because the class action device is supposed to enable people to recover on claims that are too small to litigate individually, class members ought to recover on claims that are settled.[81] The problem with this argument is that its premise is ambiguous. Is the class action device a means of enabling people to recover on all claims, or only on valid claims? If the latter, then the device will serve its intended purpose if compensation is paid to class members whose grievances are supported by convincing evidence and rationalized in terms of adequate theories of wrongfulness. Since in most cases both facts and theories are poorly developed at settlement, and since the rules of evidence are largely ignored during the pretrial discovery process, very often there is little reason to think that a settled claim is valid. Unless one is willing to contend that the purpose of the class action device is to enable people to collect on all claims, including those which are largely unproven, one cannot argue that class members are entitled to settlement payments simply by virtue of their participation in a class action.

At this point, one might argue that it is impossible to know before trial whether allegations are valid, and that it is inappropriate to penalize people who possess potentially valid claims for settling rather than pressing on with a lawsuit. This argument is very disturbing. Its force stems from the

[81] "In re Folding Carton Antitrust Litigation," *Federal Reporter* 2d, vol. 744, p. 1258. Judge Flaum was confused because he failed to see the effect adjudication has on class members' legal rights. He cited "Boeing Co. v. Van Gemert," *United States Reports*, vol. 444 (1980), p. 482, one of the few class actions ever to be won at trial, for the proposition that class members are the equitable owners of settlement funds. When a class wins at trial its members acquire rights to compensation. It is therefore true that they are entitled to payments. However, when a class action settles, the validity of members' claims is never proved. Consequently, class members may not be the equitable owners of shares in a settlement fund and *Boeing* is off point.

assumption that at least some members of settling classes have legally valid claims, for only if one assumes that a class would have won at trial does it make sense to say that members are penalized when they are denied settlement payments. But, of course, this assumption is inconsistent both with the law of settlements and with a basic principle of our legal system – the principle that plaintiffs' claims are not presumed to be valid unless proven to be.

At this point one might fall back on the weaker line that class members who can present a prima facie case for their claims should be permitted to share in a settlement. This argument is akin to the statement often heard from the bench that only class members who possess colorable claims against a defendant may participate in a distribution.[82] Obviously, this gambit leaves open the possibility that some class members – those who cannot make a prima facie showing – may reasonably be denied settlement payments. For this reason, the argument does not justify the current practice of dividing settlement funds among class members in all cases. Moreover, this move would require judges to decide questions of fact and law, tasks that, as we have seen, they are ill-placed and legally forbidden to do at this stage of a proceeding. And if it is suggested that a minihearing on the merits should be held prior to settlement, then one must ask how great the savings from settlements will be, whether an adversarial presentation of views could reasonably be expected, and what threshold of legality would entitle plaintiffs to compensation. If, as seems likely, the savings would be small and the hearing a sham, then this suggestion ought to be rejected. Further, it is possible that any standard short of full legality would fail to justify compensation. Many plaintiffs who ultimately lose at trial successfully demonstrate the prima facie plausiblity of their claims, for example, by defeating motions for summary judgment. These plaintiffs are denied compensation nonetheless. Therefore, were a court to use a summary judgment standard at a minihearing on the merits, it would not follow that plaintiffs who prevailed would deserve to be compensated.

Thus, the argument that class members are entitled to settlement payments because settlements confer partial recognition on their grievances fails. This is not surprising. After all, the argument fails even to explain why plaintiffs who settle ordinary, nonclass actions are entitled to payments. As we saw above, their entitlements stem from the contracts that end their cases. Plaintiffs can contract around their disputes and bargain for settle-

[82] "If the spouses and children of the veterans were 'completely without any colorable legal claims against [the] defendants, it would [be] an abuse of the court's discretion to allow them to share in the settlement fund.'" "In re Agent Orange Product Liability Litigation," *Federal Supplement*, vol. 611, p. 1411 [quoting "In re Chicken Antitrust Litigation American Poultry," *Federal Reporter* 2d, vol. 669 (Fifth Circuit 1982), p. 238].

ment payments because it is an established policy that trials are to be discouraged, not because settled claims are valid claims. It is only because judges unthinkingly went about distributing benefits to members of settling classes that they now find themselves engaging in specious arguments about the partial validity of members' claims. We think the time has come to admit that neither class members' unproven allegations nor the policy of encouraging settlements *entitles* them to share in class action settlement funds.

B. *Should class members be compensated for the loss of the right to sue?*

As we mentioned above, judges sometimes argue that since each member of a class forfeits the right to sue when a case is settled, each should be compensated for the loss of that right. The intuitive appeal of this argument is apparent. It raises several related questions. First, do class members forfeit the right to sue when class actions settle? Second, if class members' rights are extinguished, do they have claims in justice to compensation? Third, if class members are entitled to compensation, how much compensation should they receive? We will consider each of these questions in turn.

(i) Do settlements deprive class members of legal rights?

The argument that class members are entitled to settlement payments in compensation for the loss of the right to sue obviously presupposes that members in fact forfeit that right on the settlement of a class action. It is certainly true that class action settlements are binding on class members in the sense that they preclude members from continuing to sue, and from launching separate lawsuits, on settled claims. Is it therefore also true that settlements deprive class members of the right to sue? Not necessarily; it depends on how we think about the nature and scope of the relevant right. The content of the right to sue may just be that one can sue or settle. Consider what happens when an ordinary lawsuit is settled. A plaintiff files a complaint, agrees to withdraw it in return for a payment, and is barred from bringing another action on the settled claim from that point on. One way to construe this series of events is to say that a plaintiff who settles forfeits the right to sue on a claim. Another, equally plausible reading is that the plaintiff was entitled to sue or to settle, but not both. In other words, instead of saying that a plaintiff *forfeits* the right to sue by settling, one could say that a plaintiff *exercises* the right to sue by settling. By analogy, class members can be said to have fully exercised their rights to sue when a class action is settled. Their rights entitle them either to sue as a class or to settle as a class, but not both. If this description of the content of class members' rights is accurate, it is false that settlements deprive class members of the right to sue. Settlements merely deprive class members of the opportunity to sue, an opportunity they have no legal right to exploit given that their case was settled.

At this point the reader may wonder whether we have undermined the case against dividing settlement funds among class members by suggesting that the right to sue is exercised when a plaintiff settles. After all, on the construction of the right to sue that we have offered, does not that right entitle class members to settlement payments in the event that the option of going to trial is foreclosed? To ask this question is to miss the point of the discussion entirely. Judges have argued that justice requires that class members be compensated because they *forfeit* the right to sue when a case is settled. Our reply to this argument is that class members may not forfeit a right (even if they pass up an opportunity) and that, therefore, they may not have a claim in justice to compensation. Of course, the practice of dividing settlement funds among class members endows them with rights to share in those funds. We do not mean to deny this fact. We mean to deny only the arguments given in support of the practice of dividing settlement funds among class members. One such argument is that settlement plans that confer legal rights on individual members to share in a settlement are justified as compensation for the loss of the right to sue. This is the claim with which we take issue. If the right to sue as a class is understood as the right either to sue as a class or to settle as a class, then in settling no individuals' rights have been forfeited. Instead, the right to sue, correctly understood, is fully exercised. Current compensatory schemes might nevertheless be justified, but not on the ground that they are required in order to compensate for a forfeited right. In our understanding of the right to sue, settlement and trial are both options within its ambit. Choosing to settle is to avail oneself of one option and necessarily to forgo others. But it is not to forfeit the right. It is to exercise it.

But suppose we are wrong to argue that the content of the right to sue is that class members can sue or settle. Would it then be true that class members forfeit a legal right when a case is settled? Again, not necessarily; the fact that settlements bar class members from suing on a claim can be construed as the effect of a voluntary transfer of either the right to sue itself or the authority to exercise that right, rather than as a forfeiture. In paradigm cases potential class members are given an opportunity to exclude themselves from a class before the class is certified. It is therefore both plausible and consonant with the case law on class actions to say that class members voluntarily transfer the right to sue to a class, or that they voluntarily empower a class to exercise the right to sue on their behalf, by failing to opt out. Both the authority to exercise legal rights and legal rights themselves are often alienable, and, as innumerable cases on contracts suggest, the conditions under which transfers occur vary widely. All we are suggesting is that a voluntary transfer of the right to sue, or of the power to exercise that right, may occur when class members fail to exclude themselves prior to class certification. If this view is correct, then class members' inability to sue on a settled claim is the natural consequence of their having voluntarily transferred their rights, or the power to exercise their rights, to a class, not an indication that members forfeit the right to sue on the settlement of a class action.[83]

(*ii*) *Does the loss of the right to sue entitle class members to compensation?*

Suppose that both the suggestion that class members' rights are exercised when a class action is settled and the suggestion that class members voluntarily transfer their rights to a class by failing to opt out are mistaken. In this event, it would be correct to say that class members forfeit the right to sue and that the occasion of their loss is the settlement of a class action. Even so, it would still be reasonable to ask whether the loss of the right to sue is the kind of loss that gives rise to a claim in justice to compensation. Corrective justice, the principle that people ought to be compensated for losses that are wrongfully inflicted upon them, does not require that compensation be paid every time anyone suffers an injury. For example, a pedestrian who picks up a loose $5 bill thereby deprives other passers-by of the opportunity of doing so, but the loss the others suffer is not one for which in justice they ought to be compensated. No compensation is required because the loss is not wrongfully inflicted.

To establish that a loss is compensable as a matter of corrective justice, then, one must show that it is a wrongful loss. A loss may be wrongful if it is occasioned by a harm illegitimately imposed or wrongfully inflicted. Several reasons for counting the loss of the right to sue as compensable come to mind. The first is simply that it is wrong to extinguish an individual's legal right or, alternatively, that doing so is justifiable only if compensation is paid.

Are class members injured wrongfully when they are stripped of the right to sue? By itself, the fact that they forfeit a legal right does not show this to be the case. There are lots of instances in which people are properly deprived of legal rights and are neither entitled to nor paid compensation for the loss. For example, plaintiffs who wage conventional lawsuits can select their attorneys, veto settlements unilaterally, and decide on forums in which to sue. Class members have none of these rights. However, they are not compensated for these losses and there is no reason that they should be. The rights mentioned are procedural rights. They enable people to invoke the

[83] It is consistent with the view that the right to sue, or the power to exercise that right, transfers from class members to a class on certification (rather than at settlement) that individual class members cannot sue on claims on which a class action is already pending, although people who have opted out of a class may do so. Moreover, since class members retain the right to settle with a defendant individually at any time during the pendency of a class action, the most appropriate reading of the facts seems to be that, by remaining in a class, members grant the class the nonexclusive authority to exercise their right to settle. That is, they empower a class to settle on their behalf if they do not do so themselves.

law on their behalf. In ordinary lawsuits these rights serve important purposes. But in class actions, they are entirely out of place. Their exercise by individual class members would render class actions unmanageable and inhibit the pursuit of justice. It is therefore appropriate to deprive class members of these legal rights, and the fact that they suffer a loss does not entitle them to compensation.

Substantive legal rights may appropriately be extinguished, too. As more and more states raise the legal drinking age, people who were once free to purchase alcoholic beverages lose the right to do so. The passage of the Antipeonage Act in 1867 deprived masters of the legal right to compel indentured servants to perform labor contracts. Manufacturers who were once free to constrain trade are now denied the right to do so by the antitrust laws. Civil rights laws deprive employers of the right to discriminate in hiring and promotions. Convicted criminals are denied an extraordinary variety of legal rights. The list could be extended indefinitely.

Thus, the claim to repair requires more than just a showing that class members are deprived of a legal right; in addition, it requires a showing that it is wrong to deprive class members of the right to sue. But is it? An argument that it is wrong might run as follows. The right to sue is a property right protected by the Fifth Amendment to the Constitution. The Fifth Amendment provides that no one shall be "deprived of life, liberty, or property, without due process of law." But to deprive class members of settlement payments is to deprive them of a property right without due process. Therefore, class members who are stripped of the right to sue are injured wrongfully and have a claim in justice to compensation.

This argument is based on a confusion about due process. It is one thing to say that class members cannot be deprived of the right to sue without due process of law. It is quite another thing to say that, when their rights are extinguished, due process entitles class members to compensation. Although the former is true, the latter is clearly false. When class actions are lost at trial, all members are afforded due process of law, but none is compensated for the loss of the right to sue as an individual litigant. This outcome accords with due process because due process requires only that class members' interests be adequately represented. It does not require that class members be compensated if they lose the right to sue notwithstanding the fact that their interests are adequately represented.

Likewise, due process does not establish that class members who lose the right to sue when a case settles are injured wrongfully. To the contrary, due process impels one toward the conclusion that there is nothing wrongful about this loss. As *Newberg on Class Actions* states, "The Supreme Court has held that a class action . . . satisfies due process . . . as long as the class has been adequately represented."[84] This requirement is often met when class actions settle. When classes are certified it must be shown that a representative's claim is typical of the claims of a class, that class counsel are experienced, that an adversarial relationship obtains between the parties, and that class members' interests are otherwise adequately protected. When class actions are settled, it must be shown that negotiations have been free of collusion, that sufficient discovery was conducted to enable counsel and the court to act intelligently, that objectors are few in number and that their complaints lack merit, and so forth. What this means is that when a class action is settled, class members receive all the process to which they are entitled. It is therefore wrong to say that class members are denied due process of law when, on the settlement of a case, they are barred from launching another lawsuit. And since class members receive due process, the Fifth Amendment cannot be invoked to show that class members were injured wrongfully. Supporters of the practice of dividing settlement funds among class members must look elsewhere for evidence that class members have a claim in justice for compensation.

It could also be argued that class members' loss of the right to sue is wrongful because they are deprived of the right without their consent. Ordinary lawsuits cannot be settled over a plaintiff's objection, but class actions are often settled in the face of opposition from class members. It might be claimed, then, that class members are forced to forfeit the right to sue regardless of their wishes and that their loss should therefore be regarded as wrongful.

This objection raises two issues: are class members deprived of the right to sue without their consent and, if they are, are they therefore injured wrongfully? Both questions must be answered in the negative. When considering the first question, one must keep in mind that the law takes many different things as evidence of consent. For example, partial performance of an obligation is often said to evince a contractor's consent to an exchange, even in the absence of an express agreement. In class actions, absent members are deemed to consent to representation and to all that it entails unless they opt out of a class. The law employs what one judge called "the Book-of-the-Month Club" technique of implying consent from silence.[85] Thus, as far as the law is concerned, class members who fail to exclude themselves from a class agree to be bound by existing class action pro-

[84] *Newberg on Class Actions* (Colorado Springs, Colo.: Shepard's/McGraw-Hill, 2d ed. 1985), sec. 10.05.

[85] See Judge J. Joseph Smith's opinion in "State of West Virginia v. Chas. Pfizer & Co.," *Federal Reporter* 2d, vol. 440, p. 1091.

cedures, one of which empowers a judge to permit a settlement over class members' objections.

In response to the claim that class members consent to representation, it could be argued that actual, full-fledged consent and legally implied consent are two different things. The idea here is that although judges may imply consent right and left, a person can truly be said to consent only under certain conditions, for example, when he or she is fully informed of all relevant contingencies and options, is free to withhold consent, is of mature years, and so forth. This line of argument is, then, that although judges say that class members consent to representation for legal purposes, for purposes of justice it is inappropriate to hold that merely by failing to respond to a notice a person can consent to representation.

Although it may make sense for some purposes to distinguish full-fledged consent from consent implied at law, we think that judges are right to hold that class members who remain silent consent to representation. Class members cannot be expected to monitor paradigm class actions closely or to develop sophisticated views of the legal issues their cases present. Often their claims are too small to motivate them even to respond to notices of settlement. Moreover, if the "positive" consent of all class members was required before a case could settle, class actions would be unmanageable and uneconomical. In some cases, the cost of tracking down members and mailing them notices would use up a sizeable portion of a settlement fund. And if a unanimity rule was in effect, class members would have an incentive to withhold their consent in an effort to garner a larger share of a settlement for themselves. Since members of paradigm classes are usually uninformed, and since class actions would be unworkable if members were required to indicate their consent affirmatively, judges are right to imply members' consent from their silence.

Even if the use of the "Book-of-the-Month Club" technique is inappropriate, however, one would still have to show that the failure to gain class members' actual consent before settling a case imposes a wrongful loss on them before one could claim that members are entitled to compensation. Not all nonconsensual forfeitures of rights qualify as wrongfully inflicted losses. Convicted criminals, for example, are not injured wrongfully when they are imprisoned, although they are deprived of many rights without their consent.

It is difficult to see that class members are injured wrongfully even if they are stripped of the right to sue without their consent. As the following replies to notices of the settlement reached in the *Antibiotics* case[86] indicate,

[86] "North Carolina v. Chas. Pfizer & Co.," *New York Civil Court*, vol. 69 (Southern District of New York 1970), p. 839.

members of paradigm classes usually take little or no interest in their lawsuits, hold unsophisticated views of legal issues, and are unable to monitor class counsel effectively.

> Dear Mr. Clark: I have your notice that I owe you $300 for selling drugs. I have never sold any drugs, especially those you have listed; but I have sold a little whiskey once in a while.
>
> Dear Sir: I received this paper from you. I guess I really don't understand it, but if I have been given one of those drugs, nobody told me why. If it means what I think it does, I have not been with a man in nine years.
>
> Dear Sir: I received your pamphlet on drugs, which I think will be of great value to me in the future. I am unable to attend your class, however.
>
> Dear Mr. Attorney General: I am sorry to say this, but you have the wrong John Doe, because in 1954, I wasn't but three years old and didn't even have a name. Mother named me when I got my driver's license. Up to then, they just called me Baby Doe.[87]

Even if justice requires that people who are well informed be deprived of their legal rights only with their consent, this requirement may not apply when people are largely ignorant of relevant information. It seems especially unlikely to apply to members of paradigm class actions because their interests will be protected even if they are deprived of the right to sue without their consent, indeed, even if a lawsuit is conducted entirely without their consent. It is, then, far from clear that a wrong is committed when a paradigm class action settles and class members are made to forfeit the right to sue without their consent.

Another reason for thinking that the loss absorbed by each class member who forfeits the right to pursue a claim further in litigation ought to be compensable is that the forfeiture frustrates legitimately held expectations. The market value of these expectations is their expected value. Thus, each class member is entitled as a matter of justice to a payment that reflects the relative expected value of his or her claim in court. There are several problems with this line of argument.

One problem is that from the fact that a claim has a particular expected value at trial, it does not follow that the person who holds that claim has any expectations at all. The claim-holder may know neither that the claim exists nor that under existing laws the claim stands a chance of being vindicated in court. As the responses quoted above suggest, class members are usually

[87] The sample replies are quoted in *Newberg on Class Actions* 2d, sec. 8.39, where it is suggested that they "typify the misunderstanding attendant such notice."

completely in the dark as to the nature and legal merits of their claims. If this is so, then class members' expectations cannot be frustrated when they are deprived of the right to sue because they have no expectations to begin with. In this respect, class members differ from contractors, and the arguments that are normally advanced for compensating contractors whose expectations are dashed cannot be invoked in defense of the practice of giving class members settlement payments. For example, one could not claim that class members ought to be compensated because they, like contractors, rely on their expectations to their detriment. Nor could one argue that class members ought to be compensated because, like contractors, they will act in inefficient ways if their expectations are ignored. These approaches fail because contractors, unlike class members, actually have expectations about things that may happen in the future.

Notwithstanding the fact that, in paradigm cases, most class members usually know next to nothing about their claims and the lawsuits that are brought on their behalf, in every lawsuit some class members may be well-informed and may have definite expectations about the outcome of a trial. Does the disappointment these individuals experience when a suit is settled entitle them to compensation?

Before answering this question directly, it is worth noting that if a frustrated class member has a claim to compensation, justice would require only that compensation be paid to class members who are in fact disappointed. It would not require that settlement funds be divided among all class members or that members be paid amounts that reflect the putative size and strength of their claims. In other words, the disappointment some class members experience cannot justify the practice of paying all class members amounts that reflect the putative size and strength of their claims.

Moreover, disappointment occasioned by frustrated expectations is rarely a sufficient condition for recovery at law or in morals. Buyers who lose at auctions are not entitled to payments from buyers who win. Frustrated gamblers have no legal claim to compensation even though their fondest hopes may be staked on a losing spin of a roulette wheel. Even people who reasonably and rationally rely on their expectations often have no legal claim to compensation when they are disappointed. An individual who visits a post office and finds it closed cannot recover in the courts. Nor are plaintiffs who rely on a hope of winning at trial entitled to compensation when they lose. More importantly for our purposes, class members who find that a settlement gives them less than they expected to receive cannot sue to recover for the pain of disappointment. When a settlement and a plan for distributing benefits are approved, class members are deemed to have received everything they are legally entitled to, their personal views on the adequacy of their payments being of no moment.

In short, class members may in fact have no expectations, the frustration of which could conceivably call for remedial relief. Moreover, even if they had *conditional expectations*, that is, expectations which they need not actually have at any time, but which they would have if they attended to the relevant circumstances, it still would not follow that failure to compensate for those frustrated expectations constitutes an injustice. Not every expectation, not even every legitimate expectation, gives rise to a claim to repair in the event of its frustration. The case for compensation, then, must rely upon the relevant expectations being secured by, or associated with, a legal right. But then it is the loss of the right, not the fact of disappointment alone, that is fundamental to the claim to compensation, and we have already shown that lines of argument resting on this fact fail to support the prevailing practice.

Is there any other reason to think that class members are injured wrongfully when, on settlement, they are stripped of the right to sue? As far as we can tell, no other reason exists. This may seem surprising, but it should not. After all, no one claims that the reason plaintiffs who settle ordinary cases are entitled to payments is that they suffer wrongful injuries when they are deprived of the right to sue. Plaintiffs who settle conventional lawsuits are permitted to bargain for and to receive payments because it is public policy to encourage settlements, and because the truth is that conventional lawsuits will settle only if plaintiffs are paid to end them. In other words, the policy of permitting settlement payments to be made in conventional cases is rationalized on the ground of economy, not on the ground that justice entitles settling plaintiffs to compensation for the loss of the right to sue. In view of this, it is odd to think that any justification other than economy could be found for the practice of compensating class members when their claims are settled. And, as we have seen, since paradigm class actions will settle even if members are paid nothing, even economy gives us no reason to divide settlement funds among all class members.

To the contrary, if we want to conserve resources, we ought to abandon the practice of paying members of paradigm classes amounts that reflect the putative size and strength of their claims. The requirement that settlement funds be distributed in this manner causes judges and lawyers, and sometimes even class members, to waste a lot of time, money, and energy figuring out who is entitled to how much and implementing the plans they devise. Judges must hold fairness hearings, write opnions in support of the plans they adopt, and oversee the claims-filing and distribution processes. Lawyers must estimate the value of claims that may allege different injuries and that may confront different obstacles to proof; they must formulate plans for distributing scarce settlement dollars; they must appear in court and argue for those plans; and they must compose and distribute notices, locate absent class members, and serve as administrators until all the proceeds are paid out or all claims are satisfied. If unclaimed funds remain in a settlement fund, and they usually do when class members' claims are small, litigation over the ownership of those funds may erupt and class counsel will again be drawn into court. On occasion, even class members get into the act, though admittedly, and expectedly in view of the size of their claims, this is a rare event. In the *Agent Orange* case, for example, thousands of veterans attended fairness hearings and spent many hours telling Judge Weinstein how they wanted the settlement fund to be used.[88] In our view, the resources consumed during the process of designing and implementing distribution plans could often be more usefully invested in other projects.

That these resources are wasted becomes even clearer if one keeps in mind that the payments distributed are often vanishingly small. In the *Hilton Hotel Telephone Surcharge* case, future guests at Hilton and other hotels received a discount of fifty cents a day on their room rates as a result of the settlement.[89] In *Ohio Public Interest Campaign v. Fisher Foods*,[90] residents of several Northeast Ohio counties received $1 food coupons redeemable at the rate of two every six months for five years. The settlement of *Grossman v. Playboy Clubs Int'l, Inc.*,[91] a state court case, entitled each lifetime member of the Playboy Club in California to receive an $8 chit redeemable over a two-year period.[92] The settlement approved in the *Barbri* antitrust case gave class members, the bulk of whom were practising attorneys, $9 in cash, a $25 transferrable discount coupon for an exam preparation course, and $50 in book discounts.[93] It strikes us as odd that so much work should be done, so much expense incurred, and so many arguments twisted, to provide people with so little.

(iii) If class members are entitled to compensation, how much compensation are they entitled to?

To this point, we have argued against the view that class members forfeit the right to sue on the settlement of a class action, and also against the view that class members are entitled to compensation in the event that such a forfeiture occurs. In this section we will assume that the views we have argued against are in fact correct. That is, we will assume that class members

[88] *Federal Supplement*, vol. 611, p. 1396; see also Schuck, *Agent Orange on Trial.*

[89] "Colson v. Hilton Hotels, Inc.," *Federal Rules Decisions*, vol. 59 (Northern District of Illinois 1972), p. 324.

[90] "Ohio Public Interest Campaign v. Fisher Foods," *Federal Supplement*, vol. 546, p. 1.

[91] "Grossman v. Playboy Clubs Int'l, Inc.," Civil No. 882939 (L.A. Super. Ct. 1970).

[92] This case is discussed in Handler, "The Shift from Substantive to Procedural Innovations in Antitrust Suits," p. 10.

[93] "Phemister v. Harcourt Brace Jovanovich," No. 77C39, slip opinion (Northern District of Illinois Sept. 14, 1984). We thank Victor Freedman of the law firm of Fried, Frank, Harris, Shriver & Jacobson for bringing this case to our attention.

are deprived of the right to sue when a class action settles and that this loss, because it is wrongful, gives rise to a claim in justice to compensation. We now want to ask how much compensation class members ought to receive, given that they suffer a wrongfully inflicted loss when a class action settles. In particular, we want to know whether the amount of compensation class members are entitled to varies with the size and strength of their claims, as the current gloss on Rule 23(e) suggests.

It should be apparent that, by itself, the principle that people must be compensated for wrongfully inflicted losses establishes only that class members must be paid *something* for the loss of the right to sue, not that they are entitled to payments that vary with the size and strength of their underlying claims.[94] The amount of compensation a class member is entitled to depends on the extent of the injury that person suffered when stripped of the right to sue. However much that turns out to be, there is no reason to think that it will always, or ever, be a function of the size and strength of that member's claim. This is so because the right lost is not a right to the expected value of a claim at trial.[95] The right lost is a right to sue on a substantive claim, and from the fact that one is legally entitled to sue it does not follow that one is legally entitled to a payment based on one's estimate of how one would fare at trial. One may be able to bargain for such a payment when one settles a case, but what one can get and what one is legally entitled to are two different things. Thus, even if it is admitted that class members ought to be compensated for the losses they incur when a case is settled, it does not follow that the payments they receive ought to vary with the size and strength of their substantive claims.

In response to this it might be suggested that the expected value of a claim at trial is an objective measure of harm occasioned by extinguishing the right to sue. That is, one could argue that even if class members are not legally entitled to payments that vary with the size and strength of their claims, these variables accurately measure the harm they suffer when they are stripped of the right to sue the defendants, and justice may be said to require that people be compensated for the losses they endure.

It may be helpful to think about this argument in the following way. In a world without transaction costs and in which plaintiffs could freely alienate their claims, claims would fetch roughly their expected value at trial. Given this, the objective loss a person suffers when deprived of the right to sue should also be measured in terms of the expected value of a claim at trial. In other words, since the size and strength of a claim would determine its price

[94] We assume for now that extinguishing the right to sue imposes a wrongful loss on class members. We dispute this assumption below.

[95] We will use the phrases "expected value of a claim at trial" and "size and strength of a claim" interchangeably.

in an open market, the same variables should determine the size of the payments class members receive when their claims are settled.

Suppose we admit that, in the absence of transaction costs, the size and strength of claims would affect their retail value. Does it follow that we ought to use these variables as *legal measures* of the loss a class member suffers when stripped of the right to sue? No. The price at which a good trades is only one of many possible objective measures of the injury a person suffers by being deprived of that good. Correlatively, a rule that ties the level of compensation to the market value of a good is only one of many possible compensation rules. For example, in tort law the cost of producing a good is often used as a measure of the loss incurred when a good is accidently damaged or destroyed, and the same measure is often incorporated into appropriate damage rules. In the class action context one could formulate an alternative measure of loss by asking how much one would have to pay to deter class members from opting out of a class. In other words, instead of looking to the prices claims would fetch in open markets, one could ask what class members' real opportunity costs are. The opportunity cost of remaining in a class is the value of the next best alternative available to a class member. That alternative is to opt out of a class. But, since class members' claims are small, we know that it is uneconomical for them to press their claims individually. This means that any nonnegative payment would persuade them to remain in a lawsuit. In turn, this means that if the opportunity cost of remaining in a class is taken as a measure of loss, members who lose the right to sue are entitled to little or nothing by way of compensation, and the amounts they ought to receive do not vary with the size and strength of their claims.

Since at least two measures of loss and an equal number of compensation rules exist, an argument must be given for taking the expected value of a claim at trial, rather than the opportunity cost of remaining in a class action, as the legal measure of loss. Can a suitable argument be made? The rationale usually advanced for expectation-based damage rules is that they promote efficient behavior of some sort. An expectation-based contract remedy, for example, is said to encourage people to breach agreements only when it is socially wealth-maximizing to do so.[96] By analogy, it may be possible to argue that paying class members the expected value of their claims at trial would encourage them to act efficiently in some respect. The two most likely applications of the argument are that payment plans that take into acount the size and strength of members' claims would stimulate efficient initiation and

[96] See, for example, A. Mitchell Polinsky, *An Introduction to Law and Economics* (Boston: Little, Brown & Co., 1983), p. 29; and Jeffrie Murphy and Jules Coleman, *The Philosophy of Law: An Introduction to Jurisprudence* (Totowa, NJ: Rowman & Allanheld, 1984), p. 243.

settlement of class actions. Unfortunately, neither application seems promising. As indicated above, the incentives that influence the rates at which class actions come and go operate whether benefits are conferred on all class members or not. Lawyers' fees and the interests of named plaintiffs are the strongest inducements to both activities, and their lure is unaffected by the decision to allow each individual class member to share in a settlement fund.

Moreover, whether one can invoke efficiency at this stage of the argument turns on one's reason for thinking that people should be compensated for wrongfully inflicted losses in the first place. If one thinks that people should be compensated because a system of compensation encourages efficient investments in accident-avoidance, then one may appropriately fall back on efficiency as a reason for paying members of a settling class the expected value of their claims at trial. However, if one thinks that people who are harmed should be compensated because it would be unjust not to compensate them, one cannot now shift to the argument that to encourage efficient rates of class action initiation and settlement we ought to pay members of a settling class the expected value of their claims at trial. One can argue only that it would be unjust to pay class members anything less than the expected value of their claims because the size and strength of a claim uniquely measure the loss a person suffers when deprived of the right to sue on that claim.

In arguing for the division of settlement funds among class members, judges have appealed to considerations of justice, not efficiency. Arguments from efficiency, therefore, cannot now be invoked in their defense. Of course, there is no reason to prevent the judges from changing horses in midstream, and if they were to do so, the argument for efficient initiation and settlement of class actions would be in order. Still, the new horse is unlikely to carry the argument very far. Given that the rates at which paradigm class actions are brought and settled are determined by things other than the size of class members' settlement payments, the argument from efficiency has little chance of success. Moreover, as we indicated above, in view of the amounts class members stand to receive when paradigm class actions are settled and the cost of distributing settlement payments, it is likely that efficiency is poorly served by the practice of dividing settlement funds among class members.

(3) What ought to be done with monies paid in settlement of class actions?

What we have shown in Part II of this paper is that justice, the principle that people should be compensated for losses that are wrongfully imposed upon them, does not require that class members receive payments when their cases are settled. Neither the existence of their underlying claims nor the fact that settlements deprive them of the right to sue drives one to the opposite conclusion. Another way to put the matter is to say that justice does not preclude the possibility that settlement funds may be used in ways that do not benefit class members at all. There may be other reasons for paying class members when cases settle[97] but if only justice is at issue, we are free to consider all of the uses to which money can be put, and that is a large number of uses indeed.

Although we are far from the point of dismissing all other options, we think it is plausible that monies paid in settlement of class actions should escheat to the federal government. The argument for escheat is simple. If we are right that class members are not entitled to compensation, then although a class as an entity has a claim in contract (by virtue of a settlement agreement) to receive a payment from a settling defendant, neither individual class members nor class members as a group have any claim to class action settlement funds. If this is correct, then it seems reasonable to treat class action settlement funds as unclaimed funds that have been left on deposit with a federal court. Under existing federal law,[98] unclaimed funds escheat to the United States Government five years after their deposit with a court.

The escheat option has a variety of attractive features, chief among which is that it economizes on the cost of devising and implementing plans for distributing benefits among class members. However, we put forward escheat merely as a proposal. Justice, efficiency, or some other principle entirely may weigh against the use of the escheat statute. In this paper we mean to show only that the practice of dividing settlement funds among class members in amounts that reflect the size and strength of their claims, as intuitively plausible as it seems, cannot be defended on the ground that class members are entitled to compensation. We have suggested an alternative way of disposing of monies paid in settlement of class actions that seems to us to be defensible, but we do not wish it thought that even that proposal has our unqualified endorsement.[99]

CONCLUSION

We have raised doubts about policies that encourage people to settle lawsuits and about the practice of dividing settlement funds among class members. In neither case have our arguments been conclusive. The argu-

[97] See Silver, "Using Class Action Settlement Funds Justly and Wisely," for a discussion of other reasons that could be given in support of the practice of dividing settlement funds among class members.

[98] 28 U.S.C. 2042.

[99] Richard Epstein has raised the concern that the proposal to escheat settlement funds to the federal government would blur the distinction between public civil proceedings and private class actions. Under this proposal, defendants who settle private class actions would pay money into public coffers, just as they do when they lose or settle public proceedings. But, Epstein's objection continues, if what we want to see is the payment of money into public coffers, what role remains for private class actions? In other words, by denying class members settlement payments, have we not obviated the need for class actions altogether?

If it were true that the escheat option would blur the distinction between private and public lawsuits, it would be a real question whether a private form of action should be available. It would not follow, however, that merely because the categories of public action and private action were merged that private class actions would cease to serve any purpose. It might be reasonable to make both public and private proceedings available, for example, because the plaintiffs' bar is better than the government at monitoring some kinds of illegal activities. Thus, even if it would be appropriate to conceptualize class actions as public proceedings in the event that settlement funds were not divided among class members, it may still be reasonable to empower private citizens to bring class actions.

More to the point, the distinction between private and public actions would remain even if class members were denied settlement payments. After all, class actions can and occasionally do go to trial, and when classes prevail at trial their members acquire rights to damage payments. Since class actions can go to trial, a difference between class actions and public proceedings would remain even if the practice of dividing settlement funds among class members were abolished. The difference would be that class actions could sometimes result in civil recoveries, whereas public proceedings can result in only fines and penalties.

Further, it is in any event wrong to think of payments made in settlement of civil suits as fines. As mentioned above, when class actions settle, ordinarily no findings of guilt, liability, or wrongdoing are made. By contrast, a fine is paid after a public proceeding only when a defendant is adjudged guilty of an offense. The difference between fines and settlement payments is important both morally and legally. From a moral point of view, settlement payments carry none of the opprobrium associated with fines and penalties because they do not indicate that a norm of behavior has been violated. From a legal point of view, a settlement payment is a good faith attempt to buy peace of mind, not an admission of guilt, and the obligation to make a settlement payment arises under a contract, not under public law.

The only possible reason to lump settlement payments together with fines and penalties is that the former have the same effect as the latter on defendants' behavior. From a defendant's point of view, it may make little difference whether money passes into public coffers or the hands of individual defendants. The economic result is the same in either event because in both cases a cost is associated with an activity as a result of a lawsuit. For the same reason penalties and fines may deter people from violating the securities laws, the prospect of having to make a settlement payment may deter a manufacturer from producing a new and potentially defective product line.

It seems likely that defendants view settlement payments like fines and adjust their behavior to minimize both. This is not, however, a good reason to put fines and settlement payments in the same category. To the contrary, it is a reason to keep the two kinds of payment distinct. When the prospect of a fine dissuades a person from violating the law, a form of behavior is deterred which, according to prevailing social policy, ought to be deterred. However, when the prospect of a settlement payment causes a person to refrain from an activity, there is less reason to be happy with the result because the behavior that is deterred may, in light of social policy, be desirable. For example, suppose we want to encourage manufacturers to market innovative products that increase social welfare, while, at the same time, we empower people who are injured by defective products to sue for compensation and to settle when they like. If the prospect of having to make settlement payments deters manufacturers from marketing products that are sound, fewer new products will be made available to the public than is desirable under this policy. Thus, if settlement payments have the same affect as fines on people's behavior, there is added reason to be concerned about the level of settlement activity in our society, the reason being that settlements may deter people from acting in desirable ways.

ments against settlement merely question the widely held view that settlements are always preferable to trials; they do not show that that view is wrong. The arguments against dividing settlement funds among class members demonstrate only that the practice cannot be defended on the grounds that are usually given for it, not that the practice is indefensible. But even though we have shown only that the waters are deeper than the proponents of settlements suspect, we are satisfied with the result. Litigation is, after all, the primary and often the sole means by which people can use political authority to work for justice. It is therefore appropriate that the advocates of settlement bear the burden of justification. Our job is to see that the burden is carried, not shirked.

Law, Political Science, and Philosophy of the Social Sciences, Yale University
Law, Yale University

WRONGFUL LIFE AND THE COUNTERFACTUAL ELEMENT IN HARMING[1]

By Joel Feinberg

I shall be concerned in this paper with some philosophical puzzles raised by so-called "wrongful life" suits. These legal actions are obviously of great interest to lawyers and physicians, but philosophers might have a kind of professional interest in them too, since in a remarkably large number of them, judges have complained that the issues are too abstruse for the courts and belong more properly to philosophers and theologians. The issues that elicit this judicial frustration are those that require the application to borderline cases of such philosophically interesting concepts as acting, causing, and the one that especially interests me, harming.

I first became interested in the concept of harming in my work on the moral limits of the criminal law, where I had to come to terms with John Stuart Mill's famous "harm principle" – the principle that it is always a good reason in support of a criminal prohibition, indeed, the only legitimate reason, that it will prevent harm to persons other than the actor. I could not very well criticize that principle until I decided what the word "harm" must mean in its formulation. I gave what I took to be the requisite analysis of harm in my book *Harm to Others*.[2] Here I wish to improve that analysis, examine its implications for civil as well as criminal liability, and test it on conceptually hard cases, especially cases of *prenatal harming*, that is, cases in which the wrongful causative conduct occurs before the victim's birth, and the harmed state that is its upshot consists in being born in an impaired condition.

HARMING AND INTERESTS

For the purposes of the harm principle, we must think of harming as having two components:

(1) It must lead to some kind of adverse effect, or create the danger of such an effect, on its victim's *interests*; and

[1] Numerous paragraphs in this paper have been taken with only small revisions from my "Comment: Wrongful Conception and the Right Not to be Harmed," *Harvard Journal of Law and Public Policy*, vol. 8 (1985). This essay can be considered an expansion and development of the earlier one.

[2] Joel Feinberg, *Harm to Others* (New York: Oxford University Press, 1984).

(2) It must be inflicted wrongfully in violation of the victim's *rights*.

There is a broader, ordinary sense of "harm" in which that word refers to *any* state of adversely affected interest, whatever its cause. In that broader sense, people are often harmed by microbes, unforeseeable eruptions of nature, innocent actions of other persons, and actions of other persons to which they have freely consented. These are all examples of nonwrongful setbacks to interest, or "harms that are not wrongs" to those who suffer them. If the word "harm" as it occurs in Mill's harm principle had that broad sense, it would be quite implausible.

Similarly, just as one can be harmed (in the broad sense) without being wronged, so one can be wronged without being harmed, that is, without having one's interests adversely affected, though examples of this are harder to come by. Perhaps a wrongly broken promise that redounds by a fluke to the promisee's advantage is one kind of example. Again, I trust that no argument is needed to show that the harm principle for determining the limits of the *criminal* law would be implausible if its use of the word "harm" were broad enough to include such "harmless wrongs." What I concluded then was that for purposes of the harm principle, "harming" must mean adversely affecting another party's interest in a way that wrongs him or, alternatively, wronging him in a way that adversely affects his interest.

It is a necessary element in all harming, then, that it have an effect on someone's interests. The term "interests" is best left undefined here, except to say that interests are distinguishable components of a person's good or well-being. The language of interests is useful because it allows us to acknowledge the complexity of a person's good, how it contains various components, some of which may be flourishing while others languish at a given time, some of which might be advanced while others are set back by the same cause. Some interests are more basic or vital than others (I call these the "welfare interests") in the sense that when they are severely set back, no other interests in a person's interest-network can advance. Thus, the interest in having a certain minimum of food to eat, for example, is more basic or vital than the interest in being widely admired. Despite the diversity of component interests in any person's interest-network, and their different degrees of importance to one's overall good, our concepts seem to commit us to the view that interests can be summed up or integrated into one emergent personal interest. Suppose that Jones's act sets back one of Smith's interests thirty units but advances another of his interests twenty units. That would be a net loss of ten units. If interests can be related in such ways, then we can speak of *offsetting benefits*, and also *net harms*, or harms on balance, as opposed to *component harms*, or harms to component interests that can be offset by advancing other component interests. Thus, we speak not only of what promotes or sets back this or that particular interest of a person, but also of what promotes or sets back his self-interest as a whole, and we speak as if overall self-interest could in principle be plotted on a graph, like the profit-and-loss chart of a business corporation.

If we employ the "interest graph" as a kind of metaphorical model, it will be easy to see that there are various distinct ways of "adversely affecting" a person's self-interest. In my book I described some of these ways as follows:

> All of them involve a kind of directional metaphor [up or down on the interest chart]. To *set back* an interest is to reverse its course, turn it away, put it back toward the point from which it started. In terms of its associated goals, it is to reverse its progress, to put it in a worse condition than it was formerly in. To *defeat* an interest is to put it to utter rout, to set it back conclusively and irrevocably by destroying the conditions that are necessary for its advancement or fulfillment, as death for example can set back some interests once and for all. To *thwart* (or block or frustrate) an interest is to stop its progress without necessarily putting it in reverse; to successfully oppose it, and prevent it, at least for the time being, from making an advancement or improvement. To *impede* an interest is to slow its advancement without necessarily stopping or reversing it, to hinder or delay. Common to all these notions is the idea of a starting point or "baseline" from which the direction of advance or retreat is charted and measured.[3]

To complicate the picture further, the determination of harms and benefits is unavoidably affected by the prior locations, high or low, of interest states on the graph, their directions of movement at a given time, and their "momentum." If the current point of the interest curve is already near the top of the graph, then an event which has the effect of merely keeping it there has a protective or preservative influence and can be thought of as beneficial. If the point of the interest curve, however, is near the bottom of the chart, then the conduct of another which prevents it from improving can itself be harmful. When a person's situation is bad enough, simply to maintain it there when one could let it improve, may be to harm that person. Similarly, if another's conduct has the effect of only weakening upward momentum without actually stalling or reversing it, then I suppose its effect is harmful, though not seriously so, and correspondingly, to weaken an interest's downward momentum is to confer a benefit of a minor kind. What these examples show is that when we take prior condition, direction, and momentum of movement into account, an interest can be benefitted without

[3] *ibid.*, p. 53.

actually being advanced or promoted, and harmed without actually being thwarted or set back.

HARMING IN THE NORMAL POSTNATAL CASE

I shall mean by the phrase *harmful condition* a state in which a person is handicapped or impaired, a condition that has adverse effects on his whole network of interests. All states of harm, I think, are harmful conditions in this sense, but not all of them are *harmed conditions*. I reserve the latter term for states of harm that are the product of a prior act of harming. In most moral–legal contexts, we are interested in states of harm only when they are also products of acts of harming. To be sure, there is a sense in which "state of harm" is the more fundamental concept, since there can be no act of harming unless a state of harm is its product, whereas we *can* have a state of harm without there being any prior act of harming as its cause. Still, more is required of an act, for most legal purposes, if it is to be considered an act of harming than that it had a state of harm as its product, else we would assimilate human acts of harming to natural events that incidentally produce harmful effects. I shall now present a rough analysis of harming in this legally relevant sense, and also, derivatively, of a special sense of "victim" that goes along with it, namely, that in which *B* is a victim of *A* when and only when *A* has harmed him in this full sense.

In the sense of the verb that is of interest and use to the law, *A* harms *B* if and only if:

1. *A* acts (in a sense wide enough to include omissions and extended sequences of activity).
2. *A*'s action is defective or faulty with respect to the risks it creates to *B*, that is, it is done either with the intention of producing the consequences for *B* that follow, or similarly adverse ones, or with negligence or recklessness in respect to those consequences.
3. *A*'s acting in that manner is indefensible, that is, neither excusable nor justifiable.
4. *A*'s action is the cause of an adverse effect on *B*'s self-interest (a "state of harm").
5. *A*'s action is also a violation of *B*'s right.[4]

There is in addition to these explicit requirements a further condition of great importance. This additional requirement might at first sight be thought

[4] This fifth condition might be redundant because implied by conditions 3 and 4. That seems plausible to me, but I make the condition explicit anyway because I cannot prove that it is implied by the others, and some might doubt that it is. I think it is implicit in the others in virtue of the principle that *any* adverse effect on a person's interest caused by another's unjustified and unexcused act is a violation of his right.

to be implied by the terms "adverse effect" and "cause" as they are used in the fourth requirement, but we shall see that it is in truth an entirely independent condition. We can call this requirement "the counterfactual test," for it is formulated as follows:

6. *B*'s personal interest is in a worse condition (usually but not always lower on the interest graph) than it would be had *A* not acted as he did.

The subjunctive phrase – "had *A* not acted as he did" – is the counterfactual clause, for it means "*if*, contrary to fact, *A* had not acted as he did."

The counterfactual test should be distinguished from what might be called the "worsening" test, which is *not* always required for an act of harming. The worsening test can be put as follows:

6X. *B*'s personal interest is in a worse condition (lower on the interest graph) than it was before *A* acted.

The counterfactual requirement and the worsening requirement do not amount to the same thing, even though they are often satisfied together. There are numerous examples in which *B*'s condition is harmed by *A* even though it is not worsened. (We can think of worsening as putting an overall personal interest down at least one unit on the interest graph.) In these examples of harming, the counterfactual test is satisfied but the worsening test is not, for example, in cases of thwarting or impeding interest without actually setting it back, or in depriving someone of a gain without actually imposing a loss. Suppose a professional model (*B*) is wrongfully detained by *A* on the eve of the Miss America contest, in which, let us suppose, she would otherwise have won a prize worth over a million dollars in subsequent engagements and opportunities. By the worsening criterion, she is not harmed because she is no worse off than before the detention, but she is much worse off than she *would have been if* she had not been detained. So by the counterfactual test, she *is* harmed, but judged by the worsening requirement, she is not.

Not only can one harm a person without worsening his condition; our analysis also implies that one can harm a person by behavior that actually improves his condition (on the overall interest graph). Suppose that Doctor *A*, in giving patient *B* medical treatment, improves his condition but not to the extent that it would have improved had the doctor performed up to a higher standard, as he should have. That aspect of *A*'s behavior which consists of his failure to perform up to a reasonably expected standard *did* adversely affect *B*'s interest. *A*'s subpar performance, however, was better than no performance at all, and *B*'s health is in a better condition than it would be in had *A* not acted at all. *A*'s negligence adversely affected *B*'s interest even though *B* is better off from what *A* did than he would be had *A* not been on the scene. The sixth condition in the analysis of harming supports the judgment that *A* harmed *B*, provided we interpret "as he did" to refer in part to the defective aspects of *A*'s actions. The example then shows that one can be harmed by an act that does not set back one's interest on balance, but also does not promote that interest as much as it could and should have done.[5]

CAUSAL OVERDETERMINATION AND THE COUNTERFACTUAL CONDITION

The analysis of harming as it stands is vulnerable from another direction. In cases of causal overdetermination there can be harming that fails to satisfy the counterfactual test itself. In these cases, causing an adverse effect may not be to make a person worse off, on balance, than he would otherwise be. Suppose two schoolyard bullies both race after another child with the intention of inflicting a beating on him. One of the bullies gets to his victim a half minute before the other, pummels him, thereby inflicting various bodily injuries, and leaves him bloodied and beaten on the ground before the other bully can arrive on the scene. But if, contrary to fact, the first bully had not acted as he did, the victim would have been no better off, at least not for long, for the second bully would then have inflicted at least as bad a beating. (Indeed, the victim may actually be better off if the first bully's beating was less severe than the beating the second bully was prepared to inflict.) According to our analysis of harming as it is thus far developed, the victim was not harmed by the first bully's beating because the bully's action fails to satisfy the counterfactual test. It is false that the "victim" (and the word must for the time being appear in quotes) is worse off than he would otherwise be, and yet common sense would attribute an act of harming to the first bully anyway. Something seems to have gone wrong.

Jurisprudential writers have long been familiar with such examples of the overdetermination of harm. Examples are legion in the literature of both torts and crimimal law. A businessman in Sydney takes a taxicab to the airport with the intention of boarding his plane to Perth. On the way to the airport the reckless driving of the taxi driver causes a collision with a truck. The businessman, severely injured, is rushed in an ambulance to a hospital, and thus misses his plane. The plane, however, develops engine trouble and crashes shortly after takeoff, killing all the passengers. Questions of liability aside, did the cab driver *harm* the businessman by causing him to be injured? Common sense seems to say "yes," but our analysis of harming, with its

[5] So the counterfactual condition should perhaps be revised to read: *B*'s personal interest is in a worse state than it would be had *A* acted as he should have instead of as he did.

counterfactual condition, seems to say "no," since the businessman's interest would not have been better off on balance had the cab driver driven more carefully. In fact, he would have been worse off, so it seems, and not simply "not better off," suggesting that the cab driver's negligence actually benefitted him on balance.

There is a short way with our problem. We could hold that neither the counterfactual condition nor the worsening condition is necessary for there to be an act of harming, since we can think of examples of harming that fail to satisfy one or the other of them, but that the two conditions should be combined into one disjunctive condition. Acts of harming, we might say, must satisfy conditions 1–5 and *either* the counterfactual condition or the worsening condition. That is a tempting solution since, while it is easy to think of harmings that do not satisfy the worsening condition (e.g., deprivations of gain), and easy to think of harmings that do not satisfy the counterfactual condition (e.g., cases of causal overdetermination), it is much more difficult to think of harmings that satisfy *neither* the counterfactual nor the worsening condition.

Difficult, but not impossible. Suppose that *A*'s gang abducts *B*, the beauty queen, on the eve of the Miss America contest, as in the earlier example, but that if they had not done so, then *C*'s gang, in a quite independent conspiracy, would have abducted her only a few minutes later. In any case, *B* does not win the contest. It appears, according to the common sense notion of harming (if there is such a thing), that *A*'s gang harmed *B*, not by setting back her interest on the whole, but by having a different sort of "adverse effect," namely, preventing her from advancing her interest or depriving her of a gain. Yet neither the counterfactual nor the direct worsening test appears to be satisfied by this example. The potential Miss America is not worse off than she would have been had the abduction not occurred, for in that event she would have fallen into the clutches of *C*'s equally resolute gang; and she is not worse off than she was before the abduction, at least not in her professional and financial interests, which in this artificial example we may suppose to be the only interests substantially affected. The abductors did not directly impose a loss on her in their effort to deprive her of a gain. If this story is a reasonably clear example of an act of harming, it shows that even our disjunctive test is not satisfied by every example of harming.

But that preliminary point leaves a great deal unsaid about the riddles of causal overdetermination. What remains inadequately explored is the possibility that the counterfactual condition is satisfied in cases of causal overdetermination, first appearances to the contrary. Let me begin a very brief probe in that direction by calling attention to three different measures of what might be called the "gravity" of an act of harming. The gravity varies, first, with the extent of the adverse effect, what we might call "the degree of adversity." Thus, two broken legs are more adverse than one, and both are less adverse than bodily paralysis or death; and deprivation of a large gain is more adverse than deprivation of a small one. Second, the gravity varies with the duration of its adverse effect on personal interest. Obviously, injuries that take six months to heal are more grave than those that take six weeks, and those with lingering aftereffects are more grave, *ceteris paribus*, than those that can heal completely. Third, the gravity of an act of harming varies with the extent of the period during which the interest is in a worse condition than it otherwise would be in.[6] In the playground bully example, the victim's interest is in a worse condition than it would be had the first bully not acted as he did for about half a minute (the time it would have taken for the slower bully to get to the victim and begin *his* pummeling). The businessman's interest is in a worse condition than it would have been had the taxi driver not driven as he did, but only for about half an hour, that is, until the plane crash. In each case, the counterfactual condition is satisfied (only in the limiting case of simultaneous causes would it not be satisfied for *any* duration), but the gravity of the act of harming in the circumstances must be discounted by the brevity of the period during which it is satisfied.

Most of our problem cases seem to have a common form. The first harmer, H_1, harms a victim, V, by putting him in a state worse than he would otherwise be in for a period t. After t, a second harmer, H_2, would have caused equal or greater harm. H_1 is V's harmer, partly in virtue of his satisfying the counterfactual condition for time t. But V's injuries linger on well beyond time t. Long after his plane has crashed the businessman is still hospitalized in a severely impaired condition, and aftereffects may linger for years. The problem is whether we should ascribe to H_1 full resonsibility for the harms he initially caused even though the duration of V's harmful state extends well beyond the period during which he is worse off than he otherwise would be.

This issue is usually addressed in the civil process when the amount of damages is assessed, not at the earlier stage when the harmer's liability in the abstract is determined. That harmful effects linger beyond the period when the counterfactual condition is satisfied is not usually taken to be a serious difficulty. The law, I think, implicitly assumes a distinction betwen the harm actually caused to V by H_1 on balance (which is determined in part by the counterfactual test) and the harm that H_1 is justly answerable for. The

[6] Thus, when a small boy falls from a cliff towards a certain death on the rocks below, but is electrocuted instantly when his hand touches an uninsulated wire through which the electric company has negligently allowed current to run, the company's negligence has harmed the boy by causing his instant death (a very adverse effect on his interest), but there was only the tiniest interval, perhaps one second, during which the boy was "worse off than he otherwise would have been," and that severely discounts the gravity of the harming. As the court put it in a case of this sort, the victim was deprived of a life "too short to be given pecuniary allowance." Dillon v. Twin States Gas and Electric Co. 85 N.H. 449, 163 A. 111 (1932).

harmful state that *V* remains in is a kind of "causal residue" directly resulting from the harm that H_1 *did* cause. It is unquestionably a *harmful* condition but strictly speaking after the passage of interval *t*, it is not a *harmed* condition, i.e., not a net harm produced by H_1's act of harming. Nevertheless, it is perfectly just to hold H_1 liable for the full damages, including those beyond what he actually caused, because only an unforeseeabe fluke of chance (e.g., a plane crash) accounts for the brevity of the period during which the counterfactual condition continued to be satisfied. In short, H_1 harmed *V* because there was some period, however brief, during which the counterfactual condition was satisfied, and he is justly answerable for the effects of the harm he originally caused, since it was only a fluke of chance, not anything he can claim credit for, that limited the scope of his harming. The harmful residue has to be paid for by someone, and it seems less unfair to charge it to the original wrongdoer than to the hapless victim.

Another possible way of reconciling the counterfactual test with cases of causal overdetermination is to reformulate that test itself. We could say that *A* harms *B* only if his wrongful act leaves *B* worse off then he would be otherwise *in the normal course of events insofar as they were reasonably foreseeable in the circumstances*. With that doubly counterfactual formulation we can say that the taxi driver harmed the passenger to the full extent of his injuries, for "in the normal course of events" the airplane would not have crashed, and had the taxi collision been avoided *in those circumstances*, this new passenger would have been much better off than he is now in his hospital bed. This is another way of normativizing the concept of harming for legal purposes, but it has the advantage of not suggesting a kind of strict liability in which wrongdoers are held liable for harms beyond those which they actually caused. Given this reformulation of the counterfactual test, the taxi driver's negligence harmed the passenger to the full extent of his injuries, and the subsequent plane crash does not get him off the hook. His responsibility is more than a fiction in the interest of justice; it is a logical consequence of the analysis of harming with its reformulated counterfactual condition.

CIVIL LIABILITY FOR PRENATAL HARMING

So much for background. We come now to our central concern, prenatal harming. I shall begin with relatively unproblematic types of tort suits for prenatal harms and work up gradually to the wrongful life cases that generate the most acute philosophical perplexities. Consider first, cases in which the harming action occurs between conception and birth, and the infant is born in a harmed condition. A negligent motorist, for example, runs over a pregnant woman, directly injuring the fetus and causing it to be born in a permanently handicapped condition. After birth, the infant sues in her own name for damages. She charges that the defendant caused her injuries directly, not just that he allowed her to be born given that there would be injuries. Traditionally, I believe,[7] it was held that there is no right in the fetus actually to be born, but a "contingent right," assuming that it will be born, to be born unharmed. Assuming that the child will be born, the law seemed to say, various interests that she will come to have after birth must be protected from damage they can incur before birth.

In a second class of cases, the harming act occurs before conception, and the infant is born in a harmed condition. There are various familiar legal examples. A pharmaceutical manufacturer who carelessly prepares medicine six months before an infant's conception will be answerable to that child fifteen months later if the medicine taken by the mother damaged the embryo, and the fetus survived until birth. In another example, a blood transfusion gives a woman syphilis. One year later she conceives, and her child is born syphilitic. *He* will recover damages for negligence from the hospital. Finally, for a clincher, consider a fanciful hypothetical example from the criminal law. A wicked misanthrope desires to blow up a school house in order to kill or mutilate the pupils. He conceals a bomb in a closet in the kindergarten room and sets a timing device to go off in six years. It goes off on schedule, killing or multilating dozens of five year old children. It was the evil action of the wicked criminal six years earlier, *before they were even conceived*, that harmed them. It set in train a causal sequence that led directly to the harm.

The only problem with these two relatively unproblematic categories of prenatal harming is that they seem to involve legal duties to not yet existent persons. I am not impressed by the difficulty. There are at least two possible responses. Both have some cogency, but I prefer the second. First, one can argue in the negligence cases (the negligent motorist, the pre-pregnancy medication, and the hospital blood transfusion) that the negligent party had a duty to the mother (or the woman who was to become a mother), and his breach of *that* duty led to a later derivative harm to another party, the child not yet born or conceived – a "third party victim" on analogy with the "third party beneficiary" in other branches of the law. The second response is to affirm that a person has a duty of care toward *anyone* who is likely to be harmed as a consequence of his conduct (a "foreseeable victim"), and in the case of some actions, that includes persons not yet born nor even conceived. I prefer this second response because it includes the first, but is more comprehensive and general. It would cover the school bomb example, for instance, whereas the third-party victim analysis would not. One of its implied consequences, incidentally, is that when you are dealing, medically or commercially, with a woman of a certain age, you've got to think of her as

[7] See William Salmond, *Jurisprudence*, 5th ed., P. J. Fitzgerald (London: Sweet & Maxwell, 1966), pp. 303–304.

potentially pregnant, and her merely potential future child as a "foreseeable victim" of your transaction with her now.

We come now to more philosophically puzzling categories of tort suits: wrongful birth, wrongful pregnancy, and, most puzzling of all, the so-called "wrongful life" suits that will be our main concern. Let me explain this terminology and give examples. First, *wrongful birth* actions are brought by parents, usually against medical providers, for compensation for their own costs and suffering, occasioned by the birth defects of their newly born infants. In a very typical kind of case, a woman contracts *rubella* in her second month of pregnancy. Her doctor says, "Don't worry, there is no danger of birth defects." Then her child is born defective. The doctor's negligence did not *cause* the defects (the *rubella* did that), but the parents might have chosen a legal abortion otherwise. They were in effect deprived of the opportunity to abort, and now they want compensation for the many years of heartbreak, expensive care, and suffering caused to *them* by their child's handicapped exisence. In other cases, abortion is not involved. The doctor (say) fails to advise the parents of the likelihood of a harmful hereditary condition, depriving them not of the opportunity to abort but, rather, of *the opportunity not to conceive* in the first place.

Second, what are called "wrongful pregnancy" suits (also "wrongful conception" and "failed contraception") are brought by parents against medical providers for negligence leading to contraceptive failure and unwanted pregnancy, *even when the emergent infant is fully normal and healthy*. Again there are familiar examples. Pharmacists are sued for negligence in filling prescriptions for oral contraceptives; physicians are sued for negligence in performing sterilizations or abortions. Wrongful birth and wrongful pregnancy are similar actions in that both are brought by the parents of the child, but they differ in that the damages for wrongful birth are typically much greater, and this for obvious reasons: the costs (economic and psychological) of a severely defective child are greater than the costs of a merely unwanted one.[8]

[8] Wrongful pregnancy suits may be "relatively unproblematic," but they are far from noncontroversial. Many judges have argued that the "intangible benefits of having a child offset the expenses of raising a child." Rieck v. Medical Protective Company of Fort Wayne, Indiana, 64 Wis. 2d 514, 219 N.W. 2d 242, 1974. Others have claimed that an offsetting benefit is shown by the parents' retention of the child when there is the option of putting it up for adoption. Typically, the action is brought by parents who have acted in reliance on medical assurances that a vasectomy or tubal ligation has made pregnancy impossible, and then have had their new life plans dashed by the birth of an unexpected child. Normally they sue for the costs of raising a child to the age of eighteen years. Compromise settlements in which plaintiffs are allowed to recover only the costs of the unsuccessful operation, "compensation" for pain and suffering, medical complications, the costs of delivery, and lost wages and consortium during pregnancy are now common. For a definitive survey of cases, see Anne C. Reichman, "Damages in Tort for Wrongful Conception Who Bears the Cost of Raising the Child?" *The Sydney Law Review*, vol. 10 (March 1985).

We come now to the most interesting and controversial category. A *wrongful life* suit is brought by the infant himself, usually against medical providers, but sometimes against the biological parent(s), for wrongfully allowing him to come into existence at all, given that it was known, or should have been known, that he would probably be born with severe afflictions. The 1980 California case of *Curlender v. Bio-science Laboratories*[9] is one of the very few successful wrongful life suits to date. An infant was born severely impaired as a result of a medical testing laboratory's negligence in conducting genetic tests on the parents (Mr. and Mrs. Curlender). If properly done, the tests should have revealed a high probability of inherited Tay-Sachs disease. The parents then would have had amniocentesis early in pregnancy in order to check, or they might have opted not to conceive at all. (Tay-Sachs disease, as I understand it, is carried by a recessive gene. Only when both parents are carriers is the probability of transmission high.) Little Shauna Curlender lived in intense pain for four years, severely retarded, with extensive loss of motor reactions, including an inability to feed orally.[10] In addition, her attorney's list of harms included "deprivation of 72.6 years of her life," but that, I think, is a logical confusion.[11]

MISGIVINGS OVER WRONGFUL LIFE SUITS

Misgivings of at least five distinct kinds have been expressed over wrongful life suits.[12] I think that reassuring replies can be given to at least four of them. It is said, first of all, that they are *unnecessary* given the possiblity of wrongful birth suits by the parents, that there is a kind of wasteful redundancy in permitting either or both, child or parents, to sue for the same wrong and the same harm. In fact, the two kinds of action *are* usually brought together, so some commentators might well wonder whether "wrongful

[9] Curlender v. Bio-Science Laboratories, 106 Cal. App. 3d 811, 165 Cal. Rptr. 477 (1980).

[10] Bonnie Steinbock describes the usual course of the disease: "The child appears well at birth and develops normally for six to eight months when progressive psychomotor degeneration slowly begins. By eighteen months the child is likely to be paralyzed and blind, unable to take food by mouth, suffering from constipation and decubitus ulcers. There are increasingly frequent convulsions which cannot be controlled by medication. The last few years of the child's life are usually spent in a vegetative state." See her "Wrongful Life," *The Hastings Center Report*, vol. 15 (April 1986), p. 17.

[11] The argument is based on there being a life expectancy of 76.6 years for white females. Shauna lived only for four years, so her disease deprived her of the other 72.6 years. But either the testing laboratory would be negligent, in which case she was destined to a life of only four years, or it would not be negligent, in which case she would not have been conceived and born at all. In neither case would she have lived 76.6 years!

[12] I am indebted to Nora K. Bell and Barry M. Loewer. See their valuable article "What Is Wrong with 'Wrongful Life' Cases?" *The Journal of Medicine and Philosophy*, vol. 10 (May 1985), pp. 127–146.

birth" might be sufficient for both. Surely there would be fewer philosophical problems that way. And in either case, the bills would get paid by the harming party.

One might give three different replies to this first kind of misgiving.[13] The first is to point out that the courts are sometimes very tough on the parents who bring the wrongful birth cases. Judges often find it hard to agree that the parents have themselves been harmed on balance by the birth of an impaired child. They often say that the birth of a child – any child – is a "blessed" event" whose benefits to its parents far exceed its burdens.[14] In *Becker v. Schwartz*[15] the judge made a more modest claim that seems quite undeniable: "Parents may yet experience a love that even an abnormality cannot dampen." That kind of consideration is often meant to show that the parents, on balance, are unharmed. This attitude encourages, indeed requires, suit by the child plaintiff. *Her* injuries are plain and less controversial. In some cases there would be no recovery at all unless the infant sues in her own name.

The second reply is that sometimes the biological parents themselves, or one of them, are the defendants in wrongful life suits. Suppose that *B*, who is mentally defective, is raped by *A*, who is wealthy, or that *A* seduces her in reckless disregard of the chance of pregnancy. *B* becomes pregnant, and it is subsequently determined that the baby is likely to inherit genetic defects from the mother. Suppose, finally, that abortion is either illegal (as it still is in many countries) or considered morally beyond the pale. The child is born out of wedlock to a helpless and indigent mother and with very costly medical needs. If we add to the example that the mother dies in childbirth, it will become more clear that there is no one to bring suit against but the biological father, and no one to bring suit but the infant.

The third reply to the redundancy objection is the most important one, namely, that in any case there is a basic difference between the indirect harm to the parents and the direct harm to the child that is produced when medical negligence permits the birth of a severely damaged baby. These are distinct harms and different in kind and degree. As Bell and Loewer put it, "While it might be true in some cases that the benefits to the *parents* of having an afflicted child may outweigh the burdens ["Better an afflicted child than none at all" might be their attitude] that doesn't address the issue of whether in some cases the burden to the *child* of being born so afflicted outweighs the benefits to *him*."[16] It is quite conceivable that *that* question has

[13] I borrow heavily here from Bell and Loewer, *ibid.*, p. 131. Bonnie Steinbock gives still additional replies to this first misgiving in "Wrongful Life."

[14] We have seen (*supra*, note 8) that this sort of thing is commonly said in wrongful conception cases, but it is also said in wrongful birth cases where *prima facie* it is less plausible.

[15] Becker v. Schwartz, 46 N.Y. 2d 401, 413 N.Y.S. 2d 895, 386 N.E. 2d 807 (1978).

[16] Bell and Loewer, "What Is Wrong," p. 131.

an affirmative answer, so that a wrongful life suit might be more plausible (and more lucrative) than a wrongful birth one, and not merely a dispensable redundancy.

The second misgiving over wrongful life suits has been expressed as a conceptual objection to all alleged cases of prenatal harm. This is the claim that a legal duty to the not yet existent is impossible. We have already encountered it, and replied that a duty of care to any foreseeable victim, including the not yet existent, is a perfectly coherent notion.[17]

The third misgiving is an especially serious philosophical one. It is thought by many people that the counterfactual comparison normally used to determine whether *A* has harmed *B* is logically inapplicable in wrongful life cases because the question of whether *A*'s wrongful conduct made the emergent child worse off than he would otherwise have been reduces to the question of whether the child would have been "better off had he never been born." Since it is necessary to *be* if one is to *be better off*, it is a logical contradiction to say that someone could be better off though not in existence.[18] If *A* had prevented *B*'s birth by contraception, abstention, or abortion, *B* would not have been better off as a result, for *B* would not have *been* as a result. Nonexistence would not have been a better condition for *B* to be in, for it would have been no condition of *B* at all.

Obviously, the counterfactual test must be reformulated (yet again!) if it is to serve as an adequate test and measure of harming in wrongful life cases. I think this can be done. Instead of asking whether *B* would be better off if he had never been born, we could ask what most of us really mean when we use this idiomatic phrase intending it to convey sense instead of paradox. When a miserable adult claims that he would be "better off dead," for example, surely he is not making some subtle metaphysical claim implying that there is a realm of being in which even the nonexistent have a place. What he is saying is that he *prefers* to be dead, that is, not to *be* at all. Similarly, when we claim that some grossly deformed, impaired, and suffering infant would have been better off unborn, we are expressing, belatedly, our belief that that state of affairs is preferable. If we speak in the first person, we may be expressing the *wish* (not a desire) that we had never come into existence — "Would that I had never been born." When that wish is expressed in terms of being "better off not having come into existence," it is to be understood not simply as a wish, but as a claim that the preference implied in the wish is understandable and justifiable, rationally based on the nature of the

[17] That is not to say that problems do not remain, especially in specifying the correlative right-holder. See my discussion of "birthrights" below.

[18] Improving the lot of the no-longer-existent may be an exception to this. See my *Harm to Others*, pp. 79–83, and Aristotle, *Nicomachean Ethics*, Book One, Chap. 10. Improving the lot of the not-yet-existent, though, does seem to be logically impossible.

speaker's present plight. When one party says that another would have been better off had he never been born, he is claiming that the preference for the one state of affairs over the other is a rational preference. Whether true or not, this is an intelligible claim without contradiction or paradox. What we must ask, then, in wrongful life cases is "whether nonexistence or nonlife is preferable to life attended by certain hardships."[19] If nonexistence in a given case would have been objectively preferable to existence, as judged for example by the law's convenient "reasonable person," then any wrongful act or omission that caused (permitted) the child to be born can be judged to have harmed the child.

That brings us to the fourth misgiving. The question now becomes this: Is nonexistence in fact ever rationally preferable to a severely encumbered existence? Surely, in most cases of suffering and impairment we think of death as even worse. This is shown by the widespread human tendency to "cling to life at all costs." And even for severe genetic handicaps and inherited maladies, most competent persons who suffer from them will not express regret that they were born in the first place. The persons who might be expected to have the contrary view in their own case are often so badly off that they are not even competent to form the opinion or express it, and it must be expressed on their behalf by others. In the most extreme cases, however, I think it is rational to prefer not to have come into existence at all, and while I cannot prove this judgment, I am confident that most people will agree that it is at least plausible. I have in mind some of the more severely victimized sufferers from brain malformation, spina bifida, Tay-Sachs disease, polycystic kidney disease, Lesch-Nyhan syndrome, and those who, from whatever cause, are born blind and deaf, permanently incontinent, severely retarded, and in chronic pain or near-total paralysis, with life-expectancies of only a few years.

Even if we can judge that *A*'s breach of duty was the cause of *B*'s being born (although not the cause of *B*'s impairment) and that *B*'s nonexistence would have been preferable to him coming into existence so impaired, and hence that *A* harmed *B*, we might still reject wrongful life suits on the ground that there is no possible way of determining damages for the harmed party. This fifth misgiving makes the strongest objection to wrongful life suits.

I think it must be conceded that so long as we think of damages as representing *compensation* (in certain senses) for the harm, then it cannot make sense to order their payment to a victim of wrongful life, for the simple

[19] Williams v. State, 18 N.Y. 2d at 485, 276 N.Y.S. 2d at 888, 223 N.E 2d at 345 (Keating, J. concurring). Judge Keating goes on to say that "it is impossible to make that choice," but surely that overstates the point. Experience as a bastard in contemporary America, a key harm in the case in question, clearly is preferable, *certeris paribus*, to nonexistence.

reason that his harms are not (in those senses) compensable. Consider the various things that have been meant by "compensation":

1. Bringing the plaintiff back to where he was (repairing the damage). No money payment could do this for the person who is so extremely and irreparably harmed that his life is not worth living. Apparently only death itself – which is not one of the permitted tort remedies – could do that.

2. Market compensation. The required payment would be the amount of money the plaintiff would have freely agreed to in advance as his price for submitting to the harm. But the plaintiff in our examples did not even exist "in advance." Before the harmful act that assured his existence he had no values formed, and therefore no order of priorities is retroactively ascribable to him now. If we nonetheless ascribe "normal values" supposititiously to his preexistent self, then presumably we would judge that no conceivable amount of money would be a sufficient price for taking on a life not worth living.

3. Diversionary displacement. This is best illustrated by a story. George, a successful 40 year old engineer, was badly burned in a car accident in which he was blameless. After countless skin grafts, he recovered his health and resumed his job, but now he was quite grotesque in appearance, his face a maze of wrinkled scar tissue. He was deeply depressed until he won a settlement of four million tax-free dollars. Some of this paid his ongoing medical bills, but most of it was pure "profit." The effect of this infusion of wealth was to divert George from his depression. He no longer looks in the mirror each morning; now he looks at stock market figures, thinks about investments (a fascinating game hitherto unknown to him), and also cultivates his new interests in sports cars and gourmet restaurants. For people like George, life has its consolations (displacements of interest) if one has enough cash, even though no amount of cash would have seemed worth it in advance. We can contrast the extremely impaired and cognitively undeveloped spina bifida or Tay-Sachs baby. There is no way to make her feel better about things and no amount of money could divert her attention and console her. (The cognitively unimpaired adult quadraplegic, however, might find playing the stock market or contributing to worthy causes sufficiently diverting to make his life worth continuing, even though he would not have agreed in advance to *any* price for his paralysis, and he would happily trade all his wealth, if he could, to recover his health. That would be an example of "compensation" rendering a life worth living that would not otherwise be so, but that is not the kind of example we find in the wrongful life cases.

4. "Compensation for pain and suffering." Often awards for pain and suffering have a disguised punitive role, functioning primarily as a way of getting back at the wrongdoer, but in what way do these damages "compensate" for suffering that has come and gone? They don't annul or obliterate pain, or make it as if the pain or suffering never were, or make one mind the pain less in retrospect. In some cases they can divert competent persons from their depression, but they would hardly console the wretched Tay-Sachs child.

5. Payment of maintenance costs (hospital fees, medicine, food). This is the only sense of compensation that seems applicable to an infant whose life is so terrible it is not worth living. But even if the child sues in her own name, *she* is not the one who is in any primary way benefitted. Rather, those who would otherwise have to pay are relieved of their burden. Their financial costs will now be paid by the defendant, thus compensating *them* for out-of-pocket costs, not the actual plaintiff whose costs would otherwise have been paid somehow by someone (in the last resort, the state). Perhaps, then, there should not be tort actions for wrongful life at all, but only maintenance suits, as, for example, in paternity suits. There could even be administrative tribunals assigning the costs of support to the most appropriate party. But *if* justice would make the assignment of those costs to the party most at fault (which is not necessarily true), that question is best settled by traditional procedures of tort litigation, and that would mean, in cases of this kind, wrongful life suits.

SOME SPECULATIVE CONSEQUENCES OF THESE REASONINGS

1. Applying the counterfactual test in wrongful life cases. In the special case of harming by bringing into existence, as we have seen, a reformulation of the counterfactual test is required. For these cases we should say that *B* is in a harmed state if, because of *A*'s breach of duty, *B* comes into existence in a condition such that *it would be rational to prefer nonexistence to that condition.* This test does require a comparison of the usual kind between *B*'s actual condition and a state of affairs alternative to it (that which would have obtained had *A* acted rightly), but that is not a comparison of two possible conditions of *B*. When we speak for *B*, we do not say "I would rather be in that condition than in this one"; rather, we say "I would rather not be at all than be in this condition."

It may seem objectionably *ad hoc* to revise the general account of harming to accommodate the one kind of case that it does not seem to fit. Revising a generalization to cover a recalcitrant special case, however, is only sometimes objectionably *ad hoc*. Consider a clearer example of an illicit *ad hoc* revision. Scientists in Melbourne conclude from an experiment that under circumstances *C*, electrons behave in a certain way, *x*. The experiment is repeated in Bundoora and fails to yield the same result. Undaunted, the scientists amend their theory to say that electrons behave in way *x* under circumstances *C except in Bundoora*. This is unsatisfactory, of course, because of the well-founded expectation that if electrons don't behave *x*ly in Bundoora, then they do not elsewhere either. That is, we assume that there is nothing special about Bundoora that would uniquely affect the behavior of electrons there. There is, however, something very special about the context of "harmful conception" that might lead us to expect that its peculiarities will not be repeated elsewhere. It is the only example we can have of a person's being harmed by the very act that brings him into existence.

2. How do we decide what is "rationally preferable"? Further philosophical difficulties are raised by the phrase – "It would be rational to prefer nonexistence to that condition." Two questions in particular require answers: (1) Rational for whom? and (2) In which sense of "rational," "dictated by reason" or merely "consistent with reason"?[20] I shall consider the former question first.

The phrase "It would be rational to prefer," as it stands, is vague and elliptical. Rational for *whom* to prefer? There are three possibilities. Perhaps we mean that it would be rational for the seriously impaired infant to prefer not to have been born. But if he is impaired to the point where it is plausible to suppose that his life is not worth living, then he may be incapable of having, now or ever, such a preference. He may never be capable of forming the concepts of existence and nonexistence. Hence, it seems to make no sense to say that he should prefer one or the other, or that it would be rational for *him* to have such a preference. Would it be rational for a jellyfish to prefer saline to fresh water, nonvoracious to voracious neighbors, a rising to a falling barometer, existence to nonexistence? If that makes no sense, what are we to say of similar statements about the hypothetical rationality of the preferences of a human neonate with (say) only half a brain? It is easy to tumble into a paradox here. The statement about the impaired infant is of even more doubtful intelligibility than that about the jellyfish. We can say that jellyfish are not rational beings, since they lack brains altogether, but if, contrary to fact, a jellyfish were a ratoinal being, everything else the same, then it would be rational for it to have the preferences mentioned above (including the metaphysical one). It is also true that the seriously impaired infant is not a rational being, since it is both immature and possessed of only half a brain. But if, contrary to fact, he were older and possessed of a full normal brain, then, everything else the same, it might *not* be true that it would be rational for him to prefer nonexistence to his present (not so impaired) condition. For if he were rational enough to make a choice at all, he might be sufficiently unimpaired for his life to be worth living after

[20] I am indebted to Thomas McKay of Syracuse University for reminding me of this distinction.

all. What can we mean, then, by the claim that it would be rational for *him* to prefer not to have been born?

Suppose that the statement is interpreted in a different way. The second possible interpretation is that an infant is in a harmed state if he comes into existence in a condition such that it would be rational for some other person (you or me or any "reasonable person"?) to prefer his own nonexistence to his continued existence if he were in that condition. This interpretation leads into a thicket of metaphysical entanglements. It requires someone to say that *if I were he*, it would be rational for *me* to prefer nonexistence to the condition I would then be in. When I say "if I were he," I imagine that somehow he (as he is now) is mixed with me (as I am now). This can be a strong mixture (most of my present properties and only some of his) or a weak mixture (most of his present properties and only some of mine). It would be my rational capacities, values, and principles mixed with his pain, impairment, and dim prospects. If such a composite person were possible, then *he* would prefer nonexistence to his present condition. Perhaps, however, such a composite would be logically impossible, on the one hand having, let us suppose, only half a brain – that is the source of the painful impairment and the dim prospects – but also my full and normal brain. Thus, the first interpretation's paradox threatens to return.

Now consider the third and final categorial possibility. Suppose that the impaired product of a wrongful conception is not *rationally* impaired, but largely paralyzed and in constant pain. Suppose that he doesn't bring suit until he is (say) twenty years old. He then claims both that his life is and has never been worth living and that he himself is competent to make that judgment, being aware of his plight and understanding his options. Now to say that some medical provider or parent harmed him by permitting him to be born is to say that that person put him in a condition which is such that (1) he in fact prefers nonexistence to that condition, and (2) it is rational for him, or for anyone in his shoes, to have that preference. It is likely, however, that rational persons in that condition might reasonably differ in their preferences. We should therefore revise the claim of the competent twenty-year-old to say that it is *not irrational* (or not unreasonable) for him to have that preference, not that it would be irrational not to have it. The test of the rationality of the actual preferences of a competent person is the weak one of "consistency with reason."

For the competent subject, then, the paradoxes of the first two intepretations do not seem to arise. But that fact is itself paradoxical, for it is precisely the incompetent subjects who seem most clearly in a position to claim that their lives are not worth living. How can we make sense of this claim? The only interpretation that remains open to us is that it would be rational (now in a much stronger sense) for a *proxy chooser*, any representative of the best interests of an extremely impaired infant, to express on the infant's behalf the preference for nonexistence. The judgment, once more, is not that the infant would be better off dead, as if death were a possible condition for him to be in, but, rather, that the preference for death over impaired present condition would be, in a strong sense, rational if it were expressed by a party concerned not to promote the infant's future good so much as to bring to an end his present harm. There is no need for a hypothetical mixing of selves in the proxy chooser's imagination. He need only represent the interests of the incompetent party. To be sure, that party may not yet have any values, goals, ideals, or aspirations, the stuff of which interests are made. But the proxy chooser is not therefore required to substitute his own, ascribing them hypothetically to the infant. Rather, he exercises his judgment that *whatever* interests the impaired party might have, or come to have, they would already be doomed to defeat by his present incurable condition. Thus, it would be irrational – contrary to what reason decrees – for a representative and protector of those interests to prefer the continuance of that condition to nonexistence. The proxy might also express the retroactive preference, on the incompetent's behalf, not to have been born at all. Parents with dangerous genetic disorders express the preference not to have children beforehand, and exercise that preference for the sake of the impaired children they might otherwise produce. "It wouldn't be fair to bring a child into existence in such a condition," they might say. If parents can express this preference intelligibly beforehand, how is the same judgment, made on the same grounds after the fact, any less rational?

It is not possible to prove conclusively that a preference, prospective or retrospective, for oneself or for another, *can* be rational in the strong sense of "required by reason," but an experiment in the imagination may serve to make that proposition seem more plausible. Suppose that after the death of your body a deity appears to you and announces that, contrary to the simplistic teachings of many moral theologians, he has far more alternatives for the afterlife than heaven, hell, and purgatory. There are infinite subtle gradations in human character, he explains, not just unqualified good and evil. Corresponding to these are a range of complex rewards and punishments tailored to each individual's complex deserts. In your case, he continues, he proposes to give you an option. You can be born again after death (reincarnated), but only as a Tay-Sachs baby with a painful life expectancy of four years to be followed by permanent extinction, or you can opt for permanent extinction to begin immediately. I should think you would have to be crazy to select the first option. Self-interest clearly dictates that you leave well enough alone and quit while you are still ahead. Similarly, if the deity required you to make a choice between the same alternatives for a loved one, say your spouse or child, someone for whose good you truly cared, you would not hesitate, insofar as you are rational, to opt once more for immediate nonexistence.

In summary, the judgment that his nonexistence would be (or would have been) preferable to his existence in such and such condition, if made by a competent adult or mature older child, is correct provided (1) he does in fact have a free and informed preference, prospective or retrospective as the case may be, for nonexistence, and (2) that preference is rational in the weak sense, that is not contrary to reason, even though other equally rational persons in his circumstances might not share it. A preference for nonexistence over continued existence with a cut finger is clearly contrary to reason; a preference for nonexistence to inescapable hideous tortures might be required by reason; but in between is a range of options about which reasonable persons might differ, for example, whether nonexistence is preferable to life as a permanently hospitalized quadraplegic.

On the other hand, the judgment that nonexistence would be (or would have been) preferable to existence in an extremely impaired condition, if made by a proxy on behalf of an incompetent infant, is correct if and only if it is rational in the strong sense, that is, "required by reason" of anyone who is concerned to protect the interests of the incompetent subject.

Finally, let us suppose that we agree, for the sake of the argument, that because of another party's negligence, a certain infant is in a condition such that nonexistence would have been preferable (in the appropriate sense) to being born in that incurably impaired condition. Would not the appropriate remedy be simply to give that infant a painless injection that would cause its death? Would not that solution make more sense than complex litigation over costs? (The harming party might still be civilly liable to pay all the infant's costs up to now – hospitalization, treatment, medication, legal fees, even the costs of the instruments of euthanasia.) Ideally, I think, euthanasia would be the most just and humane solution, but the conceptual riddles we are attempting to resolve here arise against a background of current legal practice, and for better or worse, we have an inflexible rule against homicide that is not likely to be relaxed in the foreseeable future. Moreover, a wise legislator would have to be assured that the substitute pratice he is to vote upon is free of the possibility of mistake and abuse, an assurance that is not imminently forthcoming. Another complication is that it may not be inconsistent for a subject, either himself competent or else competently represented by proxy, to judge that not to have been born would have been preferable to being born but that, nevertheless, now that he does exist he prefers not to die. If that combination of rational preferences is possible,[21]

[21] I find this to be a difficult question that requires an examination of the instinct of self-preservation, and the concepts of weakness of will and voluntariness and their relations to rationality. I am skeptical, but in the absence of detailed examination, I prefer to leave it an open question.

then the ideal solution may after all be to make a wrongful harmer liable for the damages of a life that ought never to have been allowed to begin, while withholding the means to its abrupt termination.

3. A new interpretation of a birthright. If the creation of a baby whose life is not worth living is to count as a *harming* of that baby, one more requirement in our analysis of "harming" must be satisfied: *A* must *wrong B* and not merely affect his interest adversely. The duty toward *B* that was breached must be a duty that was logically correlated with *B*'s right against *A*. The right in question, I suspect, is a very special kind of right indeed, since it seems in some sense to attach to a merely potential being, and to be violated only at the moment its possessor is allowed to come into exsitence. I shall try to show, however, that prospective rights of this kind are not as mysterious as they may first seem.

Before the fetus becomes a person, it is a potential person with the potential attributes, including possession of rights, of a person. If it should be the case that the potential person has an unalterable destiny of extreme impairment and suffering, and if it is true that one of the rights he will have at birth (at the presumed onset of personhood[22]) is the right to be free of these total impediments to development and fulfillment, that is, a right to *some* opportunity for a tolerable life, then the potential rights at the very moment they are actualized are violated. A grossly impaired infant comes into existence not simply with rights, but with rights already violated. From the moment such an infant is born he has a grievance – a claim that he has been wronged. There are rights that are affirmable from the moment of birth (or the onset of personhood, whenever that is), and some of these birthrights have been violated from the moment they are initially assertable. In my book, I note that a new interpretation of the idea of a "birthright" is suggested by this point, namely that

> . . . if you cannot have that to which you have a birthright then you are wronged if you are brought to birth. Thus, if the conditions for the eventual fulfillment of the child's future interests are destroyed

[22] In the account I sketch in the text, I refer to birth as the "presumed onset of personhood," and the rights that become actual at that point as "birthrights." But if the reader believes that the onset of personhood is earlier than birth, he should substitute "personhood-inception rights" for my "birthrights," and locate their origin at whichever developmental stage he wishes. I use the point of birth as an example only. I do not mean to beg any controversial questions in the abortion debate. There is one acknowledged implication for that debate, however, in my account: If the only way to prevent a child from being born into a life not worth living, and thereby being severely harmed, is to abort, and if we can know this in advance (a big IF), then it would seem to follow that the mother has a moral duty to submit to an abortion. See my "Wrongful Conception and the Right Not to be Harmed."

> before he is born, the child can claim, after he has been born, that his *rights* (his present rights) have been violated. Moreover, if before the child has been born, we *know* that the conditions for the fulfillment of his most basic interests have already been destroyed, and we permit him nevertheless to be born, we become a party to the violation of his rights. It bears repeating that not all interests of the newborn child should or can qualify for prenatal protection, but only those very basic ones whose satisfaction is known to be indispensable to a [minimally] decent life.[23]

In those extreme cases, then, in which a child is negligently or deliberately permitted to be born into a life not worth living, the infant is both wronged and put into a state of harm, and therefore *harmed* in the full sense.[24]

4. Criminal liablity for wrongful life? Up to now I have been discussing mostly the law of torts, even though my interest in questions about prenatal harming arose in the course of a book on the moral limits of the criminal law. But now, just for completeness, I shall consider whether it could ever be feasible to impose criminal liability for wrongful life. Civil suits for wrongful life, as we have seen, are in principle acceptable, though in fact perhaps of limited utility given the possibility of wrongful birth suits by parents, and the limited applicability of meaningful notions of compensation to incompetent infants. Statutes permitting criminal prosecutions for wrongful life could also be legitimate in principle, since they would be aimed at the prevention of genuine and serious harms. Wrongfully permitting or enabling an infant to be born into a life not worth living would not be a so-called "victimless crime." There are numerous decisive reasons against such statutes, however, and no legislature has ever even considered passing such legislation. The fault in most wrongful life cases is negligence, and that is a rather problematic ground for severe criminal liability. Moreover, vulnerability to criminal prosecution would have a chilling effect, with diverse deleterious consequences, on the medical professions. Reckless and intentional causing of pregnancy in the face of known risks of abnormal birth are very often crimes under some other name, like rape or fraud, and new legislation is not needed to cope with them. Moreover, deliberate failures to undergo abortions are usually motivated by the conviction that abortion is morally wrong, hardly a suitable state of mind for criminal punishment. Even the question of whether a given handicapped life is worth living is one on which reasonable persons can and often do conscientiously disagree, creating further difficulties of an intractable kind.

[23] Joel Feinberg, *Harm to Others*, p. 99.

[24] I must therefore repudiate my position in *Harm to Others*, p. 102.

Still, it is possible to conceive of instances of deliberate and wrongful life creation that would be plausible targets of criminal legislation, though at present we must resort to examples from philosophical science fiction. Imagine an evil scientist who does genetic research on fetuses and newborns in the hope of creating a super-race or alternatively, a slave-race. He creates test-tube embryos through *in vitro* fertilization from chemically altered sperm and ova. Then he reimplants them in a natural womb of a willing subject. The emergent infants have horrible afflictions and no oportunity of ever having normal lives, but the scientist respects their "right to life" and keeps them under observation until their lives mercifully sputter out. Perhaps there is a crime with some familiar name that is already applicable to this sort of behavior, but if not, a bill carefully defining "criminal wrongful life" might well be in order. At present, fortunately, there seems to be no need for it.

WHEN THE NEWBORN IS NOT SO SEVERELY HANDICAPPED THAT HIS LIFE IS NOT WORTH LIVING

The class of examples I shall consider now are cases in which the wrongdoing is flagrant (in the most interesting cases deliberate or reckless, rather than merely negligent), and done by one or both of the biological parents, rather than by some medical provider. In an ingenious example of Derek Parfit's,[25] a woman is warned that if she gets pregnant while she suffers from some temporary illness, her baby will be born in a defective condition. Nonethelesss, whether through intentional perversity or reckless impulsiveness, she heeds not her physician's warning, and gets pregnant at the dangerous time. If her emergent child is so defective that his life is not worth living, then he would have a strong case for wrongful life damages against the mother. He would surely have a *moral* grievance against her. "But for your wrongful conduct," he might say (or his lawyer might say for him), "I would never have been conceived much less born, and nonexistence would surely be preferable to my miserable state." By the counterfactual test, reformulated for wrongful life cases, this wretched infant has indeed been harmed: he is in a condition so bad that even nonexistence would have been preferable to it. Moreover, his birthright has been violated from the moment he came into existence, since the conditions for a minimally decent life had already been destroyed. His interests have been adversely affected and he has been wronged, so it follows that he has been harmed in the full sense, and his impaired state can be understood as a harmed state, i.e., a state of harm that is the product of a prior act of harming.

In Parfit's example, however, the inherited defect is *not* so severe as to

[25] Derek Parfit, "On Doing the Best for Our Children," Michael D. Bayles, ed., *Ethics and Population* (Cambridge, MA: Schenkman, 1976).

render the child's life not worth living. The child never regrets that he was born, but only that he was born (say) with a withered arm – a serious handicap but surely not such that nonexistence would be preferable to it. Therefore, when we apply the counterfactual test as reformulated for wrongful life situations, it turns out that the mother did not harm her child. She had only two options with respect to his birth. One was to do what she did, which led to his being born with the withered arm. The other was to obey the doctor, which would have led to his never having existed at all, which even the child acknowledges was the worse fate. Hence, she picked the option which had the best total consequences for the child that eventually emerged. Hence, her act did not harm that child (at least by the revised counterfactual test). Thus, the child's impaired condition is not a *harmed condition*, that is, not a state of harm that is the product of a prior act of harming. It clearly is neverthelesss a state of harm, however we characterize its causal antecedents, since it does have adverse effects on the child's interests. I prefer to call it, therefore, a *harmful condition* rather than a harmed condition.

Did the mother *wrong* the child by causing him to come into existence in a harmful (handicapped) condition? I do not think the child can establish a grievance against her so long as he concedes that his handicapped existence is far preferable to no existence at all. For if he were to claim that she wronged him by doing what she did, that would commit him to the judgment that her duty to him had been to refrain from doing what she did; but if she had refrained, that would have led to his never having been born, an even worse result from his point of view. There is no doubt that the mother did act wrongly, but it does not follow that her wrongdoing wronged any particular person, or had any particular victim. She must be blamed for wantonly introducing a certain evil into the world, not for harming, or for violating the rights of, a person.

If I am right about this, there may be a case against tort liability in this instance, since the wrongful act of the defendant did not harm (on balance) the plaintiff. To hold her liable anyway, would be (at least with respect to the harm element) something like holding a rescuer liable for injuries he caused an endangered person that were necessary to his saving that person's life. He may have caused the imperiled party's arm to be broken in the rescue effort, but the alternative, let us suppose, was to let him die. So the broken-armed plaintiff suffered a harmful condition with respect to his arm, but the rescuer-defendant did not cause a condition that was harmful on balance, offset as it was by the overriding benefit of rescue, and he cannot be said, therefore, to have *harmed* the plaintiff (in the relevant full sense) at all.[26]

[26] For all this to be true, we must assume that the rescuer was not himself responsible for the other party's peril. If he put that party in the precarious situation in the first place, he himself is responsible for the costs of rescuing him, including the costs of repairing the broken arm.

Similarly, a statute imposing criminal liability on the mother for her behavior in Parfit's example would not appear at first sight to be legitimate, at least not according to the liberal doctrine that there should be no criminal liability without a proper victim. Such a statute would create a victimless crime, and could be justified only on the grounds that wrongdoing deserves punishment even when it harms no one and violates no one's rights (the illiberal doctrine of "legal moralism").

Nevertheless, I shall investigate in the space that remains the possibility that criminal and/or tort liability for wrongful life might be justified even in cases where the harmful condition is not so severe as to make the wrongfully created life not worth living. And we shall have to ask what consequences these cases might have for the liberal condemnation of victimless crimes, and for the way in which we apply such terms as "harm," "wrong," and "victim" to the infants who are plaintiffs in civil suits for wrongful life.

CRIMES WITHOUT VICTIMS

If "negligent conception" (as we might call it) were more common, and impaired infants began to appear in increased numbers, it might not seem unjust even to a liberal's conscience to create a class of "victimless crimes." In an example of Gerald Dworkin's, we are asked to suppose that when the barometer falls to *X*, any baby conceived under those meteorological conditions will be born with some serious impairment, much worse than cleft palates, club feet, or withered arms, but not so severe that his life will not be worth living. Imagine that nearly every bedroom has a barometer on the night stand, and that all radio and television stations broadcast warnings when the barometric pressure reaches the dangerous point. A criminal statute forbidding unprotected intercourse at such times would seem, at least at first sight, to create a victimless crime, since babies born with these handicaps, severe as they are, would not be wronged/harmed by their negligent or self-indulgent parents. And yet, in the example a certain amount of avoidable misery might be introduced into the world if we do not pass the statute. Surely, one might argue (on grounds that *resemble* the liberals'), the prevention of unnecessary suffering is a legitimate reason for a criminal prohibition. Still, on the other side, we can imagine a child born with the handicap in question who feels positively lucky that his parents negligently conceived *him* (of all people) against huge odds. He does not rejoice in his handicaps, but since he does not regret having been born, handicaps notwithstanding, he does not *feel* like a "victim," and he might resent the injustice of treating his parents as criminals.

We can strengthen the case for the legitimacy in principle of criminal legislation by imagining hypothetical examples of "wrongful conception" that are not merely negligent, but deliberate, malicious, and sadistic. In conducting this experiment in the imagination, it is important to notice that there is a great conceptual, though perhaps not as great a moral, difference between the case in which a woman takes a drug *after* she is pregnant, causing her fetus to be born later in a harmed condition, and the case in which she takes drugs first and then, after she is herself in a condition that would be perilous for a fetus, she has intercourse and becomes pregnant. If a woman takes thalidomide while already pregnant, knowing its well-publicized effects, then the child that is born months later is her victim. The counterfactual test for harming yields a clear and unequivocal judgment in his case. He is much worse off than he would have been had his mother not taken the dangerous drug. This case is on all fours with that of the negligent motorist who runs over a pregnant woman, causing her child, months later, to be born in an impaired condition. Since it is criminal liability we are considering, however, let us imagine that the mother's fault is much more serious than mere negligence. Suppose she deliberately damages her fetus in this way because she wants the experience later of mothering a child that will be more completely dependent on her, and for a longer period, than a normal child would or, even worse, because she wishes to glory sadistically in a child's frustrations and sufferings. Now we have a picture of a parent who is morally indistinguishable from a serious criminal. Criminal liability for her, given her culpability and her real on-balance victim, does not seem illegitimate.

But now change the example in only one small respect. Suppose the mother has already been taking some dangerous drug for a long time when she chooses to become pregnant. Suppose she is, as a consequence, in a bodily condition such that any fetus conceived while she is in that condition will develop in the manner typical of thalidomide fetuses. Knowing full well the dangers, she deliberately choses to become pregnant, precisely in order to have an overly dependent child whose sufferings she can enjoy. She is precisely as culpable morally as the woman in the other version of the story, but she does not harm her child since, had she behaved otherwise, her child would never have existed; and since the thalidomide-type impairments are preferable to nonexistence, the counterfactual test for harming is not satisfied, and there is no proper victim. The advocate of criminalization might argue that so trivial a diffference between the two cases as the order in which the pill-taking and the act of conception took place cannot support so momentous a moral difference as that between criminal liability and no criminal liability. If criminal prohibition would be legitimate in the one case, he might conclude, then it must equally be legitimate in the other, whether there is a victim or not.

Of course, there are powerful reasons against criminalizing the behavior in the highly artificial examples we have been driven to in this section.

Criminalization would not be necessary in the barometric pressure example because people can be presumed to have more than enough incentive to avoid producing impaired infants, quite without gratuitous threats from the state. And deliberate conception of foreseeably handicapped infants for selfish or sadistic reasons would be so rare and extraordinary that surely more economical means of dealing with it could be used than the cumbersome apparatus of the criminal justice system. But these rejoinders miss the point. The examples do not show that there are some imaginable circumstances in which criminal legislation would be justified as good public policy. Rather, these examples, contrived and unlikely though they be, are designed to show that there are conceivable circumstances in which criminalization even without a victim would be *legitimate in principle*, even if unjustifiable, for practical reasons, on balance.

It is beyond question that the severe handicaps of wrongfully conceived children (where the wrongful conceiving follows rather than precedes the event that causes the impairment) constitues a great evil. Moreover, that evil, unless so widespread as to be a public harm, is a "non-grievance evil," lacking deteminate victims who can complain that their rights have been violated. As non-grievance evils go, however, this one carries a great deal of moral weight, enough to command even the liberals' respect. The evil is not the basis of any one's legitimate personal grievance but it is not an evil that is unassociated with human interests and well-being. A criminal statute designed to prevent such evils would be a departure from strict liberal legitimizing standards, but it would not be contrary to the animating humane spirit of the liberal's harm principle. The liberal can be expected to combat harmful conditions of other human beings even when they are not harmed conditions. Such conditions may be non-grievance evils but their connection to human suffering puts them in a special category of non-grievance evils, having much greater moral weight, for example, than consensual taboo infractions, unnatural matings, beetle squashings, defamations of the ancient dead, evil thoughts, even nonconsequential species extinctions.[27] They have as much weight, in fact, as it is possible for a non-grievance evil to bring to the legislative scales, and for some liberals that might even be enough, *ceteris paribus*, to warrant criminal legislation. I do not think that such liberals can be charged with making an *ad hoc* exception (in the illicit sense) to liberalism. The case is an exception, but on the other hand, the circumstances truly are special and not likely to recur indiscriminately. For those who suffer con-

[27] This is a partial list of "free-floating evils" from my "Legal Moralism and Free-Floating Evils," *Pacific Philosophical Quarterly*, vol. 61 (1980), pp. 130–63. I have changed my usage, however. I prefer now to distinguish "grievance evils" from "non-grievance evils" as generic classes, and then distinguish two species of non-grievance evils, the welfare-connected ones (like impairment stemming from wrongful conception) and the free-floating ones (like those listed above in the text). In the earlier article, I used "non-grievance evil" and "free-floating evil" as synonyms, but that was a mistake.

genital defects, the evil of their condition does not "float free" of their interests, even though it has not set back those interests on balance nor violated their rights. I can concede, then, that non-grievance evils do have *some* weight, simply as evils, but no other non-grievance evil has as much weight as this one derived from avoidable, nonconsensual suffering. Liberalism must bend to permit an exception in this special kind of case. I think it can bend without breaking.

TORTS WITHOUT VICTIMS

Given our analysis of harming, the infant in the Parfit story has not been harmed by his parents in the sense of "harming" that involves a genuine grievance in the victim against the party whose conduct put him in a harmful condition. If, nevertheless, we wish to argue that tort actions in such cases, practical difficulties aside, would be legitimate in principle, we can attempt to do so in either of two ways. We can argue for an enlarged conception of "harming," "grievance," and "victim," such that the woman in Parfit's example did, after all, harm the child, who is after all her victim, and has, after all, a legitimate grievance against her. Or we can hold fast to our analysis of harming, which does neatly fit the normal cases of postnatal harming, and abandon the view that liability can be legitimately imposed only when the harm principle is satisfied. The second course seems the wiser to me. A person can be justly held answerable for the harmful condition of another, in some circumstances, even when that condition, strictly speaking, is not his doing.

If we take the first course, however, and insist that there is some relevant sense in which the infant in Parfit's example has been *harmed* by his mother, that could have the unfortunate consequence of legitimizing wrongful life suits for such harmful states as illegitimacy, ugliness, below average intelligence, and the like, all of which are "harmful conditions," but which, since all are rationally preferable to nonexistence, are not harms on balance. Therefore, if a writer were to advocate a special sense of "harming" just to permit wrongful life suits in cases like Parfit's to be legitimized by the harm principle, the proposal would founder on these other examples where the harms are relatively insignificant. Minor harms could be awarded relatively minor but appropriate compensation, and the courts would be flooded with plaintiffs airing fancied "grievances" against their parents for providing them with disadvantageous environments or poor genetic inheritances.[28]

[28] Cf. the opinion in Zepeda v. Zepeda, 41 Ill.App. 2d 240, 190 N.E. 2d 849 (1963): "What does disturb us is the . . . related suits that would be encouraged. Encouragement would extend to all others born into the world under conditions they might regard as adverse. One might seek damages for being born of a certain color, another because of race; one for being born with a hereditary disease, another for inheriting unfortunate family characteristics; one for being born into a large and destitute family, another because a parent has an unsavory reputation . . ."

It would be better in these exceptional cases that traditional tort rules requiring harming be suspended, as they have been elsewhere. Instead of requiring that the defendant violated the plaintiff's rights, we might require only that her conduct was indeed seriously wrongful, and instead of requiring that she harmed him, we could require that she was responsible for his coming into existence in a seriously harmful condition. There would be fault aplenty in these examples, and harm too, even though the fault does not give the plaintiff a personal grievance, and the harm is not the product of an act of harming. This would be a "victimless tort," that is, not a tort at all in the traditional sense, but perhaps justice would support it anyway, as it supports various kinds of strict and vicarious liability. It might not be fair to make a person pay damages to another whom she has not directly wronged, but it may be more unfair still to make the miserable impaired party pay, or do without the aid he needs. In that case, however, I would prefer changing our practices to changing our concepts, dropping the requirement that the defendant must have harmed the plaintiff to inventing a new sense of "harming" tailored to the case at hand.[29]

There would be no point, of course, in the child in Parfit's example suing his own mother, since her care and funding would probably be forthcoming anyway, and there would be no actual gain in support from a judicial award of damages (unless she were to put him up for adoption and wash her hands of him, but I put that possibility aside). Imagine, then, a twist on the Parfit story. Suppose that the woman's lover is none other than her gynecologist. In

[29] I have not had time to revise this essay to accommodate an important suggestion made by Wayne Sumner at the Ann Arbor conference at which this paper was read. Sumner, accepting an invitation I made to the audience to help me "better preserve my liberal purity," suggests a way in which I might avoid, at least in Parfit-type cases, the view that liability without a properly harmed victim is morally legitimate after all. All that stands in the way of saying that the Parfit child has been harmed, he points out, is my counterfactual test for harming. Sumner therefore proposes that we modify that test (as I did, e.g., in cases of overdetermination) by casting it in an *impersonal* form. In the Parfit case, Sumner writes, "the child is worse off than *the child the woman would (or might) otherwise have had* would have been, had she acted otherwise." This is an attractive suggestion to me because, in permitting me to be steadfast in support of the liberal doctrine of "no liability without a harmed and wronged victim," it contributes to the greater overall coherence of my political philosophy, and on Sumner's alternative account of harming, the Parfit baby *is* a "harmed and wronged victim." The disadvantage of Sumner's suggestion is that it seems to make a rather sharp departure from the concept of harming–wronging as it is normally and naturally employed. "How can I have wronged you when you admit that you are better off for what I did than you would otherwise be?" asks the Parfit mother. "Yes," Sumner would have her child reply, "but I am not better off than the child you would have had a month later if you had waited." This reply has the merit of establishing the child's grievance, if that's what we antecedently wish to do, but we might have some sympathy with the mother's further reponse if she questioned what relevance *that* counterfactual has to the question of whether she harmed (wronged) the child by bringing him into existence. Still, I think the Sumner suggestion deserves further serious exploration. As my argument now stands, I seem to prefer (relative) linguistic purity to the (relative) moral purity required by my initial liberal commitment.

this version of the story, he knows that if the woman gets pregnant now (instead of, say, next month), she will conceive a child with severe defects, though not so severe as to render his life not worth living. Instead of warning the woman, however, he conceals the information, seduces her, and recklessly runs the risk of pregnancy. Nine months later the severely impaired baby is born, much to his mother's distress. Somebody will have to pay the heavy costs of raising this handicapped child. Why not the person at fault, the wealthy gynecologist, even though his fault did not consist in a violation of the child's rights, and the child, therefore, was not his "victim"?

Some readers will want more than this. They will not be content with civil liability created by useful and just public policies for the more extreme Parfit-type cases. They will also insist that there *is* a victim in these cases whose right has been violated and who therefore has a genuine moral grievance against the wrongdoer. I am willing to go part of the way to meet this objection. The impaired person (plaintiff) is indeed in a special moral relation to the wrongdoer that makes a certain kind of negative attitude towards him appropriate and understandable. I think the best word for that attitude is "resentment." The specific type of righteous moral indignation that stems from an awareness that one has been personally wronged by another is not quite the same thing as generic resentment, since it is closely linked with perceived right-infraction, and resentment need not be. Neither must resentment imply imputation of guilt, charges or claims, or other such legalistic postures. "Having a grievance" is a vague phrase that might conceal the difference between resentment and the feeling that one has been personally wronged. To be sure, there is something personal in the disapproving sort of ill-will we call "resentment." We do not resent everything that we disapprove of. But it is sufficient for resentment that the attitudes or behavior we disapprove of be directed at a class we feel part of, or can identify with, or somehow feel associated with.

The plaintiff in the hypothetical stories we are considering may come in time to resent his biological parent, not for violating his right by an act that made him worse off on balance than he would otherwise be but, rather, for being the sort of scoundrel he or she is, a person who has manifested an indifference to the possibility of human suffering and is prepared to bring people into existence with harmful impairments for no morally respectable reason. The plaintiff recognizes that he is a member of a class of possible persons, those that might have come into being through the defendant's wrong act, toward whom the defendant's hateful unconcern was directed. Only in that way is there anything "personal" in his resentment. He is in a position similar to that of a black in the presence of an honorable bigot who never violates the rights of blacks, but shows by his behavior that he is the sort of person who always prefers the well-being of whites to blacks, other things being equal. He always roots for the white boxer, for example, when watching televised contests between a white and a black, and he gives generously to worthy white charities but nothing at all to worthy black ones. (It is possible to have that sort of bigoted character while also being a resolute Kantian determined never to violate anyone's rights.) The white person's attitude does not by itself give the black person a personal grievance in the absence of any right-infractions, but the black person's resentment, as a member of a group whose welfare is valued less than others', is well-grounded and understandable.

One final point. For that class of cases that are similar to Parfit's example in that the life wrongfully produced is worth living, but different in that the parties at fault are medical providers rather than biological parents, there is less obviously a need for radical departure from those traditional tort rules that require wrongful harming. If a physician negligently fails to diagnose a married woman's illness as Parfit's disease, so that without the warning that it was her right to receive from the physician she gets pregnant during the dangerous period and gives birth, to her surprise and distress, to a son with a withered arm, then she should have a cause of action against the physician for wrongful birth, even though her son, on traditional tort grounds, has no cause of action for wrongful life. In this kind of case the physician directly wrongs the parents and causes them to suffer the indirect harm of having a handicapped child. *They* would clearly have been better off had the physician not been negligent, for then they would have waited for the prescribed interval before conceiving a child – a different child to be sure – who would have been healthy. The parents in this example have been harmed in the full sense (adversely affected and wronged)[30] even though the child himself, the person who comes into existence in a directly impaired condition, has not been wronged or harmed by the physician, since the only alternative for him would be nonexistence which he does not, and rationally could not, prefer. Moreover, allowing the parents to recover damages in this case would give them the wherewithal to care for their child's special needs (if they are the child's legal guardians), and thus fulfil*some* of the functions of a wrongful life suit in the child's own name.

CONCLUSION

This paper has been concerned with both conceptual and policy questions. The chief problems of the former kind concern the application of the

[30] This is the judgment that would seem clear when made from a prospective vantage point at the time of the harming, even though *now*, years later in retrospect, it might be admitted that love of *this* particular child "offsets" the harm. I think it is the prospective judgment, however, which should control. After all, the parents, but for the negligence of others, could have had another child that they would have loved every bit as much as this one, but without the heartbreaking handicaps.

concept of harm employed in J. S. Mill's "harm principle" to cases of prenatal harming, and in particular to the most difficult of these, that in which the act said to cause an infant's impaired condition is the very same as that which brought him into existence. Because of the counterfactual condition that must be part of the analysis of harming, whether prenatal or postnatal, I concluded that an infant is harmed by a wrongful act responsible for his coming into existence only if that act causes him to be born in a condition so bad that he would have been "better off if he had never been born at all." The paradox implied in this wording is eliminated, I claimed, if we analyze it in terms of rational preferability, a notion that is not without its own difficulties, but which, I claimed, is coherent and actually applicable to the preference for nonexistence over some extremely severe impairments. More typically, however, infants are born with impairments that are *not* such that nonexistence would be rationally preferable to them. These unfortunate children suffer the continuing residual harms caused by the acts that produced their existence, but even when those acts were negligent or more seriously wrongful, the child cannot claim that he was wronged or harmed on balance by them, so long as he admits that he prefers his present impaired existence to the nonexistence that was its only alternative for him. I think that he has no grievance against those responsible for his existence, since they did not violate his rights, but that his resentment of them, in some circumstances, would be understandable and justified.

The policy questions in this essay are largely derivative from the conceptual ones. How can we apply the liberal doctrine ("liberal" at least when applied to *criminal* law) that it is morally illegitimate to impose liability without a wronged/harmed victim to cases of wrongful life and their (largely hypothetical) analogues in criminal law? When the impairment of the infant is so severe that his life is not rationally preferable to nonexistence (or as we say, is "not worth living"), and it was produced by another party's negligence or deliberate wrongful conduct, then criminal liability would be legitimate in principle, since the harm principle would be satisfied, but I could illustrate such cases only with science fiction examples which are at present no threat. Wrongful life tort suits, where the life is worse than no life at all, are conceptually coherent, and legitimate in principle, but in most of the familiar senses of "compensation," there can be no compensation for a life that is so terrible that nonexistence would be preferable to it. Tort suits can only achieve a transfer of the costs of maintaining such a life to a more appropriate party.

When the infant's impairment is serious but not so bad that nonexistence would have been preferable to it, the liberal's policy problems are even more difficult. Here the liberal may have to concede grudgingly that criminal prohibitions of some wrongful acts are legitimate in principle (though rarely justified in fact) even though they do not have victims, that is, persons who are wronged and harmed on balance by them. These prohibitions would be legitimate only when an interest-connected nongrievance evil is extreme. This result appears to be a departure from the strict letter of the liberal's doctrine, but I have claimed that it accords with the animating humane spirit of that doctrine. Similarly, I concluded, wrongful life suits against a biological parent could conceivably be legitimate, even for harms that are not worse than nonexistence. That is partly because in the civil, as opposed to the criminal law, a party may be justly answerable for another's harmful condition, even though that condition is not, strictly speaking, his doing.

Philosophy, University of Arizona

CONTRACT REMEDIES AND INALIENABLE RIGHTS*

By Randy E. Barnett

I. INTRODUCTION

Two kinds of remedies have traditionally been employed for breach of contract: legal relief and equitable relief.[1] Legal relief normally takes the form of money damages.[2] Equitable relief normally consists either of specific performance or an injunction – that is, the party in breach may be ordered to perform an act or to refrain from performing an act.[3] In this article I will use a "consent theory of contract" to assess the choice between money damages and specific performance. According to such a theory, contractual

* I wish to thank the following people for their most helpful comments on an earlier draft: Larry Alexander, Stuart Deutsch, Richard Epstein, David Gerber, R. H. Helmholz, Marty Malin, Emilio Pacheco, Ellen Frankel Paul, and Christopher Wonnell. Financial support for this research was provided by the Marshall D. Ewell Research Fund of I.I.T. Chicago-Kent College of Law.

[1] Legal relief was relief available in "courts of law." Equitable relief was extraordinary relief originally available from the King, then from the King's Chancellor, and finally from the Chancery courts or "courts of equity." See Dan B. Dobbs, *Handbook on the Law of Remedies* (St. Paul, MN: West Pub. Co., 1973), pp. 24–34 (describing the historical development of courts of equity and the distinction between legal and equitable relief); E. Allan Farnsworth, *Contracts* (Boston: Little, Brown & Co., 1982), pp. 818–824 (same). These were not, however, the only court systems that coexisted in England. See Harold Berman, *Law and Revolution* (Cambridge, MA: Harvard U. Press, 1984), p. 10 (stressing the importance of competing courts to the Western legal tradition).

[2] The historical picture is not quite this clear-cut. For one thing, medieval English common law courts may not have had as strong a preference for money damages as is commonly assumed. See Frederick Pollock and Frederic Maitland, *The History of English Law, Vol. II* (London: Cambridge Univ. Press, 2d ed., 1898), p. 595 ("[E]ven when the source of the action is in our eyes a contractual obligation, the law tries its best to give specific relief.") For another, during most of the medieval period, the effective remedy for breach of most contracts in the common law court was enforcement of a penal bond. See generally, A. W. B. Simpson, *A History of the Common Law of Contract* (Oxford: Oxford Univ. Press, 1975), pp. 88–125. Thus, every sort of obligation could be reduced to a monetary one or a "debt" by the party in breach. Beginning in 1283, a debtor's liability to pay could be enforced by imprisonment; see Simpson, p. 87.

[3] A variety of different contractual remedies have traditionally been available – for example, replevin, reformation, recission, cancellation, or specific restitution. See D. Dobbs, *Handbook*, pp. 1–3; E. Farnsworth, *Contracts*, pp. 815–816. Damages, specific performance, and injunctions, however, are the types of remedies most commonly used to *enforce* a contract. In contrast, recission and cancellation are used to *avoid* enforcement of a contract and reformation is used to *change* the terms of a contract.

obligation is dependent on more fundamental entitlements of the parties and arises as a result of the parties' consent to transfer alienable rights.[4]

My thesis will be that the normal rule favoring money damages should be replaced with one that presumptively favors specific performance unless the parties have consented to money damages instead. The principal obstacle to such an approach is the reluctance of courts to specifically enforce contracts for personal services. The philosophical distinction between alienable and inalienable rights bolsters this historical reticence, since a right to personal services may be seen as inalienable.

I will then explain why, if the subject matter of a contract for personal services is properly confined to an alienable right to money damages for failure to perform, specific enforcement of such contracts is no longer problematic. Finally, I shall consider whether the subject matter of contracts for corporate services is properly confined to money damages like contracts for personal services, or whether performance of corporate services can be made the subject of a valid rights transfer and judicially compelled in the same manner as contracts for external resources.

II. REMEDIES FOR BREACH OF CONTRACT

1. The Present Law Governing the Choice of Contract Remedies. The present rule governing legal and equitable remedies can be simply stated: Legal relief – money damages – is available as a matter of right. Equitable relief – specific performance or injunction – is available at the discretion of the court upon a showing by the party seeking enforcement that legal relief is somehow "inadequate." Put another way, money damages are the presumptive form of remedy for breach of contract. Specific performance orders and injunctions are exceptional forms of contract remedies. While the rules governing the choice of remedies can be complex,[5] the following summary should suffice for purposes of this discussion.

Money damages are said to be inadequate when they fail to fully compensate the victim of the breach, as, for example, when the item contracted for is "unique" and therefore unavailable from another source, or when the amount of monetary damages is difficult to prove. Traditionally, land is presumed to be unique and specific performance has therefore come to be the presumptive form of relief in such cases. For contracts involving other

[4] See Randy E. Barnett, "A Consent Theory of Contract," *Columbia Law Review*, vol. 86 (1986), pp. 269–321.

[5] Two excellent articles describe in some detail and critically assess the present law governing this subject. See Anthony Kronman, "Specific Performance," *University of Chicago Law Review*, vol. 45 (1978), pp. 351–382; Alan Schwartz, "The Case for Specific Performance," *Yale Law Journal*, vol. 89 (1979), pp. 271–306.

types, of property, the burden traditionally has fallen on the victim of the breach to prove uniqueness of unavailability. Finally – these rules and presumptions notwithstanding – specific performance has traditionally been unavailable to enforce contracts for the provision of personal services, even if these services can be shown to be unique and damages therefore are in fact inadequate.

Courts have given two reasons for their reluctance to award specific performance. First, they have sought to avoid the task of administering specific performance decrees.[6] It is sometimes difficult for a court to monitor the quality of performance or to assess claims that performance is not being appropriately provided.[7] Second, specific performance decrees for breaches of personal services contracts have been thought to pose moral problems as well, "because they are perceived to be substantively unacceptable limitations on personal freedom."[8] Forcing someone to perform a contract strikes courts as involuntary servitude and is said by judges to be against "public policy."[9]

Finally, a fundamental premise of contract damages has traditionally been that, while victims of a breach should be fully compensated for the injury caused by the breach, they should not be *over*compensated – that is, they should not be placed in a better position than they would have been in had the contract been performed. If most victims would be completely and more efficiently compensated by money damages, and if specific performance was generally perceived by contract breakers as a more onerous sanction, then there is a risk that a general presumption favoring specific performance

[6] But see Schwartz, "The Case for Specific Performance," pp. 292–296 (disputing the claim that specific performance decrees generally and unavoidably create administrative problems).

[7] Partly for this reason courts have been somewhat receptive to imposing injunctions on parties in breach. "Instead of ordering that the act be done, as a court would in granting specific performance, the court orders forbearance from inconsistent action." E. Farnsworth, *Contracts*, p. 824. For example, a person who promised to work for another might be barred from obtaining alternative employment elsewhere. In the analysis that follows, I shall not separately consider such orders. If a contract itself specifies that the party in breach should refrain from performing a given act — as it did in the famous injunction case of *Lumley v. Wagner*, 1 DeG. M. & G. 604, 42 Eng. Rep. 687 (Ch. 1852) — then an injunction is a form of specific performance. If there is no such term (either expressed or implied-in-fact) in the agreement then there is no consensual basis for such relief.

[8] Kronman, "Specific Performance," p. 372. See also Schwartz, "The Case for Specific Performance," pp. 296–298 (discussing specific performance and liberty).

[9] See E. Farnsworth, *Contracts*, p. 838 (specific performance "may be refused on the ground that, though the act or forbearance that would be compelled is not against public policy, the use of compulsion to require that act or forbearance is against public policy.") A "public policy" rationale usually obscures rather than illuminates the true reasons for a judicial decision. While the involuntary nature of court-ordered labor or "servitude" is obvious, it is less clear exactly why such an order is unjustified when the commitment being enforced was originally consensual. In Part III, the philosophical distinction between alienable and inalienable rights will be employed to provide support for this longstanding judicial sentiment.

would give many if not most victims the ability to extort a premium in return for accepting money damages.[10]

2. Problems With the Present Approach. Given that no system of proof is perfect, the allocation of the burden of proof has an important effect on allocating the costs of error.[11] The current approach to contract remedies places two burdens on victims of breach. First, to receive money damages, victims must prove with a fair degree of certainty that an injury has in fact been sustained and that the injury has a determinate value. But it may sometimes be difficult to prove what injuries have been sustained or to place an accurate monetary value on those injuries which can be proved. Therefore, a fully compensatory judgment may be hard to obtain.[12] In contrast, by giving the victim what he bargained for, specific performance may in many cases better assure that the victim is fully compensated.

Second, to get specific performance, victims must somehow prove that money damages are inadequate. When money damages are in fact inadequate, but inadequacy cannot be proved or the court errs in assessing the evidence, the victim of breach suffers under the current approach. Suppose instead that the burden was reversed and the party in breach had to show why damages were adequate. With such a rule, the party in breach would suffer when damages are in fact adequate, but proof of adequacy cannot be made out or the court errs in assessing the evidence.

The burden of proving the existence of a contract and the fact of breach is properly placed on the victim of a breach. But when the victim has met these twin burdens and it comes time to choose among remedies, justice would seem to require that – as between the party who has been proved to have breached a contract and the innocent victim of the breath – the former should bear the greater risk of adjudicative error.

Moreover, a requirement that all victims of breach (except breaches

[10] See Schwarz, "The Case for Specific Performance," pp. 284–291 (explaining the alleged problem with such *ex post* negotiations and questioning its significance).

[11] The phrase "costs of error" refers to "enforcing contracts that should not be enforced and . . . not enforcing contracts that should be enforced." Richard A. Epstein, "Unconscionability: A Critical Reappraisal," *Journal of Law and Economics*, vol. 18 (1975), p. 300. Such errors of judgment are an inevitable product of using general rules of conduct, burdens of proof, and fallible factfinding. For example, by requiring more evidence that a contract existed before granting relief, fewer "false" contracts will be erroneously enforced. At the same time, however, more "true" contracts will erroneously go unenforced. Conversely, by making the burden of proof less stringent, fewer "true" contracts will erroneously go unenforced and more "false" contracts will erroneously be enforced. See generally, George Sher, "Right Violations and Injustices: Can We Always Avoid Trade-offs?" *Ethics*, vol. 94 (1984), pp. 212–224.

[12] See Schwartz, "The Case for Specific Performance," p. 276: "[I]n many cases damages actually are undercompensatory."

involving land) show that money damages are inadequate may conflict with the reasonable expectations of many, if not most parties to contracts. Persons with common sense – that is, those who have not taken a first-year contracts class (or been counseled by a lawyer who has) – would naturally assume, for example, that when a good is purchased the purchaser obtains a right to the good. They would not assume that the seller has an *option* to deliver or pay damages – if damages can be proved – unless the victim can prove that the good is unique.

When such persons enter a contract, the terms of their bargain are unlikely to reflect the increased risk of enforcement error that, unbeknownst to them, contract law imposes on them. This becomes a problem when one party *is* knowledgeable about contract law and obtains the commitment of the ignorant party at a lower price than would be obtained if the rules of contract remedies better comported with common sense. While some disparity of information between parties is inevitable and irremediable, information disparities concerning the law of contract itself should be minimized.

Finally, placing the burden of showing inadequacy of damages on the victim of a breach means that those victims who need specific performance must pay a higher price to obtain justice than those victims requiring only money damages – a burden that is magnified in a legal system that does not compensate successful parties for their legal expenses. One reason for such discrimination might be higher costs associated with enforcing a specific performance decree. But enforcement costs will not necessarily be higher for some categories of contracts – for example, contracts calling for the delivery of identifiable goods.[13]

Why not, then, simply reverse the presumption? Why not make specific performance the presumptively favored form of relief as some have proposed?[14] Notwithstanding the problems of administration and overcompensation discussed above, giving all victims of breach a presumptive right to specific performance might, on balance, be preferable to the present rule. Given the often serious problems of assessing the true extent of injuries arising from contract breaches and the other inefficiencies of obtaining contractual enforcement through the legal system, victims of breach would be better protected by a rule making specific performance more generally available.[15] And by having chosen to break their contracts, parties in breach

[13] See *ibid.*, p. 294. (When efficiency gains of specific performance are included in an analysis of its costs, "it is impossible to say whether these gains would exceed the increase in administrative and judicial opportunity costs that the availability of specific performance would engender.")

[14] See, e.g., *ibid.*

[15] *ibid.*, p. 291. "[E]xpanding the availability of specific performance would produce certain efficiency gains: it would minimize the inefficiencies of undercompensation, reduce the need for liquidated damage clauses, minimize strategic behavior, and save the costs of litigating complex damage issues."

can be said to have brought upon themselves whatever difficulties a reversal of the presumptive remedy would create.

There is one important obstacle to such a reversal. Such a rule would seem to at least presumptively require the specific enforcement of personal service contracts. Even if an "exception" of the sort that currently exists were created to exempt such contracts from specific enforcement, many judges are understandably reluctant to respect *ad hoc* and vague "public policy" limits on their power to grant relief to apparently deserving victims. As a result, when personal services are unique (as they often are) and money damages are therefore truly inadequate, courts are always sorely tempted to compel performance.[16]

We might, however, resolve this obstacle to specific performance if we better understood why specific performance is appropriate in contracts involving the sale of goods and inappropriate in contracts involving personal services. In the balance of this paper, I hope to show how a "consent theory of contract," which looks to an underlying theory of entitlements to explain contractual obligation, assists such an understanding.

III. A CONSENT THEORY OF CONTRACT

A property rights conception of entitlements suggests that rights are best construed as enforceable claims to acquire, use, and transfer resources in the world – claims to control one's person and external resources.[17] A consent theory of contract specifies that an enforceable contract requires the satisfaction of at least two conditions. First, the *subject* of a contract must be a morally cognizable right possessed by the transferor that is interpersonally transferable, or "alienable."[18] Second, the holder of the right must *consent* to its transfer.[19] Thus, commitments will generally be enforced only if they manifest to the promisee the promisor's assent to transfer rights.[20]

[16] See, e.g., De Rivafinoli v. Corsetti, 4 Paige Ch. (N.Y.) 264, 270 (1833) (". . . a bird that can sing and will not sing must be made to sing.")

[17] See Randy E. Barnett, "Pursuing Justice in a Free Society: Power v. Liberty," *Criminal Justice Ethics*, vol. 4 (Summer/Fall, 1985), pp. 50–72 (discussing the possible basis and scope of a property rights conception of entitlements); and "Contract Scholarship and the Reemergence of Legal Philosophy" (book review), *Harvard Law Review*, vol. 97 (1984), pp. 1223–1245 (attempting to place recent interest in entitlement theories in a historical context).

[18] In contrast, the *object* of a contract is the purpose of the contract, what the parties hope to accomplish by entering into a contract.

[19] A more extended discussion of this conception of contractual obligation can be found in Barnett, "A Consent Theory of Contract."

[20] Two other ways of expressing this concept of contractual obligation are "a manifestation of an intention to be legally bound" or "a manifestation of an intention to create legal relations." Such expressions, while useful, do not stress the entitlements-dependent nature of contractual relations. Note also that there are certain instances where a consent theory would favor subjective assent over a manifestation of assent. See Barnett, "A Consent Theory," pp. 307–309.

The fact that there must be a consent to transfer *rights* suggests that the issue of contractual enforceability could potentially turn on one of two inquiries into the subject matter of the contract. First, are the rights that are allegedly being transferred to the promisee in fact held by the promisor?[21] For example, a contract to transfer rights to goods that are owned by someone else would not ordinarily be enforceable because the transferor does not possess the rights she purports to transfer.[22]

Second, unless we conclude that every right is potentially transferable, it would also be appropriate to determine whether the rights that are the subject of a purported transfer agreement are the *kinds* of rights that *can* be transferred. In other words, in determining the enforceability of an agreement, the presence of consent to transfer rights, while a necessary element of a contract, is not a sufficient ground to enforce a commitment. In certain cases, it may also be important to discern whether the rights-transfer being consented to involves *alienable* or *inalienable* rights.[23] For if the right to personal services, for example, is inalienable, then such a right cannot be made the subject of a valid, enforceable rights transfer.

IV. INALIENABLE RIGHTS

1. Defining Inalienable Rights. The distinction between alienable and inalienable rights has been widely discussed in recent years.[24] To characterize a right as inalienable is to claim that the consent of the right-holder is insufficient to extinguish the right or to transfer it to another.

> That which is inalienable . . . is not transferable to the ownership of another. So an inalienable right is one that may never be waived

[21] While I use the standard terms "promisor" and "promisee" in the text, a consent theory is inapposite to a promise theory of contract. Compare the alternative definitions of consent, *supra* note 17, which speak of "*legally* bound" and "*legal* relations" with the definition of a promise found in the *Restatement (Second) of Contracts* (St. Paul, MN: American Law Institute Pub., 1981), §2(1): "A promise is a manifestation of intention to act or refrain from acting in a specified way, so made as to justify a promisee in understanding that a commitment has been made." And the authors of the *Restatement* deny that a manifested commitment to be *legally* bound is essential to a contract. See *Restatement*, §21: "Neither the real nor apparent intention that a promise be legally binding is essential to the formation of a contract. . . ." Thus, a consent theory is distinct from most discussions of contract that emphasize the moral duty to keep one's promises; see Barnett, "A Consent Theory," pp. 304–305.

[22] Once a contract has been performed, the legal system has come to favor those who purchased goods in "good faith" over the original title holder. This issue is somewhat distinct from whether the purchaser can *enforce* such an agreement when the promisor fails to perform and, as such, is beyond the scope of this essay.

[23] A purely promise-based theory would have difficulty explaining the source of such a distinction.

[24] Much of the recent legal literature was stimulated by Guido Calabresi and A. Douglas Melamed's seminal article, "Property Rules, Liability Rules, and Inalienability: One View of the Cathedral," *Harvard Law Review*, vol. 85 (1972), pp. 1089–1128.

> or transferred by its possessor. . . . Thus what is proscribed by inalienable rights are certain *relationships* or *agreements*.[25]

Such a claim must be distinguished from a claim that a right is forfeitable. "A person who has forfeited a right has lost the right because of some offence or wrongdoing."[26] It has been noted that one who wishes to extinguish or convey an inalienable right may do so by committing the appropriate wrongful act and thereby forfeiting it.[27] But notwithstanding the "consensual" nature of such an action, it is the wrongfulness of the right-holder's act and not the consent that justifies the conclusion that an inalienable right has been foreited.

> When a person has forfeited a right, others are permitted to treat him in a way that would otherwise be inappropriate *simply because* of his *wrong actions*. But when a right has been waived, others are permitted to behave in an otherwise unacceptable manner *simply because* of the *consent* of the original possessor.[28]

2. Four Reasons for Inalienability. There are several reasons why consent might be insufficient to extinguish or transfer certain rights. First, the nature of individual rights might rule out the alienation of certain of these rights. It is usually maintained than an important part of what having a right entails is that others have a duty to refrain from violating that right. But if a person must respect the rights of others, then that person may not be able to alienate the rights he possesses that provide the *means* by which he is able to respect the rights of others.

To illustrate this, suppose *A* consents to an arrangement under which he will always unquestioningly follow the commands of *B*. If such a consensual arrangement were legally and morally binding, then *A* would violate *B*'s rights by refusing to do what *B* commands; *A* would be wrong to so refuse. Suppose, now, that *B* orders *A* to violate the rights of *C*. If such a commitment was considered to be a binding transfer of rights, two important moral consequences result.

First, *A* no longer has the right to act on his own assessment of the rightfulness of a given command. In other words, *A* no longer has the moral means to respect the rights of *C*.[29] If the transfer from *A* to *B* is valid, then *A*

[25] Terrance McConnell, "The Nature and Basis of Inalienable Rights," *Law and Philosophy*, vol. 3 (1984), p. 43 (emphasis in original).

[26] *ibid*., p. 28. See also Joel Feinberg, *Rights, Justice and the Bounds of Liberty* (Princeton, NJ: Princeton Univ. Press, 1980), pp. 240–242; and Diane T. Meyers, *Inalienable Rights: A Defense* (New York: Columbia Univ. Press, 1985), pp. 13–15.

[27] See Meyers, *Inalienable Rights*, p. 14.

[28] McConnell, "The Nature and Basis," p. 28 (emphasis in original).

[29] See Arthur Kuflik, "The Inalienability of Autonomy," *Philosophy and Public Affairs*, vol. 13 (1984), p. 286 (if the original agreement "is valid, then the autonomy-abdicating agent has no right to object, let alone to refuse.")

cannot be liable for the violation of *C*'s rights. If liability exists, it must be limited to *B*.[30] Second, there is now a conflict of rights. *A* would be acting wrongfully if he respected *C*'s rights (thereby violating *B*'s rights) and would also be acting wrongfully if he failed to respect *C*'s rights.

The validity of the first consequence is undermined by the moral principle that "ought implies can." If a person has a duty to respect the rights of another, then a person also has a right to do so. As long as the duty exists, the right must also exist, so the right to so act may not be transferred to another by consent. There would appear to be something morally defective about a theory that failed to hold a competent person responsible for his actions simply because that person had consented to shift responsibility to another.[31]

The validity of the second consequence is undermined by the "compossibility" requirement of a coherent theory of rights. That is, for logical and functional reasons, a system of rights may not recognize two conflicting rights as valid.[32] One of the alleged rights here cannot be valid, and the conflict may be resolved in one of two ways. First, we could conclude that because the original arrangement is binding, either *C* really had no enforceable right against *A* in the first place, or *C* lost his right upon the making of the contract between *A* and *B*. Second, we could conclude that the original agreement between *A* and *B* cannot be binding – that is, some of *A*'s rights are inalienable – because such a rights transfer would conflict with the valid rights of *C*.

Any rights theory that supported the rights claim of *C* (as most theories would) would have to deny the validity of the contract between *A* and *B*. Any rights theory that resolves the conflict in this way must also conclude that persons cannot alienate the right to control all of their future actions.[33] No

[30] I thank George Smith for first suggesting to me this analysis and example.

[31] Cf. Jean-Jacques Rousseau, *The Social Contract and Discourses*, trans. G. D. H. Cole (New York: J. M. Dent & Sons Ltd., 1973), p. 170:

> To renounce liberty is to renounce being a man, to surrender the rights of humanity and even its duties. . . . Such a renunciation is incompatible with man's nature; to remove all liberty from his will is to remove all morality from his acts.

[32] See Robert Nozick, *Anarchy, State and Utopia* (New York: Basic Books, 1974), p. 199 ("Individual rights are co-possible; each person may exercise his rights as he chooses."); Hillel Steiner, "The Structure of a Set of Compossible Rights," *Journal of Philosophy*, vol. 74 (1977), pp. 767–775 (arguing that compossibility is a logical requirement of a system of rights); Barnett, "Pursuing Justice," p. 58 (adding functional concerns to Steiner's logical analysis).

[33] It might be argued that the analysis in the text does not describe inalienable rights — that is, rights a person has that cannot be transferred to another by consent — but, instead, describes actions that *A* may not perform because neither *A* nor his master *B* has the right to so act in the first place. In other words, *A* need not violate *C*'s rights because neither *A* nor *B* have the right to violate the rights of another. This is true, but to recast the example in this way is to omit the issue unavoidably raised by the hypothetical agreement: Is *A*'s right to control his own person and respect *C*'s rights — a right that *A* indisputably starts with — a right that can be transferred? The analysis in the text suggests that the answer to this question is no. Notwithstanding any agreement he may have made to *B*, *A* is still under a duty to respect *C*'s rights. *A* cannot, therefore, alienate such complete control of his future actions to anyone.

matter what *A* and *B* have agreed to, *A* must retain the right to respect the rights of *C*.

The first reason for inalienability shows that the claimed distinction between alienable and inalienable rights is a plausible one. However, any agreement to obey the *lawful* (or rights-respecting) orders of another would survive the analysis thus far presented. Another reason why some rights might be inalienable would be the literal impossibility of the commitments that certain rights transfers entail. This second reason for inalienability would have far more sweeping consequences than the first.

If rights are enforceable claims to control resources in the world and contracts are enforceable transfers of these rights, it is reasonable to conclude that a right to control a resource cannot be transferred where the control of the resource itself cannot in fact be transferred. Suppose that *A* consented to transfer partial or complete control of his body to *B*. Absent some physiological change in *A* (caused, perhaps, by voluntarily and knowingly ingesting some special drug or undergoing psychosurgery[34]) there is no way for such a commitment to be carried out.

True, *A* could conform his conduct to the orders of *B*, but he would still possess control over his actions and would have to willfully act so as to conform to *B*'s order. Because *A* could not in fact transfer the control of his body to *B*, *B* would in fact be forced to rely on *A*'s actual control of his body to carry out *B*'s orders, notwithstanding *A*'s agreement.[35] *B*'s "control" of *A*'s body would, then, be metaphorical rather than actual. The argument here is not that force is "ineffective" in getting slaves or servants to obey the orders of their masters but, rather, that force would be unnecessary if the actual control of servants' bodies could be transferred to the masters.[36]

[34] Arthur Kuflik offers these examples to undercut this type of argument for inalienability; "The Inalienability of Autonomy," p. 281 ("This suggests that the impropriety of an autonomy-abdicating agreement has more to do with the impropriety of autonomy-abdication itself than with some general fact that we have no right to make commitments we know we will be unable to keep."). But arguments based on impropriety and one based on the impossibility of such agreements are not mutually exclusive. Kuflik's examples only show that this reason for inalienability is *limited* to those commitments to alienate the future control over one's person which are not made possible by mind-altering drugs, brainwashing techniques, or psychosurgery.

[35] Similarly, a promise to undergo a dependency-inducing procedure would be an unenforceable attempt to transfer an inalienable right: the right to control whether or not to submit to the operation. But third parties might have no right to forcibly interfere with someone who voluntarily undergoes such a procedure. (The claim, for example, that members of religious "cults" may rightfully be kidnapped and "deprogramed" is properly controversial.) A person who voluntarily submitted to such a procedure (assuming that such a procedure actually worked) might be committing a nonfatal kind of "suicide" (zombicide?) and the "master" or guardian *would* then become legally responsible for his ward.

[36] It may be revealing that the law governing employment relations used to be called the law of "master-servant."

This distinction between alienable and inalienable, transferable and non-transferable rights corresponds to the distinction recognized in civil law countries between contracts "to give" and contracts "to do."[37] The former transfer a right to control external resources. The latter call for some future act involving the use of one's person. Surely, the former kind of transfer is possible. What is *my* house or car could equally well be *your* house and car. But bodies are different from other kinds of things. What is *my* body cannot in any literal sense be made *your* body. Because there is no obstacle to transferring control of a house or car (of the sort that is unavoidably presented when one attempts to transfer control over one's body), there is no obstacle to transferring the right to control a house or car.[38] But if control cannot be transferred, then it is hard to see how a right to control can be transferred.[39]

Suppose, now, that the agreement between A and B were recast to read that A transfers to B "the right to use force against A to compel A to conform his conduct to B's commands." It would appear that since force *can* be used by another, the right to use force can be transferred to another and this agreement is not barred by reason of impossibility (though it might be subject to other difficulties). Upon closer inspection, however, such an

[37] See Barry Nicholas, *French Law of Contract* (London: Butterworth & Co., 1982), p. 149 (the French Code "adopts the traditional classification into (a) *donner*, (b) *faire ou ne pas faire*. It is important to note that *donner* in the technical legal sense means neither to make a gift nor to deliver (*livrer*), but to convey, to pass ownership or some other real right."); Guenter H. Treitel, "Remedies for Breach of Contract," Arthur von Mehren, ed., *International Encyclopedia of Comparative Law* (Paris: J. C. B. Mohr, 1976), vol. 7, p. 13 (in French law, the "obligation to do or not to do is contrasted . . . with the *obligation de donner* or to transfer property").

[38] Transferring ownership in animals may be seen as presenting a special difficulty. Cannot animals refuse the orders of the new master? But the problem of control here is less than meets the eye. The second owner gets no more control and hence no more rights than those held by the original owner. Suppose the promisor attempted to transfer the right to a horse that would cuddle up with you in bed. Unless the first owner actually possessed such a horse, the *right to this kind* of horse could not pass. While the failure to tender this kind of horse would not alone constitute a breach of contract, the possibility of an action for fraud or breach of warranty remains. In contrast, the issue of inalienable human rights concerns the rights an individual *retains* despite the fact that consent to transfer these rights may have been expressed. Therefore, the truly analogous problem with animals is whether or not sentient animals themselves have rights — inalienable or otherwise — in the first place, an issue that is well beyond the scope of this essay.

[39] It will not do to argue that such a right to control is transferable because a putative master can obtain legal enforcement of the agreement. Such a claim would be a *non sequitur* in an entitlement theory. According to entitlements theories, we do not have rights because our claims are in fact enforced — the view of legal positivism — but, rather, our claims ought to be enforced only because we can demonstrate that we have rights. Nor would a claim for *damages* for breach of a contract to perform services in the future necessarily entail that a right to the services themselves had been alienated. Rather, as will be discussed below, such a claim could be as well accounted for by saying that it is the right *to the money* — an indisputably alienable right — that had been transferred (conditioned on the nonperformance of the services).

agreement does not escape the problem of attempting to transfer a right of control which cannot in fact be transferred.

If *B* has the right to use force against *A*, then *A* may not rightfully resist. But *B* has the right to use force against *A* only if such force can be justified. Such force may be justified if *A* consented or appeared to consent (and did not change his mind) – for example, if *A* and *B* were prize fighters or stunt men, or if *A* was a masochist. The crucial question, however, is not whether *A*'s consent to the use of force by *B* justifies *B*'s actions, but whether *A*'s prior consent can limit his right to withhold consent in the future.

Suppose that, after promising to perform services and granting to *B* the "right" to use force to compel performance, *A* thinks better of it and revokes his consent. When *B* (or a court) attempts to enforce *B*'s command, may *A* rightfully resist? The agreement that *B* may rightfully use force against *A* entails that *A* no longer has a right to resist *B* because this right has somehow been transferred to *B* (or lost).[40] Yet *A*'s agreement notwithstanding, *A* retains his ability to resist *B*. Just as *A* cannot alienate his right to the future control of his person because his ability to control his person cannot literally be transferred, *A* cannot have transferred or lost his right to resist when he retains his ability to resist.[41] Therefore, if *A* may rightfully resist *B*, then *B* may not have the right to use force against *A*, since such a right would also impose on *A* a contradictory duty to refrain from resisting.

The implications of this analysis may appear far-reaching.[42] The legitimacy of *all* commitments to perform personal services in the future has been undercut. When a promisor who has promised to perform services in the future refuses to perform, because no right to performance has been transferred to the promisee by the promise, no right of the promisee is violated by nonperformance. But, as will be considered below, the actual consequence

[40] If *A* retains his right to resist *B*, then *A* will be acting both rightfully and wrongfully should he resist *B*. Such a conflict of rights is barred by the compossibility feature of an entitlements theory. See *supra* note 32 and accompanying text.

[41] True, as above, *A* can voluntarily submit to procedures which would eliminate his ability to resist (although it is very hard to imagine the value to a master of a slave who had lost the power to physically resist violence). The harder question would then be, in the unlikely event that *A*'s ability to resist had been alienated, can others rightfully go to *A*'s defense? This issue would perhaps be best governed by principles of guardianship. See Kuflik, "The Inalienability of Autonomy," p. 275 ("[T]o say that autonomy cannot be alienated is not to deny that one human being can be legitimately subject to the guardianship of another."); Barnett, "Pursuing Justice," p. 69, note 17 (briefly discussing the concept of guardianship in a Liberty Approach).

[42] But the analysis just presented is not as far-reaching as some might at first imagine. It neither stems from nor supports a view that the only rights we have are those which we are able to assert — that "might makes right." The analysis of inalienability in the text claims only to describe a feature of those rights which we (arguably) have: some of these rights may be alienated or transferred, others of them may not. What rights we have and how we come to have them is another story requiring additional analysis. See Barnett, "Pursuing Justice." I thank Emilio Pacheco for bringing this issue to my attention.

of such an analysis is only to limit relief for nonperformance of personal service commitments to money damages.

Suppose, now, that A attempts to transfer a right to control *parts* of his body to B – such as his blood or heart. Since a transfer of actual control of these body parts is possible, the transfer of a right to control is also possible. Accordingly, agreements to transfer body parts may not be barred by the second reason for inalienability. Some such agreements, however, may be barred by a third reason for inalienable rights.

Rights may not only arise from duties one has to respect the rights of others; they may also arise from duties owed to oneself. Suppose that it could be shown that one has a moral duty to live a good life or to pursue happiness. Such a duty may imply that it would be wrong for others to interfere with such actions, which would mean that we would have rights to be free from such interference.[43] Would not such a claim also imply that some of these rights may not be transferred to another by consent? For example, the rights we have to acquire and then use resources in the world are essential to carrying out such duties to oneself and for this reason would be inalienable. Therefore, an agreement to transfer rights to all present and future acquired external possessions would be an unenforceable attempt to transfer an inalienable right.[44]

Further, a person's consensual commitment to always obey all the commands of another (or all those commands which are lawful) might be unenforceable because it is never the case that such a commitment is conducive to the pursuit of a good life. This would be true if the good life is a "do-it-youself job";[45] i.e., even if one is doing "all the right things," one's life is truly impoverished if one is not freely choosing to do the right things. If this is true, one may never alienate the right to make all choices about one's actions – that is, slavery – because doing so will always be an inferior moral choice.[46]

According to this analysis, while one may freely and rightfully continue to obey the commands of another, what one never loses – no matter what one has consented to – is the right to change one's mind and begin pursuing the truly moral course of self-directed action. Suppose that a competent, adult

[43] Henry B. Veatch offers an account of rights based on self-regarding duties in *Human Rights: Fact or Fancy* (Baton Rouge: Louisiana State Univ. Press, 1985).

[44] Such a principle would provide a property rights basis for some limited form of "bankruptcy" laws. See Lawrence H. White, "Bankruptcy as an Economic Intervention," *Journal of Libertarian Studies*, vol. 1 (1977), p. 287, note 27 ("Perhaps some distinction among the debtor's assets in terms of alienability can be made according to a standard of subsistence . . . .").

[45] Veatch, *Human Rights*, p. 114.

[46] See John Stuart Mill, *On Liberty* (Indianapolis: Library of Liberal Arts, 1956), p. 125 (A person, "by selling himself for a slave . . . defeats, in his own case, the very purpose which is the justification of allowing him to dispose of himself.").

person commits herself to giving her heart to a dearly loved one, an action which – unlike the gift of blood – will inevitably result in her death, and that no fraud or duress is used to induce this consent. We might conclude that while the person has no duty to make such a gift – such an act would be termed supererogatory – and, indeed, the gift might be in conflict with the duty that person owes to herself (of course, it also might not), no *other* person would have the right to interavene and prevent such a sacrifice from being made.

Suppose, now, that after the commitment has been made, the person making it changes her mind and refuses to go through with the transfer. While a person may be able to transfer control over a heart to another (and arguably may not be prevented from doing so), her never-ending duty to herself prevents her from transferring a right to her heart to another such that she must convey control of the heart even if she changes her mind. The same reasoning applies with equal force to attempts to alienate a right to the future control of the rest of one's body, since doing so is always inconsistent with the duty that one owes to oneself. In fact, the most salient characteristic of inalienable rights may be that, while rights-holders may *exercise* their inalienable rights for the benefit of others, a rights-holder may never surrender *the right to change her mind* about whether to exercise such rights or not.[47]

Anthony Kronman has argued that legal prohibitions of slavery are "paternalist."[48] But while an argument for inalienable rights might be paternalist, this need not be so. Surely the account just provided is not paternalist.[49] No

[47] Cf. *ibid.*, p. 125 ("[T]here are perhaps no contracts or engagements, except those that relate to money or money's worth, of which one can venture to say that there ought to be no liberty whatsoever of retraction."). Extreme situations warranting different treatment can always be hypothesized. For example, may a pilot be forcibly compelled to complete a journey he has contracted to fly and be prevented from parachuting out of a plane? The endangerment involved in the example, however, introduces a tortious element. The better analogy would be to ask whether a pilot who safely lands a plane short of completing a designated route can be compelled to finish the trip.

[48] See Anthony Kronman, "Paternalism and the Law of Contracts," *Yale Law Journal*, vol. 92 (1983), pp. 774–776 (attempting to show that paternalist restrictions in contract law are well-accepted and permissible).

[49] An argument for inalienable rights is not paternalist simply because advocates of such rights argue that restrictions on (everyone's) options are, on balance, best (for everyone). First, such a universal argument for inalienable rights denies everyone the same option and therefore does not put advocates into any type of parental stance towards others. Second, *all* rights — not just inalienable ones — can be advocated on the grounds that individuals be permitted the liberty that rights provide because such liberty is "good" for them. See Barnett, "Pursuing Justice," pp. 50–72. And any compossible system of rights restricts somebody's options — one may not act so as to violate the rights of another. If it is not paternalist to advocate these restraints on the ground that they are good or necessary for rights-holders and nonrights-holders alike, then it is not paternalistic to argue in the same manner for restrictions on the alienability of certain of these rights.

one may rightfully interfere in the consensual sacrificial conduct of a competent adult – as a parent may interfere with a child – simply because the intermeddler knows what is truly best for the individual making the sacrifice. Rather, this argument against the enforceability of agreements to transfer control over one's body is that the law should not specifically enforce certain commitments when the party who made the original commitment thinks better of it.[50]

An inalienable right does not give others the right to think for a competent adult. Such rights simply define a category of decisions about which competent adults may rightfully override *their own* previously expressed preferences. Where *ex ante* consent and *ex post* consent are the same, there would be no breach of contract. Restrictions on alienability, then, are really rules concerning which of two inconsistent expressions of assent by the same party determines the rights of both parties to an agreement: With alienable rights, *ex ante* consent transfers rights to control resources and binds the transferor *ex post*. With inalienable rights, a right to control resources is never transferred by consent, so *ex post* consent takes precedence over *ex ante* consent.

A fourth reason why some rights may be inalienable stems from a general skepticism that agreements to transfer rights amounting to the control of one's destiny would ever (or very often) be obtained in the absence of incompetence, fraud, duress, mistake, or some other recognized contract defense. Assuming that it was theoretically possible to alienate every right (including a right to the future control of one's person), the failure of any legal system to accurately decide every case, coupled with the extremely high cost of error in evaluating the procedural validity of certain rights-transfer agreements, argues for a blanket prohibition on the transfer of certain kinds of rights.[51] For example, the high cost of erroneously deciding that a slavery contract was truly voluntary could be said to militate against *ever* permitting the enforcement of such an agreement.

The argument that epistemological uncertainty and the cost of epistemic errors might convert rights that are in point of moral principle alienable into

[50] In assessing a different argument for inalienability than that presented here, Calabresi and Melamed, "Property Rules," p. 1113, make a similar observation:

> This type of limitation is not in any real sense paternalism. . . . It merely allows the individual to choose what is best in the long run rather than in the short run, even though that choice entails giving up some short run freedom of choice.

[51] See Kronman, "Paternalism," p. 768 ("[I]f fraud is widespread, if it can be concealed with sufficient ease, and if the victims of the fraud typically lack the resources to prosecute their legal claims, lowering the proof requirement may not be enough. A more radical solution . . . is to give the victims an inalienable entitlement they cannot waive and therefore cannot be fraudulently induced to abandon."); McConnell, "The Nature and Basis," pp. 53–54 ("[T]he policy in question is one that could easily be abused, thereby resulting in harm to nonconsenting parties.").

rights that are legally inalienable is an example of indirect consequentialism.[52] Such system concerns can prove to be quite compelling in any serious effort to formulate a legal system that is truly just in its actual operation.[53]

3. What Rights Are Inalienable? We cannot conclude on the basis of the four reasons presented here for inalienable rights that *all* our rights are inalienable. Far from it. The transfer of rights to control external resources is both possible and normally compatible with the duties we owe ourselves and others.[54] Nor could it be fairly argued that the cost of erroneous adjudication of claims to external resources always "exceeds" the benefits of permitting alienation. Except in the most rare and extreme of circumstances,[55] rights to external resources are not inalienable.[56]

On the other hand, the alienability of rights wholly or partially to control the future use of one's person has been called into question. The transfer of the right totally to control one's person may conflict with the duties one has to respect the rights of others. Even if slavery agreements are limited to obeying only those commands which respect the rights of others, the costs of an erroneous decision to enforce such an agreement may create epistemic risks so great that in every case they are deemed to outweigh whatever benefits might accrue from enforcement. Further, the transfer of complete or partial rights of control might inevitably conflict with duties one owes to oneself. Moreover, the transfer of even limited rights of bodily control may

[52] See Larry Alexander, "Pursuing the Good — Indirectly," *Ethics*, vol. 95 (1985), pp. 315–332; John Gray, "Indirect Utility and Fundamental Rights," *Social Philosophy & Policy*, vol. 1 (Spring 1984), pp. 73–91.

[53] Richard Epstein has stressed the importance of epistemic problems of administration for the formulation of common law rules. See, e.g., Richard Epstein, "Unconscionability," pp. 300–303; "The Social Consequences of Common Law Rules," *Harvard Law Review*, vol. 95 (1982), pp. 1748–1749. See also Sher, "Rights Violations."

[54] For example, we transfer rights to some things in exchange for rights to other things we value more highly; and we make gifts because the good life entails acting charitably towards others. See Richard A. Epstein, "Why Restrain Alienation," *Columbia Law Review*, vol. 85 (1985), pp. 971–972 (discussing reasons why alienation is permitted).

[55] As was suggested above (*supra* note 44 and accompanying text) attempts to alienate rights to such a quantity of external resources that there would not be enough left for the transferor to survive are not enforceable. In other words, at some minimum quantity, normally alienable rights to external resources become inalienable.

[56] Other reasons for inalienability of otherwise alienable external property have been suggested, but space constraints prevent me from considering them here. See, e.g., Susan Rose-Ackerman, "Inalienability and the Theory of Property Rights," *Columbia Law Review*, vol. 85 (1985), pp. 931–969; Epstein, "Why Restrain Alienation," pp. 973–990.

be barred in principle by the literal impossibility of transferring control over one's person.

Thus, we may conclude that (a) rights to possess, use, and control resources external to one's person are (generally) alienable, and (b) the right to possess, use, and control one's person is inalienable.

V. REFORMING THE RULES GOVERNING CONTRACT REMEDIES

A consent theory of contract permits us to distinguish between the *subject* of a contract – that is, the particular rights being transferred from one party to the other – and the *object* of a contract – that is, what the parties are trying to accomplish by entering into a contractual arrangement. Only alienable rights may be the subject of an enforceable rights-transfer agreement. Obstacles in the path of a presumption favoring specific performance of all contracts may be obviated by distinguishing three kinds of contracts: contracts for external resources, contracts for personal services, and contracts for corporate services.[57]

In this section, the problems traditionally associated with specifically enforcing contracts for personal services will be shown to stem from the fact that inalienable rights may improperly be construed as the subject, rather than the object, of such contracts. In contrast, the specific performance of contracts for corporate services gives rise to no such problem.

1. Contracts for External Resources. The first kind of contract involves consent to transfer alienable rights to possess, control, and use identifiable external resources, whether land or goods. Because rights to external resources are presumptively alienable, such rights may be made the subject of an enforceable rights transfer.

If *A* contracts to "sell" a piece of land or some good like a car to *B*, most people would expect that when the contract is executed *B* has a right to the specified land or car. Therefore, when this is the normal expectation and intention, the normal or presumptive remedy for breach of contract in such a case should be that *B*'s newly acquired rights to the land or car are respected

[57] This essay does not exhaust the subject of inalienable rights, nor that of the proper choice of contract remedies. Contracts to provide employment, for example, do not easily fit into any of the three categories of contracts discussed in this paper. Determining whether such a contract may permissibly be specifically enforced might turn out to require a more extended discussion of inalienable rights.

– he gets the land or car if he still desires to receive it.[58] If not, he may elect to receive money damages.[59]

> Why not, as in both French and German law, give specific performance as to any physical object that can be found and is reachable by direct execution? It is true that wherever speed is a factor and markets reasonably organized, promisees will not often ask for it, as has proved true in Germany (and I think also in France). But why not leave this to the promisee's choice?[60]

Of course, *A* and *B* need not agree to transfer the right to the land or car itself. They might instead include an express provision in their original contract that would rebut the normal meaning of such contracts and limit recovery for breach to money damages. The *object* of such a contract might be to secure performance, but its *subject* would be a conditional transfer of a right to compensation for nonperformance. A consent theory of contract says that such an agreement would ordinarily be enforced.[61]

[58] This category corresponds to the category of contracts to give (*donner*) in French law; see *supra* note 37 and accompanying text. Consistent with the analysis in the text, French law grants specific performance as a matter of right. See B. Nicholas, *French Law*, p. 211; Treitel, "Remedies," p. 13.

[59] It is arguable that, in some cases, sellers might be permitted to show why buyers should not get the thing contracted for. For example, if a fungible replacement good is easily available to the buyer on the market, but performance would be an extreme hardship on the seller, then where the contract is silent on the form of relief, the seller might be liable only for money damages. Where these circumstances can be shown to exist, and in the absence of an express clause, it may no longer be safe to presume that sellers would have consented to specific relief. In contrast with the traditional rule, however, the burden of proof is placed on the appropriate party — the party in breach. But see Schwartz, "The Case for Specific Performance," p. 289, note 52 (arguing against the recognition of such a defense on the grounds that it is unnecessary in practice, costly to administer, and unpredictable in application). Nonetheless, Schwartz does favor a very limited defense to specific performance based on administrative difficulty: "Although such cases are rare, courts should have the power to deny specific performance where necessary." *ibid.*, p. 305.

[60] John Dawson, "Specific Performance in France and Germany," *Michigan Law Review*, vol. 57 (1959), p. 532. The common law apparently once granted a comparable right of replevin to buyers of goods, but this right was conceived of as arising from property law, not contract law; see Friedrich Kessler and Grant Gilmore, *Contracts: Cases and Materials*, 2d ed. (Boston, MA: Little, Brown & Co., 1970), p. 1000 (describing this "twin set of remedies" as "one of the curiosities of sales law as it developed in the nineteenth century").

[61] While courts are generally willing to enforce limitation of damages provisions, at present they do not generally recognize the parties' right to expressly agree to a specific performance remedy in their contract. See Ian R. Macneil, "Power of Contract and Agreed Remedies," *Cornell Law Quarterly*, vol 47 (1962), pp. 495–528 (describing the various limitations on the enforcement of agreed remedies); Anthony Kronman, "Specific Performance," pp. 369–376 (describing present law and favoring the enforcement of such clauses). Perhaps courts would be more respectful of such clauses, if it became clearer why a specific performance clause in a contract for personal services would not be enforceable.

2. Contracts for Personal Services. What should happen if *A* breaches a commitment to provide personal services by refusing to perform as agreed? Can a commitment by *A* to *B* that *A* will do something for *B* constitute a valid contract? If the right to the future control of one's person is inalienable, the personal services in question cannot be the subject of a valid rights transfer agreement. Therefore, if a promise to provide personal services is only a commitment to exercise inalienable rights, then it is unenforceable. By breaching his promise to *B*, *A* may commit a morally bad act. He has not, however, committed a legally cognizable wrong.

Alternatively, a contract "to provide personal services" might accurately be construed as a commitment to transfer alienable rights to money damages (or other alienable resources) on the condition that specified personal services are not performed as promised. Such an agreement would not purport to transfer the inalienable right to the services themselves. Rather, such an agreement would (conditionally) transfer alienable rights to the money and would be enforceable in the event that the condition was satisfied – that is, in the event that services were not performed as agreed. In essence, the true commitment in an enforceable agreement to provide personal services would be: "I'll do *X* for you and, if I fail to perform *X*, you will have the right to money damages."[62]

While the *object* or purpose of such a contract for personal services would be to assure that one party will exercise his inalienable rights in a certain way some time in the future, the actual *subject* of such a contract would be the transfer of alienable rights to the money.

> Every obligation to do or not to do (*de faire ou de ne pas faire*) resolves itself into damages in the case of non-performance by the debtor.[63]

Thus, if *A* consents to a legally binding commitment to personally paint *B*'s picture, then no matter what the contract specifies, *B*'s only right is to money

[62] Justice O. W. Holmes, Jr., suggested this approach as a general rule of contract remedies in *The Common Law* (Boston: Little, Brown & Co., 1881), p. 301:

> The only universal consequence of a legally binding promise is, that the law makes the promisor pay damages if the promised event does not come to pass.

While this passage is both famous and often criticized, it has been noted that Holmes did not assert that money damages were the exclusive form relief for all breaches, only that it was the only remedy that was always or generally available. See Mark DeWolfe Howe, *Justice Oliver Wendell Holmes: The Proving Years* (Cambridge, MA: Harvard Univ. Press, 1963), pp. 233–237.

[63] French Civil Code, art. 1142 as it appears in Nicholas, *French Law*, p. 210. Of course, any such award would be limited by the quantitative constraints placed on the alienation of external resources discussed *supra* note 44.

damages (specific enforcement of the transfer of the money)[64] – even if *A*'s performance is unique or monetary damages are inadequate for some other reason. When viewed in this manner, contracts for personal services require no exception to a remedies rule which generally favors specific performance. It is the stipulated transfer of money that will be specifically enforced in the event of a failure to perform.

Limiting the proper subject of contracts for personal services to money damages (which will be specifically enforced) produces legal results which are entirely consonant with the common law's traditional reluctance to grant specific relief for breach of personal services contracts. A consent theory of contract and a proper distinction between alienable and inalienable rights both explains and justifies this seemingly *ad hoc* "public policy" exception.

3. Contracts for Corporate Services. At first blush, it may appear that if Firm *A* legally commits itself to provide corporate services involving individual labor to a consumer or another firm, such a contract should be governed by the same rule that applies to contracts for personal services. But there is an important difference. If Firm *A* breaches its contract to provide services, it need not be the case and, in fact, it is quite unlikely that the reason for the breach is the unwillingness of the employees of the firm who are personally to provide the services. Rather, what has likely happened is that for one reason or another, the owners or managers of Firm *A* have found it inexpedient to honor their commitment. They might, for example, have found a more profitable opportunity elsewhere, or something may have occurred to make performance more costly to them than they had anticipated.

If the undesirablity of performance to the owners or management of a firm and not the reluctance of the workers supplying their labor accounts for the decision to breach, a court may still be faced with problems of administering a decree of specific performance. It will not, however, confront the issue of involuntary servitude that plagues the specific performance of personal services contracts.

> The liberty interest objection thus poses no barrier to expanding the availability of specific performance to sales of roughly fungible goods and corporate services.[65]

[64] What the contract specifies might influence which *measure* of money damages is used. For an explanation of the various possible measures of contract damages, see Robert Cooter and Melvin Aron Eisenberg, "Damages for Breach of Contract," *California Law Review*, vol. 73 (1985), pp. 1432–1465; Lon L. Fuller and William R. Perdue, Jr., "The Reliance Interest in Contract Damages," *Yale Law Journal*, vol. 46 (1936), pp. 52–96.

[65] Schwartz, "The Case for Specific Performance," p. 298.

True, as with personal service contracts, the services of the employees cannot be the subject of a valid contract because such services consist of the employees' exercise of their inalienable rights. And if an employee breaches his contract to perform services for the firm, he would only be liable to the firm for money damages. Unlike contracts for personal services, however, the subject of a valid contract for corporate services need not be limited to the payment of money damages for failure to perform as agreed. The following series of examples illustrates that another morally permissible construction exists as well.

First, suppose that *A* wishes to have his house painted and is unable or unwilling to paint it himself. *A* can contract with individual *B* that *B* will paint the house – that is, *B* commits herself to compensate *A* if she fails to paint the house. If *B* breaches this contract to provide personal services, she is liable only for money damages. Suppose, instead, that *A* decides to buy Firm *C* which is a housepainting company. As the owner of Firm *C*, *A* may then order its painters to paint his house. (If any painter refuses to do so, then that painter may have breached whatever employment contract she has with Firm *C* and, if so, she is liable to the firm for money damages.) This may mean that Firm *C* might have to pass up the opportunity to contract with individual *D* to paint *D*'s house. As the new owner of the company, the right to make this decision now belongs to *A*.

Now, suppose *A* thinks that it is both too much trouble and too expensive to buy a painting company merely because he wishes to have his house painted. The only right of ownership that *A* really wants is the right to order the employees of Firm *C* to paint his house. To secure this and only this right, instead of buying Firm *C*, *A* contracts with it to paint his house. The principal difference between the two transactions is that a direct purchase of Firm *C* gives *A* many more rights in addition to the right to direct the firm's painters to paint his house – rights which he neither desires, nor can afford to purchase. A contract for corporate services, on the other hand, may transfer only the narrow right to direct the employees to paint his house, which *A* desires, and nothing more.

A court order that Firm *C*'s employees paint *B*'s house is no different from *A* issuing this order as the owner of the firm. While one person cannot own another person, a person can own a firm. This suggests that where *A* contracts to buy corporate services from Firm *C*, *A* might have acquired a (very limited) kind of ownership right to the resources *of the firm*.[66]

[66] Cf. Steven N. S. Cheung, "The Structure of a Contract and the Theory of a Non-Exclusive Resource," *Journal of Law and Economics*, vol. 13 (1970), p. 50 ("Combining resources of several owners for production involves partial or outright transfers of property rights through a contract.")

Whether *A* has in fact acquired such a right depends entirely on the construction given the terms of the contract. A consent theory would look first to the demonstrated intentions of the parties or, if the contract is silent on this issue, to the custom of trade. (If there is no trade custom, the problem of interpreting the contract becomes more complicated.) The agreement itself or the trade custom might have only given *A* a right to money damages for breach; or it might instead have specified that *A* gets the same right to have Firm *C*'s employees directed to paint his house that he would have acquired by buying the company and becoming its owner. No matter which form of relief the parties agree to, however, there is no moral problem of the sort that exists with specifically enforcing personal services contracts.

Suppose, now, that the contract is silent on the issue and no trade custom exists. An important reason exists for favoring specific performance of a contract for corporate services, provided that the victim of the breach is an individual (as opposed to another firm). Purchasers who are legally unsophisticated – that is, unfamiliar with the common law rules governing the choice of remedy – most likely assume when they contract for performance from the firm that performance is what they can get if there is a breach, because performance is what they bargained for. If the legal rule governing the choice of remedies awarded only money damages, then such persons – who are by assumption ignorant of the legal background – would be most unlikely to insist on an expressed clause to the contrary. Their silence would not, then, reliably indicate assent to the terms provided by the legal background rule. By interpreting this silence as assent, courts would likely be giving firms a beneficial term they had not paid for.

In contrast, a firm in the business of regularly providing corporate services is, by virtue of its past experience (or legal counsel), very likely to be aware of the prevailing background legal rule and, should it not wish to be bound by this rule, it can be expected to try to insert in the contract an expressed provision to the contrary – that is, a term that mandates money damages only. This suggests that when a contract to provide corporate services which is silent on the issue of remedy is breached by the service provider,[67] and the victim is an individual (not another firm), a court should, at the request of the victim of the breach, order specific performance.[68] In short, where the

[67] The provider of "corporate services" is by definition a firm. When the service provider is an individual, rather than a firm, this is a contract for *personal* services for which only money damages for breach of contract should be obtained.

[68] Service providers might arguably be permitted to oppose a request for specific performance by showing that the services they provide are readily available elsewhere and performance is for some reason an extreme hardship. But, as with contracts for external resources, the recognition of such a defense would be controversial. See *supra* note 59.

purchaser of corporate services is an individual consumer, the reverse of the traditional rule governing contract damages should apply and specific performance should be favored.[69]

Providers of corporate services who wish to limit their liability to monetary damages would have to attempt to insert a clause to this effect in the contract. A presumption of specific performance when the recipient of corporate services is an individual forces the party with better access to the background rule (the firm) to educate the less knowledgeable party by its bargaining behaviour.[70]

VI. SUMMARY

The traditional approach to remedies for breach of contract is that only money damages are available to the victim as of right. Specific performance is an exceptional form of relief available only when money damages are inadequate. Even when damages are inadequate, however, a contract for personal services will not be specifically enforced. A consent theory of contract suggests the following rule to govern the choice of remedies for breach of contract: The only enforceable agreements are those which consensually transfer alienable rights. All such agreements should presumptively be specifically enforced.

Where a contract transfers the right to *external resources*, then transfer of these resources should be ordered by a court. If parties do not wish this result, they may agree – or trade custom might establish – that only monetary damages will be due for failure to deliver a promised resource.

[69] It may well be that the best rule for corporate services contracts when both parties are firms is the traditional one: the victim of the breach has a right to money damages, but may obtain specific performance if it can show that damages are inadequate. Assuming that money damage awards are less costly to administer and comply with, the traditional rule might best reflect the intentions of the parties when (a) the parties and trade custom are silent on the issue of remedies, and (b) both parties are firms and therefore are presumably aware of the background legal rule. Kronman and Schwartz sharply disagree with each other about what, if any, general inference of the parties' intentions can be derived from an analysis of their *ex ante* interests. Compare Kronman, "Specific Performance," pp. 365–369 ("There is . . . some basis for believing the uniqueness test reflects the typical solution that contracting parties would arrange for themselves in light of their *ex ante* interests."), with Schwartz, "The Case for Specific Performance," pp. 279–284 (criticizing Kronman's analysis and rejecting his conclusion). The incentive effects of the legal rule are less significant here than when the recipient of corporate services is an individual, because both parties are sophisticated enough to bargain for a clause which deviates from the legal background if they wish a different remedy. This assumes, however, that such a clause will be enforced, which may not be true at present. See *supra* note 61.

[70] Even an express clause in a form contract can serve to give the recipient of services notice of the remedy in the event of a breach: see Douglas G. Baird and Robert Weisberg, "Rules, Standards, and the Battle of the Forms: A Reassessment of §2–207," *Virginia Law Review*, vol. 68 (1982), pp. 1217–1262 (discussing the value of form contracts and ways to resolve disputes when the forms used by contracting parties conflict).

Since a right to *personal services* is inalienable, persons wishing to enhance the reliability of a promise to perform personal services by means of a contract may accomplish this object by making a transfer of alienable rights (to money or other property) conditional on nonperformance. Upon failure to perform the desired services, the rights transfer could be specifically enforced.

Where a contract calls for the provision of *corporate services*, the subject of the contract may either be a right to money damages or a limited right to control the firm. Since both of these rights are potentially alienable, when either right is transferred, a court may order a firm to specifically perform. Where the purchaser of corporate services is an individual, a court should (at least) presumptively award specific performance.

Law, Chicago-Kent College of Law, Illinois Institute of Technology

PRACTICAL WISDOM AND PROFESSIONAL CHARACTER

By Anthony Kronman

I

The existence of the legal profession is something most lawyers take for granted. Lawyers of course do many different things, and lead different sorts of lives, but those who make their living in the law tend to assume, without much reflection, that they have a bond or association of some sort with others who do the same and believe they share something important in common with them. It is not at all clear, however, what this common element is, and the great diversity of tasks that lawyers perform – representing litigants, counseling clients, advising legislators, administering government programs, and deciding cases – can easily make one doubt whether the search for a link leads to anything but empty generalities.

One may, of course, conclude that the main law jobs, as Karl Llewellyn called them,[1] have nothing important in common, and that the legal profession is only a name for a disconnected collection of pursuits with no substance or reality of its own. This is not, however, a very satisfying view, to lawyers at least, and is likely to provoke the quick reply that what lawyers share in common is after all quite easy to discern. All lawyers, regardless of the nature of their work, possess a general knowledge of the law which they have acquired through a specialized program of instruction; laypersons lack such knowledge and it is this, one might argue, which marks the line between those who are lawyers and those who are not and, thus, defines the scope and nature of the profession.

This view, however, also denies the existence of the legal profession, though in a less obvious way. Undoubtedly, to be a lawyer one must possess a special knowledge of the law, just as one must possess a special knowledge of automobiles to be a mechanic. But lawyers resist the idea that they are mere technicians, and nothing disturbs a legal educator as much as the suggestion that he is running a trade school operation. This reaction reflects the belief

* I would like to thank my colleague Perry Dane for his very helpful comments on an earlier draft.

[1] K. Llewellyn, *The Normative, The Legal and the Law Jobs: The Job of Juristic Method*, 49 Yale L. J. 1355 (1940)

that there is an important distinction between professionals and technicians. Samuel Huntington has rightly observed that the former notion includes, as the latter does not, the idea of an activity with a self-conscious history or tradition that serves ends widely regarded as essential to the well-being of society as a whole.[2] The notion of a profession includes something more than this, however. To be a professional is to have a certain identity or character, to be a person of a particular sort. An expert possesses special knowledge, but to call someone an expert implies nothing about his character traits or dispositions, about the sort of person that he is. When someone describes himself as a professional, he is making a claim not merely about what he knows but also about who he is; considered strictly as an expert, as the possessor of some expertise, a person has no character at all, which is why the perfect expert can never be anything but a tool or instrument for others whose ends pass through him as through an utterly transparent medium that offers no resistance of its own. When lawyers complain that they are not mere tools but professionals bound by an ethic that requires them to behave in certain ways, they are insisting, in effect, on the link between character and professional identity. To argue that the legal profession is a group distinguished by its members' special knowledge of the law, and nothing more, is to deny this link and with it the existence of the profession itself. If one is not prepared, then, either to deny that lawyers have some common professional identity despite the differences that separate their various lines of work, or to found this identity upon the possession of an expertise – which, as I have suggested, implies nothing about the ideas of character and disposition that lie at the root of what we understand a profession to be – then the search for a connecting link or common element must be continued, but in a different direction.

We may begin by taking notice of the fact – a fact whose importance is generally underestimated, in part, I think, because it is so obvious – that lawyers deal with specific problems or controversies, with cases, and not merely with abstract propositions. I shall call this characteristic of law practice its "case-centeredness." The cases with which lawyers deal always arise, of course, within the framework of general norms and a knowledge of this framework, or at least the relevant portion of it, is something a lawyer cannot do without. What gives such knowledge its relevance or meaning for the lawyer, however, is its relation to the case at hand. The case is a kind of prism which refracts the lawyer's more generalized doctrinal knowledge, and when he looks at the law he always does so from the perspective of a case and through the medium of its dense particularities. This is easiest to see in

[2] S. Huntington, The Soldier and the State 8 (1957).

the work of a judge, who is never concerned with general principles of law except in the context of a specific dispute, or a legal counselor who advises clients as to how they should conduct themselves and deal with their problems. But even those lawyers who seem far removed from cases in the work they do are in reality more case-centered than first impressions might suggest. The lawyer, for example, who acts as counsel to a legislative committee and whose job it is to put the committee's conclusions into statutory form, chooses among the phrasings available to him from the perspective of those possible future cases that are likely to test the meaning of the general language which these variant phrasings employ. A lawyer who drafts legislation must, of course, have a grasp of the aims that animate his statute and understand the political and economic theories that underlie it, but it is not his comprehension of these that distinguishes the lawyer's contribution to the process of legislation or that defines the focal point of the role he plays in it. The lawyer's special contribution to the legislative process lies in his attention to the inadequacies of language that appear only when competing statutory formulations are viewed from the perspective of those imaginary future cases which they must eventually be made to decide.

The work of lawyers, then, is case-centered; in whatever capacity they function, whether as judges, counselors, or draftsmen, lawyers are chiefly concerned to solve or to avoid specific problems, and it is these that fix both the beginning and end points of their reflections. This, of course, is a property not only of law practice but of every practical activity, a property which the term 'practical' itself denotes. Someone who is managing a business, for example, or running a country, will be confronted in his work with a series of concrete problems, and however deep his understanding of the general principles of finance or government, the relevance of these will for him depend upon their connection to the immediate problem at hand, whatever it might be. The entrepreneur or statesman, like the lawyer, always views matters from the perspective of a specific case, and it is from this vantage point that the meaning and utility of all his more theoretical knowledge will be determined. By contrast, there are pursuits – all those we call "academic" to distinguish them from the realm of practical affairs – in which the attainment of such knowledge is an end in itself whose value or significance does not ultimately depend upon its connection to some particular case or other. This is true, for example, in philosophy. Philosophers talk and write about specific cases, but their motive for doing so is generally to identify the strengths and weaknesses of the speculative theories whose assessment is their main concern. In philosophy, we might say, cases are seen from the vantage point of theory, rather than the other way around. Philosophy is not a case-centered discipline in the twofold sense that it often proceeds without any discussion of cases whatsoever and shows an interest in them, when it does, only from an independent speculative point of view. In law practice, as in every other pratical activity, just the opposite is true.

Because their work is always centered on a specific case or problem, lawyers require not only a general theoretical knowledge of the law but a facility for bringing this knowledge to bear in an effective way on the particularities of the cases they encounter. This latter skill or capacity, though it depends upon and employs a certain measure of theoretical understanding, is distinguishable from it. Aristotle puts this point with special clarity.[3] There is, he says, a species of understanding, which he calls the understanding of particulars, that is distinguishable from theoretical knowledge and that is required to bring general rules or principles to bear on specific problems of conduct, the problems that confront a person when he asks himself how he ought to act, not in general, but in this or that concrete situation. Some men, according to Aristotle, possess an understanding of particulars and others lack it, or possess it to a lesser degree. Aristotle uses the term *phronesis* to describe this special kind of understanding, and *phronismos* to denote the man whose understanding of particulars has been developed to an exemplary degree.

The Latin-speaking followers of Aristotle translated *phronesis* as *prudentia*,[4] and the original Greek term is often rendered in English simply as "prudence." Today, however, the word 'prudence' has a variety of meanings that suggest something rather different from what Aristotle had in mind;[5] a better translation of *phronesis* would be "practical wisdom" or "sound judgment." We may express Aristotle's view, then, by saying that to deal with problems of action or conduct one requires not only theoretical but practical wisdom as well. This applies directly to the work that lawyers do. Lawyers deal with cases, not abstractions, and thus must have a measure of practical wisdom in order to do their work well. Indeed, if the distinctive skill that lawyers are most often called upon to exercise in their work is the skill of forming judgments about specific problems, then the possession of practical wisdom is more than just a requirement for success in the practice of law; it is, in some sense, the central requirement, and when one goes to a lawyer for advice or to a judge for decision – rather than to a professor of philosophy or

[3] Nicomachean Ethics 1141b 1–1142a 30.

[4] Thomas Aquinas, Summa Theologica, Q. 57 Art. 4–5.

[5] Kant is in part responsible for this, having used the term prudence to denote enlightened self-interest. "The word *prudence* is taken in two senses: in the one it may bear the name of knowledge of the world, in the other that of private prudence. The former is a man's ability to influence others so as to use them for his own purposes. The latter is the sagacity to combine all these purposes for his own lasting benefit." Fundamental Principles of the Metaphysic of Morals 33 (1873).

economics – it is in the hope of benefiting from his superior practical wisdom.

In general, of course, every practical activity from cooking and carpentry to international diplomacy requires that those engaged in it possess a working knowledge of the relevant particulars, and in this sense demands of its practitioners something we might call practical wisdom. There are, indeed, certain broad similarities between the pratical know-how of an accomplished chef and the special skill in dealing with particulars that distinguishes the great statesman or diplomat from those of lesser rank; in both cases, for example, a knowledge of particulars can be acquired only by experience. Despite these similarities, however, there are also important differences in the nature of that knowledge of particulars which different practical endeavors require. One such difference is this: in some fields – cooking and carpentry are examples – a person may become an acute judge of particulars without, for that reason alone, acquiring any distinctive traits of character of a morally significant kind; in other activities, however, the development of certain traits of the latter sort, of a set of moral habits, appears to be intimately connected with the acquisition of a capacity for discriminating judgment. This is true, for example, in the field of diplomacy; when we say that someone has conducted a negotiation in a diplomatic way, we are making a remark not only about his skill in discerning the most favorable course of action under the circumstances, but also about the way in which he has behaved, about his qualities as a person – in short, about his character. To call someone a diplomat is to describe, at once, his practical knowledge of affairs and certain of his traits or dispositions. The same is true if we call someone a statesman, but not, I think, if we call him a master chef, even the greatest chef in the world. In the cases of the diplomat and statesman the nature of the connection between their practical knowhow, on the one hand, and their character traits, on the other, may be obscure – are the latter preconditions or products of the former? – But there does appear to be some general link between the two. Because the term 'practical wisdom' itself suggests a certain quality of temperament or character as well as a species of understanding, it seems most aptly used to describe the knowledge of particulars that is demanded by activities in which moral character and know-how are conjoined (whatever the nature of the link between them might be). It is difficult to say how many activities fit this description. I do think, however, that the practice of law is one such activity, and in what follows shall attempt to explain why.

I have said that the work of lawyers is case-centered and therefore requires the special kind of knowledge that Aristotle called *phronesis* or practical wisdom. I have also suggested that the practice of law is one of those activities in which a knowledge of particulars is inseparable from the possession of certain morally significant traits of character, and that it therefore belongs to that family of activities for which the expression "practical wisdom" is most appropriately reserved. If this is true, then it may be possible to construct a new and more convincing account of the lawyer's professional identity by examining closely the nature of the practical wisdom he requires in his work. To say that a lawyer must have practical wisdom or sound judgment in order to be good at what he does is to suggest, if I am right about the connection between cognition and character, that he must also have certain traits of character to attain a high level of achievement in the practice of law. In these traits we may hope to find a foundation for the belief that to be a lawyer is to be a person of a particular kind, a person one may reasonably take pride in being, rather than an expert with no particular character at all.

II

Though lawyers often speak of others in their profession as either having or lacking sound judgment, and tend generally to regard the possession of this attribute as an important professional qualification, the meaning of this and similar expressions (like "good sense" or "practical wisdom") is by no means clear. It is much easier, in fact, to say what these expressions do *not* mean than it is to give a positive account of the faculty or capacity to which they refer.

In the first place, when one lawyer says that another has sound judgment, he does not mean simply that he has a special skill or talent for dealing with ideas and is able to follow trains of thought with exceptional speed or subtlety, the sort of skill that we might call dialectical. A person may have considerable skill in this regard and be very adept with ideas, but still lack sound judgment or practical wisdom. In following out a train of thought, no matter how long or elaborate, one is only concerned with ideas and the relationship between them. Dialectical thinking of this kind never arrives at cases in their full particularity, never gets all the way down to the world of immediate experience, but remains within the domain of abstract ideas. Some, of course, are more facile in this domain than others but we do not call such facility practical wisdom or sound judgment, for these latter expressions imply an ability to deal with concrete cases that lie outside the self-enclosed world of thought. Between thinking and experience, the world of ideas and the world itself, there is an infinitely deep chasm which no train of thought by itself can span; those who have practical wisdom are able to cross this chasm with confidence and grace, but not because they are skilled dialecticians. This is the point of the oldest joke about philosophy, the joke about Thales the Miletian, who is reported to have fallen down a well while gazing at the stars: Thales may have been able to think more quickly and clearly than anyone else, but he could not get about in the world and was out of touch with the ground beneath his feet.[6]

The difference between dialectical ability and practical wisdom might also be described as the difference between a purely intellectual capacity and one that has an important perceptual component. Dialectical skill is skill in argument; it is an excellence of the intellect or thinking part of a person's soul. Practical wisdom, by contrast, always displays itself in judgments about particular cases and therefore necessarily has a perceptual character for, as Aristotle says, of particulars there can only be perception and not thought.[7] The perceptual immediacy of that knowledge of particulars which a man of sound judgment must possess is well-conveyed by Justice Stewart's famous explanation of how he was able to tell when a particular film or book is pornographic: "I know it," Stewart said, "when I see it." It is suggestive of the perceptual character of practical wisdom that we tend to employ metaphors of sight to describe it; dialectical skill, which is displayed in our ability to construct and criticize arguments, is by contrast associated with speech and hence with hearing, the most abstract and least perceptual of the human senses.

From what I have said it is tempting to conclude that practical wisdom must be a form of intuition; this is the view that is suggested, for example, by Justice Stewart's comment. Conceived in this way, practical wisdom is nothing more than a certain clarity of vision, literally, a form of insight: the man who possesses such insight is the one who can immediately see what is the right thing to do in a particular situation even though he cannot explain or give an account of his judgment. Though appealing in some respects, this description of practical wisdom is also, I believe, seriously misleading.

Practical wisdom does, as I have said, display itself in judgments about particular cases whose full concreteness can be grasped only through perception, but the claim that practical wisdom is simply a species of intuition ignores the fact that the judgments of the practically wise man are arrived at by a process which is reflective and intellectually disciplined in a way that the concept of intuition, as we ordinarily employ it, fails to convey. The person of practical wisdom is not a Buddhist sage, working to clear his mind of all the interferences and obstacles created by its reflective apparatus, so that he may see the world directly, unmediated by the illusions of his own thought. Quite the contrary, the judgments at which a practically wise man arrives are *thought out*; they are the products, that is to say, of a reflective examination

[6] Hannah Arendt's interpretation of this story is quite interesting. See The Life of the Mind: Volume One, Thinking 82 (1977).

[7] Nicomachean Ethics, 1142a 27.

which employs ideas or general concepts. The term that Aristotle uses to describe this process of examination is *bouleusis*, usually translated as "deliberation."[8] The practically wise man does not just look at a problem to see what should be done; he deliberates about it, and his excellence – the quality that distinguishes him from those who are less practically wise than he – is in part an excellence *in* deliberation. Accordingly, we do not ascribe practical wisdom to a man solely on the basis of the final conclusions that he reaches, the "inscrutable prescriptions"[9] he leaves behind (that is the way we evaluate seers and the interpreters of omens), but take into account as well the way in which these conclusions have themselves been reached. Indeed, when we are assessing the soundness of a particular judgment we cannot do so without considering the reflections that support it; the reflective aspect of deliberation thus remains an important element in the judgments or decisions to which it leads, and we are unable to evaluate the one apart from the other. Some judgments – "this milk tastes funny" – cannot be supported by arguments and must therefore be validated by a direct experiential comparison, that is, by putting oneself in the position of the person who has made the judgment and looking (or, in this case, tasting) for oneself. The judgments which are the mark of a practically wise man are not of this kind, however, but depend for their validation upon a review of the deliberative considerations that underlie them.

I can summarize these rather abstract remarks in the following way: the sort of practical wisdom that lawyers must possess in order to do their work well is neither sheer dialectical skill, on the one hand, nor blind insight on the other, but combines reflective and perceptual elements – thinking and looking – in a manner which these other two views of it conceal. Instead of identifying practical wisdom with one of these two elements, it is more illuminating to think of it as a capacity for joining them together, for effecting what (to use a Kantian expression[10]) might be called a "synthesis" between them. If this is true, then the faculty or capacity that is employed in practical deliberation and whose development to an exceptionally high degree is the mark of a man of sound judgment cannot be the faculty we employ when attempting to follow very abstract arguments – arguments, say, in mathematics – nor the faculty through which we have a direct perceptual experience of the world. The practically wise man is distinguished by his possession, in an especially developed form, of some third capacity which partakes of both these other two and which, by establishing a link between

[8] Nicomachean Ethics, 1112a 17–1113a 13, 1142a 32–1142b 35; on the translation of *bouleusis*, see J. Cooper, Reason and Human Good in Aristotle 5–6 (1975).

[9] The phrase is Henry James'. See Washington Square 1 (1984).

[10] Kant, Critique of Pure Reason, B 130.

them, makes it possible to combine elements that otherwise seem so unbridgeably distinct. What might this capacity be?

III

Some philosophers have answered that it is the faculty of imagination. Kant, in particular, assigned to the imagination the mediating role I have described, and one of the most important sections of the *Critique of Pure Reason* is devoted to an analysis of its synthetic operations.[11] Though Kant's account of the imagination is open to criticism,[12] it provides a useful point of departure for my own attempt to give a more positive account of the union of thought and perception which all practical judgments exhibit and which the practically wise man is able to effect with greater sureness and reliability than most. I shall follow Kant in referring to the faculty by which we are able to bring about a union or synthesis of this sort as the faculty of imagination, for the ordinary meaning of this term is not only consistent with Kant's main philosophical claims, but also helps us to understand them and to grasp their significance.

In the *Critique of Pure Reason*, Kant was concerned, among other things, to account for the possibility of empirical judgments of the sort, "this cup is red" or "the object on the table is a lamp." These are judgments of the most ordinary kind, judgments everyone makes all the time, and which neither require nor display the special powers of discrimination that distinguish the man of practical wisdom. Nevertheless, the prosaic judgments of which Kant sought to give an account, like the more complex and less easily copied judgments of a practically wise man, combine perceptual and intellectual elements in a way that needs to be explained. When someone says, for example, "this cup is red," he makes a judgment that joins an experience with an idea or, as Kant would say, he brings a concrete case under the category to which it belongs. Judgments of this sort differ from those that remain wholly within the realm of ideas (like the judgment expressed by the Pythagorean Theorem), since they purport to establish a connecting link between this realm, on the one hand, and an altogether different one – the realm of immediate experience – on the other. Here, at a more elementary level, Kant encountered the same general problem as the one I have just described, the problem of explaining how such a connection is possible and by what faculty or capacity it is accomplished.

Kant's suggested solution was that the connection in question is established by the intermediating agency of the imagination which, he claimed,

[11] The section called "The Schematism of the Pure Concepts of the Understanding," A 137/B 176 – A 147/B 187.

[12] See J. Bennett, Kant's Analytic 141–152 (1966).

interposes between every immediate perception and its corresponding category a *schema* able to function by virtue of its own synthetic nature as a bridge or link between the two.[13] If we regard the imagination even from a commonsensical point of view, Kant's reasons for assigning it the role he did become apparent. We often say that when we imagine something, we see it with the mind's eye. This is a metaphorical way of expressing the fact that objects of imagination – the bright red teacup that I can see when I close my eyes – are visually present to us in the way that immediate objects of perception are and abstract ideas (like the quadratic equation or Kant's categorical imperative) are not.

There is, of course, a difference between the kind of immediacy that real physical objects possess and the kind that imaginary ones do, a difference we sometimes describe by saying that the objects of imagination are "shadowy" or "wavering" or "tentative" in comparison with their real counterparts. There is, however, a strong kinship between the two. One sign of this is the ability of artists and others to translate imaginary objects into real ones (the image before one's mind into an actual painting on canvas); another is the universal experience of trying to imagine someone or something that is absent, a process which always involves an effort at visualization and succeeds only when the picture before one's mind achieves a certain level of vividness and detail.

If imaginary objects have something important in common with real ones, however, they also resemble our most abstract ideas. When we look at a real teacup, we cannot help but see it in a certain way; the real teacup exercises an irresistible power over us, a power best described simply by saying that the teacup, along with the rest of the real world, is *given* to us in experience. By contrast, the objects of imagination do not possess a similar power; we may alter or recompose them as we wish and have the ability to abolish them altogether merely by withdrawing our attention from them, an ability we most decidedly do not possess with respect to real objects. In this regard, imaginary objects are more like thoughts than things, for the existence and content of our thoughts are subject to control by us in a way that the existence and content of the world are not. The world of imagination, like the world of thought, is more our own invention than the world itself and, hence, more fully subject to our powers of revision and denial. In imagination we are free from the world to a degree that we are not in perceptual experience, and the wavering or tentative character of our imaginings attests to this freedom by reminding us of our ability to make them over in whatever way we wish.

The objects of imagination, then, share certain features both with the

[13] Critique of Pure Reason, A 140/B 179.

objects of perception and with our most abstract ideas. Like the former, they have a vividness which the latter lack, and yet, like the latter, they depend upon us for their shape and even their existence to a degree that perceptual objects do not. Imaginary objects are simultaneously concrete – in a manner of speaking, visually apprehensible – and abstract, thought-things that we have made up and that would have no existence whatsoever were it not for us. The objects of imagination, we might say, are ideas clothed in sensual form or, to put the same point the other way around, idealized perceptions. Possessing in some degree both the immediacy of perceptual reality and the abstractness of ideas, the products of imagination stand between thought and experience and join them in a kind of synthesis that appears to be unique.

IV

Even a brief survey of the various tasks that lawyers perform immediately suggests two respects in which Kant's account of the imagination must be modified if it is to provide an adequate basis for understanding the peculiar character of that form of practical wisdom which lawyers are required to exercise in all phases or departments of their work.

In the first place, the judgments that lawyers are called upon to render require them to take the interests of other persons into account; this is true, for example, both of a judge (who must consider the interests of the litigants before him) and of a legal counselor (who has committed himself to protect the interests of his client). To understand the interests of another person, to form some estimate of their importance to him and to grasp the significance of events as they appear from his self-interested perspective, one must, so to speak, put oneself in that other person's position and make an effort to see things from his point of view. This can only be done, of course, in imagination, just as it is only in imagination that I am able to visualize the view from a certain promontory where I am not now standing. In the latter case, however, though I must imaginatively assume a point of view I do not presently occupy, the point of view is my own; that is to say, it is the view that I myself with all my own interests and attitudes would have were I now standing at the place in question. To imagine how the landscape would look from that perspective, it is not necessary for me to imagine how it would look to anyone else. By contrast, when a lawyer advises his client to follow a certain course of action (to refrain, let us say, from initiating a formal divorce proceeding) he must, if his advice is to be sound, have some idea of what his client cares about or has an interest in achieving, and to form an idea of this sort he needs to put himself imaginatively in his client's intellectual and affective postion. A lawyer must, in other words, *sympathize* with those whose interests he has agreed to protect or whose disputes it is his responsibility to resolve. The sympathy that is required is neither uncritical nor complete, but presupposes a certain measure of detachment which a more perfect identification with another person's interests would preclude; as we shall see, this is what distinguishes a lawyer from a lover or friend. Nevertheless, the presence of this sympathetic element differentiates the judgments that a lawyer is called upon to make – the judgment, for example, that a disputed contract should be interpreted to contain certain implied terms which reflect the parties' true but unstated aims, or that a client should pursue a particular business opportunity despite the legal risks involved – from judgments like "this teacup is red" or "the whole valley can only be seen from the top of the cliff." Each of these judgments is empirical in Kant's sense; each, that is to say, applies general categories to a particular experience and, hence, depends upon the special mediating powers of the imagination. Only the first two, however, demand the imaginative appreciation of another person's point of view. The professional judgments that a lawyer is required to make in the course of his work thus presuppose an element of sympathy which some judgments, at least, do not, and any adequate explanation of what it means for a lawyer to be practically wise must take this fact into account.

In the second place, the deliberative processes by which lawyers arrive at judgments in specific cases typically have a dynamical character that Kant's general description of the imagination and its synthetic schemata ignores. Kant is primarily concerned, in the *Critique of Pure Reason*, with relatively simple empirical judgments of the sort, "this cup is red," and he tends to view such judgments as acts of subsumption that bring particular objects or events under an established system of categories. Kant assumes that the categories we employ in making judgments of this kind remain fixed and are not themselves subject to revision in the very process of judging by which they are brought to bear on concrete particulars. This is obviously not true, however, of the professional judgments that lawyers are required to make. Consider, for example, the process by which a judge reaches his decision in a particular case. If there is an uncontradicted precedent on all fours with the case at bar, the judge's decision may appear to involve nothing more than the subsumption of an instance under a general rule, the rule for which the precedent is said to stand. In many cases, however, there is no single and unambiguously controlling precedent of this sort (the very fact that the parties are in litigation makes this unlikely), and where no such precedent exists the judge must decide how to construe arguably relevant earlier cases and the rules they are said to exemplify. In construing them, the judge gives these earlier cases and rules a more definite meaning than they previously possessed; after his decision, more can be said about the rules in question, about what they do and do not require, than could have been said before.

Every judicial construction thus amplifies the framework of rules within which the case to be decided itself arises. Some constructions, moreover, go further and alter or abolish norms whose previous meaning was quite clear. This is most dramatically obvious in cases that simply overrule a prior holding, but the same can be said of decisions that turn the law in a direction different from the one in which it earlier appeared to be heading. In cases of this sort, and even in cases that merely develop the implicit meaning of a previously ambiguous rule, the judge's construal of the law is bound to be affected by the felt necessities of the specific controversy before him; inevitably, therefore, the pressures exerted by the facts of particular cases will influence the shape and content of the rules that we normally think of as forming the conceptual framework of the adjudicative process itself. A judge simultaneously looks to see what existing legal rules imply for the case at hand and what that same case implies for the rules themselves. His deliberations cannot, therefore, be adequately conceived merely as a process of subsumption in which particular instances are brought under established and unchanging categories. A judge moves back and forth between cases and categories, adjusting his view of cach in light of the other. This is a fluid and dynamical process which results not only in judgments about particular cases but also in the ongoing revision of the system of rules in accordance with which subsequent disputes must be decided.[14]

Though especially prominent in adjudication, this same fluidity characterizes the various deliberative processes that typify the other main branches of law practice as well. A legislative draftsman, for example, rather than taking certain categories as fixed and then subsuming particular cases under them, aims to construct a plausible and effective body of general rules by considering the possible future cases to which these rules will be applied. And a legal counselor who at the beginning of his career may be inclined to accept without criticism certain broad axioms of conduct – for example, that it is unwise to initiate a divorce proceeding until all possibilities of reconciliation have been exhausted – will,if he listens to his clients and makes an effort to understand their particular dilemmas, refine his own axiomatic assumptions to reflect the lessons of experience, a process of fluid readjustment that resembles the adjudicative refinement of established precedents.

It should be emphasized, however, that although the judgments which a lawyer is called upon to make in the course of his professional work have a dynamical character that is obscured by Kant's characterization of the process of empirical judgment as one merely of subsumption, the general account Kant gives of the role played by imagination in mediating between

[14] This, of course, is the process that Rawls describes as the movement toward "reflective equilibrium." See J. Rawls, A Theory of Justice 20 (1971).

experience and thought applies with equal force to the more fluid judgments demanded of lawyers in their various employments. Indeed, the function of imagination is, if anything, more easily discernible in judgments of this latter kind. Every judicial decision, for example, combines a specific conclusion about the case at bar with an opinion, that is, with a statement of the legal rules that support the conclusion reached; every such decision is, in this sense, a synthesis of intellectual and perceptual elements. But since the intellectual component of the decision is itself fluid rather than fixed, the range of possible syntheses that a judge may reasonably entertain in any particular case is far wider than the range with which one is presented when shown a cup and asked to name its color. If the judgment "this cup is red" requires an act of imagination, then the decision rendered by a judge does so to an even greater degree, for before a judge can decide a case he must review in imagination a wide variety of combinatory possibilities, each of which joins a specific judgment to a different account of the relevant legal norms. Adjudicative judgments and the other sorts of judgments that lawyers are called upon to make have an openness or flexibility which judgments about the color of teacups do not; if anything, therefore, it is reasonable to assume that they require an imagination of even greater breadth and suppleness.

V

Kant viewed the imagination as an intermediary, a kind of go-between which possesses certain features both of perception and abstract thought, enabling it to unite these other faculties in the way that even very simple empirical judgments require. The sorts of judgments that lawyers are asked to make in the course of their work differ, however, in two important respects from those with which Kant was primarily concerned in the *Critique of Pure Reason*, and the account of the imagination that he offers there must be modified to reflect these differences before it can be applied to judgments of the former kind. The modifications I have suggested do not invalidate Kant's main insight; they are enriching complexities that supplement without contradicting the general account he offers of the imagination as a power of synthesis whose function it is to establish a bridge between thought and experience. Nevertheless, even after Kant's view of the imagination has been modified in the ways proposed, it remains unclear what the relation between this faculty and the virtue of practical wisdom – a virtue indispensible in all areas of law practice – might be.

It is my own view that a lawyer's practical wisdom actually consists, to a very large degree, in a certain expansion or development of his imaginative powers. There are two reasons, however, for questioning this view. First, though it is reasonable to assume that the more developed a person's imagination the wider the range of solutions he can envision to any particular problem, the man of practical wisdom is not merely someone who is able to conceive alternatives but who knows how to choose the right one as well. A person who can set out a broad menu of possibilities but is unable to offer any guidance in selecting among them, or whose selections are frequently misguided, can hardly be said to possess practical wisdom. The practically wise man excels at deliberation *and* routinely makes choices that are valued for their soundness. Now it is possible to see a connection between imagination and the process of reflection that leads to choice – a process in which an impoverished imagination is a serious liability – but the connection between imagination and choice itself is more obscure. Why should we expect a lawyer with a powerful imagination to make the right decisions? If we have no reason to expect that he will, then the development of his imaginative powers can at most be a necessary condition for the possession of practical wisdom, not a sufficient one; to be practically wise, a lawyer must be able to make the right decisions in particular cases, and whether or not he possesses this ability would appear to turn on considerations having nothing to do with the strength of his imagination.

Second, the concept of practical wisdom immediately calls to mind a person of a certain disposition or temperament, someone characterized by the caution and calm sobriety which the Romans termed *gravitas* and considered indispenable in all those with some share in public affairs. As a trait of character, *gravitas* seems nearly antithetical to the easy excitability that we customarily associate with an active and powerful imagination. The person of practical wisdom is usually pictured as proceeding with a watchful deliberateness and circumspection, and a general fear of taking too large steps from the existing order, whatever it happens to be. In this respect, he stands at the opposite pole from the prophet or visionary, and it is natural to conclude that the sobriety and suspicion of dramatic change we associate (rightly, I think) with practical wisdom reflect a deficiency in those same imaginative powers whose possession enables more radical reformers to envision far-reaching alternatives to the *status quo*. There is therefore something mildly paradoxical about the suggestion that the lawyer's practical wisdom not only presupposes but resides in a certain development of the imagination. Lawyers are popularly viewed as unimaginative and dull, and it seems more reasonable to assume that these qualities – and not a superabundance of imagination – underlies the quality of *gravitas* which is in general the mark of a practically wise person and more particularly, among those who make their living in the law, a *déformation professionnel*.

These are serious objections to my suggestion that the lawyer's practical wisdom actually consists in a strengthening of his imaginative powers. In answering them I shall have to say more than I have already both about the nature of practical wisdom and the special role that imagination plays in the work that lawyers do.

The questions raised by the first objection, which concern the relationship between imagination and choice, may usefully be approached by concentrating, to begin with, on the process of adjudication, and by asking what we mean when we describe a judicial decision as sound or sensible or practically wise. When we say that the decision in a particular case shows practical wisdom we are not, I think, merely indicating our approval of the outcome of the case, of the judge's decision in the narrowest sense. Whether a decision is sound or sensible depends not only on the final result at which it arrives, but on the path by which it does so, and it is entirely possible to approve the outcome in a case but think the arguments used to support it are imprudent or unwise (as, for example, when a broad generalization with a dangerous potential for subsequent abuse is employed to justify a result that could have been given adequate support by a more circumscribed rule or principle). By the same token, when we praise a judicial decision for its practical wisdom we do so not merely because its argument has a certain property or quality (novelty, for example, or internal consistency or conceptual elegance). The claim that a decision displays practical wisdom is a claim neither about its intellectual apparatus considered in isolation from the actual upshot or outcome of the case, nor a claim about its outcome evaluated independently of the arguments supporting it. What we use the term practical wisdom and its various cognates to describe is a certain relationship between the component parts of a judicial decision, what I shall call the relationship of "suitablity" or "fit."

A particular argument may, in any given case, be theoretically applicable and lead to the right result but nevertheless be unsuitable or inappropriate. Thus, for example, a strong argument in support of the admittedly proper outcome in a case may be inappropriate if the way has not been prepared in earlier cases by arguments of a less demanding sort nor, in general, if the triviality of the case or its tangential connection to the issue being decided is likely to deprive the decision of all sentimental support. The same can be said about a case of the opposite kind, one that squarely presents for decision a fundamental question towards whose solution the courts have been working for some time: to turn away in such a case from the hard but fully ripened choice which it presents and to decide it, instead, on technical grounds shows (I should say *may* show, for everything depends on the circumstances) a similar lack of fit between outcome and argument. In these ways, and in many others, the intellectual component of a decision may be either proportionate or disproportionate to the outcome it supports; when these elements are in proportion to one another, when there is a balanced harmony between them, we may speak of the decision as possessing what I have called suitability or fit. These terms describe a certain harmonious relationship between the intellectual apparatus of a case and its factual peculiarities, a relationship in which the elements are not merely stuck together in a mechanical fashion but are synthetically united in a way that strengthens each (the facts of the case giving its abstract arguments a vivid plausibility they would otherwise lack, and the arguments in turn giving coherent intellectual form to the inarticulate moral pressure which the facts themselves exert). A judicial decision which possesses the property of suitability or fit has a self-strengthening integrity like that of a work of art. It is this relational property – and neither the outcome nor the argument of a case considered by itself – to which we are referring when we say that a decision is sensible or prudent or practically wise.

Every judicial decision combines an intellectual element (rules of law) with a perceptual one (the facts of the case), and in reaching his decision a judge must always exercise his imaginative powers, for only the imagination can join these two elements or establish a connection between them. Not all connections of this kind, however, are equally successful: there are, first of all, the real monstrosities in which rules and facts are dramatically out of proportion and, more routinely, the pedestrian opinions whose factual and conceptual elements have simply been fastened together in an external way. Decisions of this sort exhibit, to differing degrees, a lack of suitability or fit, and a judge whose decisions consistently display this characteristic must himself be either insensitive to the difference between arguments that are appropriate in a particular setting and those that are not, or indifferent to the importance of this distinction.

The insensitivity and indifference he shows with regard to matters of fit mark such a judge as a person of limited practical wisdom. It is reasonable to think that these inadequacies themselves reflect a deficiency in his powers of imagination. The more developed a judge's imaginative abilities, the broader the range of solutions he can envision to any particular problem; a judge with a strong imagination will quickly see a wide variety of different ways in which the specific case before him might be resolved, each alternative representing a different combination of rules and facts (the rules invoked and the facts emphasized changing from one imaginary solution to the next). A judge whose imaginative powers are developed in this way is certain, in one important sense at least, to be more experienced than a judge whose powers are not: he is certain to have had a wider and richer experience both of the activity of imagining itself and of its various synthetic constructs. The more experienced someone becomes in this respect, the more likely he is to acquire what I have called a sense of fit. When we say that the intellectual and perceptual elements of an imaginary solution to a problem do not fit together in a balanced or harmonious way, what we mean is that they are not, or cannot be, satisfactorily synthesized; since the faculty of imagination *is* the faculty of synthesis, and since those most experienced with its operations will be best able to discern the difference between its successes and its failures, a judge with great imaginative powers is more likely than one without them to recognize which solutions to the case at bar, whatever it may be, combine rules and facts in a genuinely synthetic way and which do not – more likely, in other words, to have a sense of fit. Most importantly, a judge with a well-developed sense of fit is likely in general to prefer those solutions whose intellectual and perceptual elements are proportionately balanced, since these offer his imagination an outlet of expression which other, less synthetic solutions do not. The stronger a person's imagination the more likely he is to take immediate satisfaction in its expression and to be pained by the obstruction of its powers; a judge with a strong imagination will therefore naturally prefer – and prefer more intensely than one whose imagination is weak or undeveloped – those adjudicative solutions that possess the attribute of suitability or fit. In this respect, an imaginative judge is like the connoisseur of art or music who is distinguished not only by his enhanced powers of discrimination but by a characteristic preference for what is balanced and harmonious, for what is beautiful. In the latter case, connoisseurship implies the possession both of certain cognitive abilities and of a taste for one sort of thing rather than another, and here it seems quite natural to assume that the two are closely related, that the development of a person's powers of discrimination leads directly to a preference for a particular class of objects, namely, those that permit the powers in question their most complete expression. My claim is that something similar is true of the great judge, of the judge with an enlarged imaginative capacity: he sees more widely than others and has a more discriminating sense of fit, and just for this reason, like the connoisseur of art, is regularly drawn to some among the things he sees and repelled by others. In sum, if the practical wisdom of a judicial decision is a function of the fit between its intellectual and perceptual components, if the judge with a well-developed imagination is more likely than an unimaginative judge to possess a sense of fit, and if one who possesses such a sense is, for that reason alone, more inclined than he otherwise would be to prefer what is fitting and suitable to what is not, then we may conclude, with some plausiblity, that the development of his imaginative powers not only expands the range of alternatives that a judge is able to entertain in any given case, but also leads him, on the whole, to choose those alternatives which exhibit prudence or practical wisdom.

This way of describing the relationship between the imaginativeness of a judge and his practical wisdom emphasizes what might be called the aesthetic aspect of the relationship. There is another aspect, however, whose primary bearing is moral in character. When the parties to a controversy appear before him and ask him to resolve their disagreement, a judge is required to do two very different things. First, he must make an effort to see the controversy from each party's point of view. A judge must treat those who appear before him with respect, and if this is to be anything more than an empty formula, it means that he must enter with a measure of sympathy into the attitudes and experiences of the parties themselves. A judge must, in other words, show compassion to those on whom he passes judgment and this he can do only by putting himself in their position and looking at the world – as much of it, at least, as the controversy draws into question – from their own point of view. The second thing a judge must do is maintain his neutrality or objectivity. When a judge decides a case, though he necessarily decides in favor of one of the parties rather than the other, he does not make his decision from the standpoint of the party who prevails; indeed, he does not decide the case from the standpoint or perspective of any of the parties involved but, rather, from a point of view which none of them occupy – an independent point of view. The perspective from which a judge is expected to decide the cases that come before him is the perspective of the law itself, what in a manner of speaking might be called the standpoint of the community as a whole. To achieve and then adhere steadfastly to this point of view requires a continuing effort of detachment on the part of a judge; it is only when a judge is able to detach himself from the self-interested perspectives of the parties to a controversy that he can decide their dispute in an impartial fashion, that is to say, in a manner that gives precedence to the interests of the whole over that of any part.

A judge, then, must be both compassionate and detached. These are the two requirements of his office: if he fails in the first respect he shows inhumanity or hardheartedness, and if he fails in the second, partiality. These requirements are not only different, however, but seem actually to pull in opposite directions. We may therefore say that a judge must not only possess the seemingly opposite qualities of sympathy and detachment, but must also have the capacity to endure the tension between them. Indeed, it is the conjunction of these two qualities and the strength to accommodate their very different demands which to a large degree defines our conception of the distinctive responsibilities associated with judicial office and, hence, our understanding of what it means to *be* a judge.

When we say that a judge has satisfied the duties of his office and conducted himself in the way he should, we are not simply approving his decisions or suggesting that they are the ones we would have reached had we been in his position (someone may behave not at all as a judge should and yet reach conclusions we support). To say that a judge has acted responsibly is to say, I think, that he has listened with comprehending sympathy to those who have appeared before him and yet maintained a scrupulous neutrality about their perspectival interests. This union of sympathy and detachment, and the ability to live with the tension it creates, is the defining feature of the trait we call judiciousness. Judiciousness is, as the term itself suggests, the first virtue of a judge, and one who lacks it – no matter how vigorously we approve the substance of his decisions – is in reality no judge at all. (To this it might be objected that the first virtue of a judge is fairness and his most basic responsibility the pursuit of justice. This way of putting things is not wrong, but merely inadequate. Fairness implies the idea of neutrality and independence; what it does not immediately convey is the counterbalancing requirement of sympathy or compassion, without which a judge's obligation to treat those who appear before him with equal respect can be met only in an external or formalistic fashion. It is not enough for a judge to be neutral or fair, though it is of course necessary that he be so; he must also be able to think and feel his way into the attitudes of the parties themselves and permit their interests, beliefs, and concerns to make an impression on him – without ever abandoning the posture of detached neutrality from which his judgment must be rendered. A judge needs not only to be fair-minded, but to remain so while reviewing the parties' claims with utmost seriousness, which means with sympathy or compassion. The real challenge of adjudication lies in the difficulty of doing both these things simultaneously, a difficulty which the idea of fairness only half describes.)

The quality of judiciousness, the first virtue of a judge, depends importantly upon the development and strengthening of the faculty of imagination. The products of imagination, it will be recalled, share certain characteristics with the objects both of perception and of thought. When we construct an imaginary picture of something and hold it before our mind's eye, the image assumes a concreteness or immediacy analogous to that which the objects of sensory experience possess; unlike a real sensory object, however, the products of the imagination are characterized by a shadowiness and instability that marks them as belonging to the realm of mental artifacts. Our imaginings are subject to reflective reconstruction in ways that the objects of direct experience are not: we can do with them as we wish. To put it differently, we possess a power over our imaginings that we do not possess over the objects given to us in experience. The more far-reaching powers we enjoy in the domain of imagination are at bottom a function of the fact that our imaginings are abstractions to a greater degree than our perceptual experiences; they are more completely things we ourselves have made and hence may unmake or remake as we choose. Because it shares in the concrete vividness of perceptual experience, the imagination enables us to make immediately present to ourselves what is in reality not present at all; and because its products simultaneously share the abstractness of pure thoughts, the imagination can at a stroke abolish or put back at a distance what it has brought close and given a kind of sensuous presence (a power of abolition which, try as we may, we are unable to exercise over the things that fill up the real world around us).

It follows that there are two ways in which a person's imagination may prove deficient. First, and most obviously, it may be deficient in its powers of visualization, in its capacity to produce anything but abstractions unclothed even by the shadowy sort of concreteness that distinguishes the works of the imagination. Second, a person's imagination may be deficient in just the opposite way: instead of producing only bare abstractions, it brings forth images of such intense vividness that the person experiencing them cannot distinguish what is imaginary in his life from what is not. Images of this sort, we might say, lack that element of abstractness that normally permits the products of the imagination to be brought forward and dismissed at our discretion and which distinguishes them from the more obdurate objects of perceptual experience. A powerful and healthy imagination suffers from neither of these defects. On the one hand, it possesses wonderful powers of visualization and is able to make vividly present even what is most remote or unfamiliar; on the other hand, it never loses the capacity to dissociate itself from its own products, however vivid they may be, but retains a sense of their abstractness and of its power over them.

It is just this combination of visualization and detachment that judiciousness requires. A judge must make an effort to visualize the controversies that come to him for decision from the perspective of each of the parties involved; he must imagine how the dispute looks from their point of view. He cannot, however, simply adopt as his own their attitudes and beliefs – make them his own to the same degree they are the parties' – for that would necessarily compromise his independence. All the time that he is struggling to imagine the case from their perspective, a judge must retain the ability to put his own imaginings at a distance and to resume the point of view from which a neutral or objective decision can be reached. If he simply cannot make the attitudes and interests of one of the parties present to himself in imagination, he shows a lack of sympathy or compassion, humanly understandable in certain situations but still a failure of responsibility on his part. By the same token, if a judge loses control over his imaginings so that he is unable to view the world from the perspective of one of the parties without making that perspective his own, he shows a lack of independence, and in this case we may just as properly attribute his failing to a weakness of imagination as when his shortcoming is an inability to comprehend sympathetically a party's interests or concerns. When a judge deliberates, he reviews the case before him from the perspective of each of the conflicting interests it involves; when he decides, he withdraws from these imaginative conjurings and pulls back to the only perspective that is truly his own, the perspective of the law. To go back and forth like this requires a strong imagination, in the twofold sense I have described; the possession of such an imagination is the distinguishing trait of the judicious man or woman and the single most important qualification for judicial office.

The connection between imagination and practical wisdom, understood first in quasi-aesthetic terms as a sense of appropriateness or fit, and second from a more directly moral point of view, as the capacity to be both sympathetic and detached regarding the concerns of other people, is easiest to perceive in the field of adjudication. I believe, however, that a similar connection exists in the other main branches of law practice as well, and although I do not propose to survey them all, a brief consideration of one will help to confirm what I have said about the role that practical wisdom plays in the professional work of judges. The branch of law practice that I have in mind is the one we usually call legal counseling.

A legal counselor advises his clients on business and personal matters. To be technically competent, he must know the law in detail and be skilled at devising strategies for accomplishing his client's goals in the legally most expeditious and least risky way. Technical competence, however, does not by itself constitute practical wisdom. The practically wise counselor is able to do two things which one with mere technical competence cannot. First, he is able not only to rank different legal strategies in terms of their relative cost and riskiness (which depends, for example, on the likelihood that they will result in litigation or leave the client's interests unprotected), but able also to advise his client as to which strategy he should pursue. To make a judgement of this latter sort, a counselor must not only know the law but understand as well his client's aims and fears, his attitudes toward risk, and the order and intensity of his preferences. Without a concrete understanding of his client's situation, it is impossible for a legal counselor to say which strategies are fitting or appropriate for him and which are not (a judgment that is different from, though of course it presupposes, an assessment of the intrinsic juridical risks associated with each strategy). The counselor's judgments of appropriateness or suitability are not mere technical conclusions, but combine doctrinal legal considerations with factual ones in a complex synthesis. To make such judgments, a legal counselor must have a sense of fit, just as a judge must, and here, too, the possession of such a sense is a large part of what we mean by practical wisdom.

Second, the practically wise counselor (unlike the mere technician) is able to act, toward his client, as a kind of critical friend. Like a friend, he takes his client's interests as his own and devotes his time and energy to helping the client realize them. To do this, he must be compassionate or sympathetic in the sense suggested earlier, that is, he must be able to put himself in his client's position and see things from the point of view of his concerns. At the same time, however, it is the counselor's responsiblity to be a *critical* friend, one who pushes the client to interrogate and clarify his own ends, questioning, challenging, and, in extreme cases, simply rejecting the client's own statement or defense of his ambitions. In order to function as an effective critic, it is necessary for the counselor to maintain some distance from his client and to retain a measure of objectivity regarding the client's situation. Strangers do not take one another's interests as their own; lovers and intimate friends often do so to such a degree that they lose the capacity (and the will) to judge one another from an independent point of view. As a critical friend, the legal counselor must be simultaneously sympathetic and detached; he must see his client's situation bifocally, both from within and from without. The counselor who is able to do this neither feels indifferent toward his client's interests – regarding them in the same disinterested way he would those of a complete stranger – nor takes the client's own account of his interests at face value, simply accepting what he has to say and proceeding from there. If he is able to meet the conflicting demands of sympathy and detachment, we say of a legal counselor, as we do of a judge, that he shows judiciousness and in this branch of law practice, too, judiciousness is a condition of all achievement beyond the level of the merely mechanical.

A practically wise counselor, then, is distinguished from a legal technician by his sense of fit and by his capacity to act as a critical friend, both of which require – for the reasons given earlier – a strong imagination. The counselor who possesses practical wisdom or sound judgment and is able to give his client prudent advice is distinguished from his more plodding counterpart by the development of his imaginative powers. Here, as in the field of adjudication, imagination is the root of practical wisdom, and the lawyer who possesses a powerful imagination will not only be able to conceive a wider range of solutions to the problems he confronts, but will be more inclined as well to make those choices that we think of as being judicious or practically wise.

VI

I want now to return to the second of the two objections set out at the beginning of the preceding section. The objection, it will be recalled, concerned the relationship between imagination, on the one hand, and those traits of character that we customarily associate with the idea of practical wisdom, on the other. The man of practical wisdom, as we usually conceive him, is a cautious man, attached to existing institutions and inclined to alter them only through a process of slow interstitial adjustment of the sort, for example, that has characterized the development of the common law. He is resistant to enthusiasms and to the fashions of the hour, and tends to take the long view of matters; in a word, the practically wise man possesses sobriety, or what the Romans called *gravitas*. Why, one may ask, should we expect the development of a person's imagination to make him sober? If anything, it seems reasonable to assume that the strengthening of a person's imaginative powers would tend to encourage character traits of just the opposite sort – visionary impatience with the established order, a general unconcern with worldly realities and the constraints they impose, a tendency toward idealism and the exuberance of the prophet or revolutionary, rather than the ardor-dampening and deal-killing caution of the lawyer.

In responding to this objection, let me begin by emphasizing the important truth that it contains. Up to this point I have treated the faculty of imagination chiefly as if it were a special power of cognition, the instrument, so to speak, by means of which we acquire a certain form of knowledge that we otherwise would not possess. I do not believe, however, that the imagination can be adequately understood in these terms alone. To be sure, the development of those imaginative powers which a lawyer requires in his work leads to greater insightfulness and in this sense to an enhancement of his cognitive capacities. But this same process also typically results in what can only be described as a change of character, a change that involves not merely what one knows or understands but who one is as well. Who a person is depends importantly upon the overall structure of his likes and dislikes, upon the habitual affective structure of those cares and concerns that tend regularly to draw him in one direction rather than another. In a way that I shall attempt to explain, the strengthening of imagination which the practice of law requires and which it is one of the principal aims of legal education to accomplish has a predictable effect on the broad structure of a person's cares, and hence on his character. When it is objected that a person with a powerful imagination is likely to be less concerned with worldly realities than someone whose imaginative powers are limited or weak, it is implicitly assumed that the development of the imagination leads not only to new possiblities of understanding, but to a distinctive set of character traits as well. I believe that this assumption is in general true and that the full significance of the role which imagination plays in the professional work of lawyers cannot be adequately grasped without taking account of the transformative effect its development has on a person's character.

Even if we assume, however, that imagination and character are connected in some important way it remains to be determined what specific traits or dispositions are associated with the development of the imagination in the particular direction demanded by law practice. I want to approach this question by offering some comments on what may at first seem like an unrelated subject, the so-called case method of instruction that is today universally employed in American law schools. The case method, as I conceive it, is essentially a training in imagination, and its overall effect is to encourage certain specific traits of character. By focusing on the aims and consequences of the case method of law teaching we can better understand both why lawyers tend to have a distinctive professional character and how the traits that form this character are related to the cultivation of the faculty of imagination.

The case method teaches legal doctrine in an indirect way by examining the application of rules and principles in the context of specific controversies. Typically, the examination proceeds by means of a series of questions and answers in which every answer that a student gives is met by additional questions that compel him to reformulate or provide further support for the answer he has already given, with no definitive judgment ever being offered by the teacher as to the correctness of the student's responses. This is what is sometimes described as the "Socratic" aspect of the case method of law teaching, and the description is indeed an appropriate one if we think of the early *aporetic* dialogues of Plato in which Socrates is depicted as an insatiable questioner and critic whose conversations with his fellow Athenians never arrive at any final conclusions but always terminate, instead, in a general state of confusion and uncertainty about the subject matter under discussion. Holmes once suggested that the principal advantage of the case method is its utility as a mnemonic device on the theory that it is easier for students to remember abstract principles that have first been presented to them in the form of concrete examples,[15] and the person traditionally credited with the invention of the case method – Dean Langdell of the Harvard Law School – seems to have regarded it as a kind of inductive procedure for identifying general rules of law (analogous to the procedure that a botanist follows in drawing generalized inferences from the examination of individual specimens).[16] The case method may, perhaps, serve the ends that Holmes and Langdell attribute to it, but these are not its central aims – or, more precisely, they are not the central aims of the Socratic method of interrogation by means of which the study of cases characteristically proceeds.

The chief goal of the Socratic method is to strengthen those imaginative powers which the students subjected to it will later require in their careers and whose possession distinguishes the practically wise lawyer from the mere mechanic; in this sense, we might say that the aim of the Socratic method is to teach practical wisdom. When studying a particular case, the

[15] Holmes, Collected Legal Papers 44 (1921).

[16] C. C. Langdell, Remarks to Alumni of Harvard Law School, *Law Quarterly Review* 123–24 (1887).

students in a law class are invited to act as spokesmen for the conflicting interests which the case involves; this is, in fact, the way in which the Socratic inquiry typically begins. To be effective spokesmen, however, the students must be able to put themselves in the position of the parties they are representing and learn to state their views more forcefully than the parties themselves. This requires considerable empathic power, especially where there is no natural fit between a student's own conception of a case and the attitude or outlook of the party he has been asked to represent. This mimetic component of the case method forces students to think about things – often very important things, and sometimes even life itself – from perspectives that may be unfamiliar or distasteful. If the discipline of this enforced representation has its intended effect, the students on whom it is imposed will eventually gain a broader understanding of areas of human experience that previously were unintelligible blanks; this does not mean, of course, that a student whose empathic powers have been strengthened by the compulsory representation of interests he finds strange or repugnant must eventually come to approve these interests or adopt them as his own, but only that his capacity for visualizing the interests in question – for making them vividly present to himself in imagination – has been deepened and intensified.

The mimetic representation of particular interests is not, however, the whole of the Socratic method, but only one of two counterbalancing parts. The student who has been asked to speak on behalf of one of the parties to a case is likely to be asked next how he thinks the case should be decided and what rule he himself would propose for handling disputes of this general sort. To answer this latter question he must be able to view the whole case objectively, despite his forced empathic identification with one or another of the interested actors involved in it; having just the moment before been a full participant in the controversy, the student who is asked for his own judgment must disengage and withdraw to the position of a spectator, assuming the role of a judge rather than an advocate or representative. These two aspects of the case method correspond, of course, to the two dimensions of imagination whose combination or synthesis is required in all branches of law practice. By strengthening both aspects, and above all by habituating the student to live with the tension between them, the case method of law study serves as a forcing ground for the imagination.

For a student to perform successfully under Socratic interrogation, it is not necessary that he give the "correct" answer to the questions his teacher asks (indeed, it is a source of considerable frustration to most beginning law students that the case method is not designed to lead to answers of this sort). The answers a student gives *can* be inadequate, however, in either of two different ways: on the one hand, they can reveal the student's inability to get beyond a blackletter statement of the relevant legal rule to the particularities of the case, which always means the particular situation of the parties and their idiosyncratic interests and beliefs; on the other hand, they may reveal a loyalty to one set of interests that is so strong and undetachable as to prevent the student from maintaining even a measure of objectivity when these interests come into conflict with others. Each of these two ways in which a student's classroom responses may prove inadequate reflects a failure of imagination, a failure either of sympathy or detachment, and it is the main function of the Socratic method of law teaching to cure these twin deficiencies (to the extent this is possible at all) through a process of slow habituation. Outside the law, either deficiency may be innocuous or even praiseworthy, depending upon the circumstances and the goals a person is pursuing. Within the law, however, they are disabilities and either is sufficient to prevent the development of those synthetic powers of imagination that lawyers require in their work. By encouraging the development of that special bifocality which is the distinguishing mark of the imagination and the foundation of the lawyer's practical wisdom, the Socratic method of instruction promotes the one skill or capacity most essential to success in the profession of law.

What affective habits or dispositional traits is it reasonable to think a student will acquire after an immersion of several years in the case method of law study? That it has some effect on character is attested to by the fact that many students worry about becoming different sorts of people – people with different cares and concerns – as a result of their legal studies. This fear is sometimes expressed as a fear of "losing one's soul," which is the way we often describe the experience of an important change in the structure of our cares or attachments. Sentiments of this sort suggest that from the perspective of those subjected to its discipline, the Socratic method is a technique not only for imparting a mastery of certain intellectual propositions but for turning people into lawyers, that is to say, into people with a distinctive set of dispositions. Some welcome the transformation; others are disturbed by it and refuse to let it proceed, tenaciously hanging on to the old souls with which they began. Whatever their reaction to the process, however, most law students recognize that the study of law does more than merely add to their previous stock of knowledge; in subtle though predictable ways, it also transforms their character, changing who they are as well as what they know.

One thing that often changes is the student's overall confidence in the ability of abstract ideas either to explain or to provide an adequate basis for criticizing social and political arrangements. Undergraduate education is for the most part devoted to the study of general ideas, and its chief aim is to familiarize the student with the main elements of our common culture.

There is nothing in the typical undergraduate program that resembles the Socratic method of instruction employed in law schools and as a result, at the end of four years of undergraduate studies, a student's convictions have rarely been examined or tested in the context of specific cases. Most of those who come to law school, therefore, come with an initial enthusiasm for ideas, with a belief in their explanatory and critical power, which the close study of cases tends typically to dampen. By permitting students to address matters of principle only in the overdetermined context of real controversies and by requiring them to reproduce, within themselves, the conflicting points of view these controversies necessarily involve, the discipline of the case method forces an awareness of the heartbreaking complexity on which every large idea in the law must eventually be brought to bear, and encourages a suspicion of those whose optimistic faith in the power of ideas is increasingly likely to seem a symptom of immaturity or inexperience.

This process, in which exuberance and enthusiasm and uninhibited idealism are replaced by a spirit of caution that is more likely to see problems and to insist upon their importance than to deny their existence or difficulty, is sometimes described as one in which the student suffers a *loss* of imagination, becoming a dried-up husk incapable of reaching in thought beyond the trivia of life. This seems to me a fundamentally wrong view. The cautious and skeptical attitude that replaces the undergraduate's enthusiastic idealism is actually the product of a great increase in imaginative powers, for it is these powers themselves that open the way to points of view too various and irreconcilable to be accommodated by any single system of ideas sufficiently simple to satisfy idealistic longings. It might be said, with greater truth, that it is the visionary who lacks imagination, who is incapable of seeing anything beyond the narrow field into which his hopes and experiences have been contracted. This special concentration sometimes leads to insight and to an appreciation of the importance of what others have overlooked or undervalued; but insight of this sort is the product of a certain kind of obtuseness or blindness, an inablity to imagine that anything else *could* matter, and the person who possesses it does so because he sees less, not more, than others – like the little boy who noticed that the emperor had no clothes. I hasten to add that while the unimaginativeness of the visionary is sometimes insightful and liberating, it is also often destructive, the source of the world-threatening belief that what one does not imagine does not exist and may therefore safely be discounted to zero in formulating a plan of social life.

The case method of instruction is a forcing ground for the imagination, and the development of the imagination, particularly in its empathic aspect, leads to a deepened appreciation of the complexity of the world and the varieties of human experience. This in turn is likely to encourage a characteristic attitude of caution and the deflationary tendency to emphasize the institutional and human difficulties that stand in the way of most programs of reform. These are the qualities that distinguish a worldy man from a prophet or revolutionary and the worldliness of most lawyers is due, I think, to the fact that their professional training and subsequent experience is case-centered and hence inevitably corrosive of the faith in abstractions on which all prophetic and revolutionary movements ultimately rest.

Closely related to the lawyer's characteristic caution is another trait or quality which might also be regarded as a symptom of his worldliness, a trait combining sympathy and detachment in a fashion well-conveyed by the Roman saying, *Homo sum: humani nihil a me alienum puto*, "I am a man: nothing human is foreign to me."[17] A lawyer has, in a literal sense, seen it all; the diet of cases on which he is trained and must later employ his professional talents exposes him to the widest imaginable range of human hopes, follies and accidents, failures and successes, and to the mix of responsible choice and luck that shapes most lives. But whether as counselor, advocate, or judge the lawyer is not permitted to adopt a posture of Olympian disdain with regard to the human interests of those he serves in his professional capacity; he must take these interests seriously, which means, as I have said before, with a measure of sympathy. The qualities of mind and character that we might reasonably expect an experience of this sort to foster are the following: a general lack of surprise at the things people do or fail to do; a calmness in the presence of what may seem to others extraordinary or idiosyncratic, a calmness based upon the fact that one's confidence in human beings has not been shaken by the disappointment of some expectation as to what they are, or are not, capable of; and, finally, a measure of sympathy or compassion which those who have been disappointed in this way are often unable to feel, seeing no human bond between themselves and those whose conduct they consider beyond the pale. "Nothing human is foreign to me": this expresses exactly the combination of sympathy and distance, the commiseration from afar, that typifies the outlook of the worldly man, and it is just this combination of contrasting moods which the bifocality of the imagination encourages by permitting us to draw close and feel, while at the same time requiring that we stand back and judge.

The lawyer whose imagination has been developed through the discipline of a case-centered education is likely to be someone for whom this motto has immediate meaning, and I believe that anyone who takes this old Roman saying to heart and finds in it an adequate expression of his own attitude toward life will find himself almost instinctively opposed to all those large

[17] Terence, The Self-Tormentor, I, 1, 25

programs of self-conscious social reconstruction whose optimistic spirit is a reflection of the belief that human nature is simple enough to be made over in accordance with a plan. One to whom nothing human is foreign will doubt this can be done; more importantly, I suspect, he will doubt that it should be done, for he is likely to have a deep sense of the diverse forms of human excellence and their inseparability from the shortcomings which the reconstruction of man would presumably abolish. In this respect, again, it is the abolitionists, the prophetic reformers, who are by comparison lacking in imagination. What they literally cannot see is that the good and bad in human life belong together, and the variety of ways in which they do: they are the simplifiers of man, those for whom certain human things *are* foreign and therefore negligible, forgettable, changeable, transcendable. They are unworldly, and the wisdom of the Roman motto is for them an obstacle, the obstacle which the world and those who belong to it always put in the way of their ideals. Lawyers, who can imagine anything, are their natural enemies: the defenders of what their visionary antagonists call the status quo but I prefer to think of as simply the world, or more simply still, the human situation.

These qualities, then – worldliness, caution, a skeptical suspicion of ideas and programs set at too high a level of abstraction, and the spirit of detached sympathy that follows from a wide acquaintance with the foibles of human beings – are the qualities which the professional experience of a lawyer, first in school and later in practice, are most likely to encourage. They are the qualities of a practically wise man and they result from or, rather, accompany the development of his imaginative powers. Lawyers *do* have a distinctive professional character, one which is in large part the expression of a strengthened imagination. It is by becoming more imaginative that lawyers become practically wise and acquire the dispositional traits, the attitudes and concerns, which distinguish them from those who are able to see a few things with prophetic intensity because they are unable to see anything else at all.

VII

A wide familiarity with human beings, with their strivings and flaws, may lead to a world-weariness of sorts, or to a refined aestheticism that regards the world as a tragicomic play that cannot be rewritten but only enjoyed from the vantage point of an appreciative spectator – in which case the whole challenge of life will be to refine one's own perceptive faculties for the sake of their immediate enjoyment. I have no doubt that some lawyers are like this, and that their professional experience has contributed to their becoming so. But there is another aspect of the lawyer's professional life which acts as a kind of counterweight to attitudes of this sort. As a lawyer, one is constantly called upon to act in the world, not merely to observe it; more particularly, one is called upon to act as the agent or ally or friend of one or another of those countless human interests which from the standpoint of the aesthete or world-weary stoic is likely to seem laughable or foolish. A lawyer cannot afford to let the world seem too ridiculous; he does so at the risk of making his own professional work pointless and stupid. One way of expressing this idea is to say that a lawyer must not break his faith with the world or retreat into a position of splendid isolation; a lawyer must be able to act effectively even on behalf of those whose situation he regards as absurd, and to do this he must retain a measure of compassion for them which the genuine stoic is likely to consider an impediment to true enlightenment. It is this requirement to keep alive one's affection for the world and the people in it while recognizing with special clarity their confusion and absurdities which is the lawyer's special challenge. The prophet who is prepared to let the world pass away so long as justice is done is immune from the tensions of the lawyer's situation, as is the novelist whose appreciative outlook on the world is infused by the coldness of the immense spaces between him and it. To have no illusions about the world and yet be well-disposed toward it: this is the direction in which a lawyer's training and professional experience incline him. Though much can act against or frustrate this inclination, it does, in my view, mark a certain tendency that is sufficiently pronounced to justify us in speaking of a lawyer's character, meaning by this an attitude, or set of attitudes, that in a peculiarly intimate way grow out of and express the professional training and subsequent experience of those who make their living in the law.

At the beginning of this essay I said that what distinguishes a profession from a mere technique or expertise is that those belonging to it view themselves not merely as possessing an estoeric body of knowledge, but also as being people of a certain type, as having a certain professional character. I believe that lawyers do in fact have a distinctive professional character, and in these last few pages I have tried to describe some of its most prominent features. My point of departure in doing so was the concept of imagination, and I have tried, as well, to bring out some of the perhaps unexpected ways in which the development of the faculty of imagination is associated with those traits which form the core of the lawyer's professional character. I hope that the connections I have suggested are plausible; but more than that, I hope the conception of character which emerges from my remarks, however vague, has some appeal, enough, at least, so that those who have made the law their profession will find in it the outlines of a worthwhile form of life – not the only one, to be sure, but one that is entitled to our admiration and respect. To feel this way is to feel a sense of professional pride, to feel that one's chosen vocation is a way that one can live, a way *in* which one can live, and at the end of the day be able to say, "I have played a part and in my work been someone of whom I can be proud." I hasten to add that pride means: the sense of belonging to a discipline that has high aspirations, not the belief that one always or even regularly meets them. I mean to hold up my conception of professional character as an ideal, not a mirror of what lawyers always and everywhere are in fact. Pride is the condition of those who belong to a community of ideals and who feel they arc making some measure of progress toward their attainment. When I say that we can be proud to be lawyers, I mean not so much to give comfort or to validate a smug self-satisfaction as to awaken those feelings of responsiblity that come only when one sees the end and knows its worth.

Law, Yale University